Other books in the *InfoWorld* series

InfoWorld's Essential Guide to the IBM PC

InfoWorld's Essential Guide to CP/M

InfoWorld's Essential Guide to the Commodore 64

InfoWorld's Essential Guide to the TRS-80 Models III & 4

InfoWorld's Essential Guide to Atari Computers

InfoWorld's
ESSENTIAL GUIDE TO THE
APPLE

Thom Hogan *and*
the Editors of InfoWorld

1817

Harper & Row, Publishers, *New York*
Cambridge, Philadelphia, San Francisco,
London, Mexico City, São Paulo, Sydney

Acknowledgements

InfoWorld thanks the following people and organizations for their assistance in the production of this book: Phyllis Adams, Laurie Coonen, John Dvorak, Paul Freiberger, Gil Hoskins, Joel Pitt, Stanford Bookstores, Donna Tondino. *InfoWorld* owes a special debt of gratitude to Bob Hoskins and Carol Person, without whose unflagging efforts this book could not have been produced.

InfoWorld and Harper & Row have made every reasonable attempt to ensure that the information contained in this book is accurate. The world of personal computers is notoriously fast moving, however: companies continually change addresses, phone numbers and product prices; companies constantly revise and update their products; product lines can be discontinued. Consequently, *InfoWorld* and Harper & Row cannot guarantee the accuracy of the contents of this book or, in particular, any product description or specification contained herein. *InfoWorld* and Harper & Row disclaim responsibility for any product's failure to conform to its description in this book. *InfoWorld* and Harper & Row cannot be responsible for any direct, indirect or consequential damage or loss of data that may occur as the result of the purchase of a product mentioned in this book. Readers should use the book as a guide to the products and services described in these pages. For the latest information on prices and other such information, readers should contact manufacturers or retailers. Anyone planning to purchase and establish a professional computing system should consider working with a professional consultant.

InfoWorld Books is a division of *InfoWorld* (The Personal Computer Weekly), published by Popular Computing, Inc., 1060 Marsh Road, Suite C-200, Menlo Park, CA 94025.

Copyright © 1984 Popular Computing, Inc.

InfoWorld Books

Managing Editor
John A. Barry

Associate Managing Editor
Carol Person

Technical Editor
Rory O'Connor

Systems Manager
Bob Hoskins

Typesetters
Roberta Edwards,
Marilyn Lombardi,
Ellen Markoff, Camille Massey

Copy and Rewrite Editors
Irene Fuerst, E.K. Hogan,
Cindy Martin, Molly Olds,
Rhoda Simmons, Laura Singer,
Jim Storey

Technical Consultants
Thom Hogan, Phillip Robinson,
Steve Rosenthal

Designer
Design Office, San Francisco,
California

Illustrations
Norman Nicholson

Product Illustration
Marc Erikson

Library of Congress Cataloging in Publication Data

Hogan, Thom, 1952-
   InfoWorld's essential guide to the Apple.

Bibliography: p. 63
   1. Apple II (Computer) 2. Apple II Plus (Computer)
3. Apple IIe (Computer) I. InfoWorld. II. Title.
III. Title: Essential guide to the Apple.
QA76.8.A662H64 1984   001.64   84-9114
ISBN 0-06-669001-3

Preface

Welcome to *InfoWorld's Essential Guide to the Apple.* This book will help you get the most out of your Apple II-family computer. Whether you already own an Apple or are trying to decide which computer to buy, we think you'll find this guide essential.

As a buying guide, it will help you get the most for your money. For example, it uncovers some of the hidden costs that you might overlook. After reading this book, you should have a good framework on which to base buying decisions.

If you already own an Apple, you'll want to keep this book next to it as a resource of additional information.

To make this guide easy to use, we've divided it into two major parts: an overview of the Apple and reviews — a representative sampling of hardware and software products. Part 1, the overview, is divided into sections, with an explanation of what's in each section. In Part 2, the reviews — which follow the well-known, well-respected *InfoWorld* format — are arranged by applications, such as Words and Numbers.

With this arrangement, you can read the whole book straight through or skip around to various areas that especially interest you.

In the back of the book, you'll find a glossary and several useful appendices.

Prepared by the editors of *InfoWorld*, noted author Thom Hogan and the *InfoWorld* product-evaluation team, this guide to the Apple II family of computers will be a valuable addition to every Apple user's bookshelf.

Contents

Part 2
REVIEWS

Part 1

OVERVIEW

Getting Started

What in the world is an Apple?

It seems a curious name for a sophisticated computer: Apple. Yet this unintimidating name is appropriate — the Apple is an unintimidating computer.

But just what is an Apple? And what can a computer such as the Apple do for you? How do you buy an Apple, and what do you get for your money?

In this section, we'll explore these questions. We'll also provide some background on the people and events behind the creation of Apple Computer, and we'll provide buying information (including a list of all those little things you may not have thought about).

The History of Apple Computer
How to Shop for an Apple

Chapter 1

THE HISTORY OF APPLE COMPUTER

Apple Computer Corporation began with the tinkering effects of two young men, Steve Jobs and Stephen Wozniak. Jobs was the organizer, "Woz" (as Wozniak likes to be called) was the designer. Woz was in his early twenties and Jobs hadn't quite reached his twentieth birthday when Apple Computer came into being.

The two Steves dubbed their first effort the "Apple I." This 1976 product consisted of only an electronics board; users had to supply everything else, from a case to a power supply to a keyboard for entering information. The mid-70s were the days of computer hobbyists, and the hobbyists didn't much mind having to put together pieces they'd garnered from several companies to form a single computer.

Apple Computer didn't produce very many Apple Is, however, mainly because Woz was already finishing up the design of the Apple II by the time the Apple I was available.

The Apple II was introduced in early 1977. For its time, this machine had phenomenal capabilities: it allowed display of information in color and had more memory than most personal computers then available, and it featured what seemed to be infinite expansion possibilities. The Apple II came packaged in a plastic case that was no larger than a typewriter case. Almost immediately, the sales of this machine became as phenomenal as its features.

Jobs and Wozniak didn't stop there, however. After the Apple II came the Apple II Plus, an improved version of the original machine. Also introduced were disk drives (such as the Disk II) and several expansion boards to fit inside the Apple. With the introduction of VisiCalc and other ground-breaking software, the Apple II's popularity gained momentum.

Next in Apple's lineup was the Apple III, introduced in 1979 amidst much fanfare. The III was essentially a jazzed-up version of the II, with faster performance, more memory, a better keyboard and several features that the Apple II didn't have. The III was Apple Computer's first attempt to create a computer solely for business use, as opposed to the home- and personal-use niches of the Apple II.

In 1983, Apple introduced the IIe, another improvement on the Apple II, and the Lisa, a revolutionary business computer using an input device called the mouse. The Macintosh (see Appendix), a portable computer incorporating many of the same features and software ideas as the Lisa, and the Lisa II, a more advanced, low cost model of the Lisa, arrived on the market in early 1984.

A simpler, portable version of the Apple IIe is known as the Apple IIc. The IIc does not have a built-in monitor, but a monitor is available as an option. This 8-pound portable computer uses the 65C02 processor and is slightly larger than the keyboard portion of the IIe. The IIc has considerably less circuitry than the IIe, but it is largely compatible with the earlier machine. Although the new Apple includes 128K of RAM, it features no expansion slots. Included with the IIc is a serial port for a modem, a port for a printer and a mouse port.

Expected from Apple is a high-performance version of the IIe, with the ability to address more memory and run the same software much faster than the IIe. From its modest beginnings in 1976, Apple Computer has become one of the fastest growing companies ever. In its first five years, Apple went from start-up to a Fortune 500 company (a first), went from no revenues to almost $1 billion (a first), and went from one of many small companies providing personal computers to become one of two dominant companies in personal computers (the other: IBM).

The significance of the Apple II product line

Compared to any other small computers currently available, the Apple II has one overwhelming advantage: software developed for the original Apple II will work on the Apple II Plus and the Apple IIe. No other small-computer manufacturer can claim this for its machines.

Indeed, Apple has shown remarkable fidelity to its original design. Simply put, six years' worth of Apple IIs have created an enormous market for Apple II software and accessories known as peripherals. At the time of this writing, Apple has sold more than 1.5 million of the various versions of the Apple II.

We cannot overemphasize the importance of this accomplishment. (Those 1.5 million Apple IIs mean that virtually every type of software or accessory already exists for the Apple II.) In addition, the Apple accessory market has had more than five years to develop; complex or sophisticated accessories that are still in the planning stages for other computers have been available for the Apple II for some time.

Some differences do exist between the various Apple II computers. Let's take a closer look at those differences.

	APPLE II	APPLE II Plus	APPLE IIe
Available	1977-1979	1978-1983	1983-present
Number sold	100,000+	800,000+	500,000+
Memory	4K to 16K+	16K to 48K 64K option	64K to 128K
Features (that differ between models)	uppercase only keyboard	uppercase only keyboard	upper/lowercase keyboard
	40-column display	40-column display 80-column option	40-column display 80-column option
	cassette tape	cassette tape or floppy-disk drive	cassette tape or floppy/hard-disk drive
	Integer BASIC in ROM, Applesoft on tape	Applesoft BASIC in ROM, Integer on diskette	Applesoft BASIC in ROM, Integer on diskette
		DOS 3.2, 3.3	DOS 3.3, ProDos

As you can see, there aren't many major differences between the various Apple II product histories. Maximum available memory increased, the keyboard and displays got better and the way the computer's instructions and information were stored evolved from cassette tape to floppy- and hard-disk drives. On the software side, the original (and minimal) Integer BASIC was stored at first within the machine at all times, then was on diskette, to be retrieved when needed. In addition, the disk-operating system evolved, acquiring more features and improvements in performance as it grew.

Here's a surprise! You can modify (upgrade) the old-time basic Apple II to make it virtually the same machine as the current IIe — at least in function and feature, if not in appearance. As you'll discover when we discuss the various hardware accessories you can purchase for the Apple II, you can get a new keyboard, more memory, a larger display, and floppy-disk drives that work with any of the Apple II clan. What this means is that, for the most part, any Apple II can do anything that any of its relatives can.

At an exhibition for dealers in late 1983, Apple showed numerous new options for the Apple II series:

☐ AppleMouse II
☐ Apple Imagewriter printer
☐ AppleWorks software
☐ Apple/Rana MS-DOS add-on

Given such continued support, Apple owners can expect their computers to be functional for many years to come, even though the II and the II Plus are no longer manufactured. Indeed, Apple is currently rumored to be working on several enhancements to the current IIe product, including the ability to run MS-DOS, new optional disk drives and much additional software.

The Apple imitators

The enormous popularity of the Apple computer has spawned several Apple imitations. These imitators generally fall into two classes.

☐ Attempts by Asian companies to clone the Apple II Plus, even down to the case
☐ Apple II Plus software-compatible machines manufactured by both American and European firms

Note that almost all of the Apple imitators attempt to emulate the Apple II Plus, not the current Apple IIe. Because the IIe offers a few price advantages over the II Plus for those persons who are interested in adding the 80-column or additional memory options, the Apple imitations might not be as cost-effective as they at first seem.

The Asian clones are easy to recognize. Some of them are legal, some illegal (they duplicate copyrighted portions of the Apple II Plus design). Most have names that are supposed to evoke the "Apple" image: Pinecom, Orange and even Lemon. In most cases, these clones look like an Apple II Plus, having a case of the same size and shape. Often, many of the internal parts also look the same. The Asian firms that create these clones don't have to do any engineering or new-product development; they simply duplicate an existing product using their low-cost labor and parts advantages (most authentic Apples sold in America are assembled at a plant in Texas). Most of these Asian clones are brought into the United States by price-conscious distributors, who sell these machines through mail channels.

Apple went to the federal government seeking a ban on the import of machines that violate any of Apple's copyrights or patents. The government concurred, and it now confiscates the illegal clones (but not the legal ones). If you're overseas and are tempted by the low prices of Apple look-alikes, don't buy until you find out whether the machine is a legal or an illegal clone. U.S. Customs will confiscate any illegal clone brought into the country, even if an individual brings it in.

The software-compatible Apple II imitators generally offer something in addition to the basic features of the Apple II Plus. Currently, the most popular software-compatible imitators are:

- □ Franklin Ace
- □ Basis 101
- □ Quadram Quadlink Apple add-on for the IBM Personal Computer

Franklin Computer's Ace series of computers is based on Apple II Plus software compatibility. This means that the Ace can use most Apple II software. Early Franklin Aces could not display color (they showed the Apple's color output as varying shades of gray); later versions added color capability. Franklin's primary advantages over the Apple II Plus are lower price and a more businesslike keyboard. When you compare a similarly equipped Franklin Ace with an Apple IIe, the price and features are quite similar, in the $1200-$1500 range for a complete system. Currently, Franklin has the most extensive distribution and sales network of any Apple imitator; thus, it is not surprising to find that Franklin has sold more Apple look-alikes than any other company. Franklin has emulated the Apple's style, although the Ace's case looks different and is slightly larger than the Apple's.

Apple sued Franklin Computer for violation of copyright, claiming that the software built into the Franklin Ace was copied from Apple's. The suit was settled out of court. Franklin agreed to change its software and came up with a new operating system.

The Basis is a fascinating, almost schizophrenic machine. Instead of merely being an Apple imitator, the Basis also includes a second microprocessor, which allows it to use the CP/M operating system without additional hardware. Thus, the use of different diskettes makes the Basis an entirely different type of machine. In addition to this advantage, the Basis adds a professional, detached keyboard. Unlike most Apple imitators, Basis has chosen to house its machine in a case that differs from Apple's. Although it's more expensive than the Apple II Plus, the Basis offers more built-in features than the standard Apple provides.

The popularity of the Compaq and Kaypro portable (actually, transportable) computers has spawned an effort by several firms to make portable Apple IIs. CompuSource has announced a 27-pound computer, named the Abacus, that runs most Apple II and CP/M software and can be upgraded to run IBM PC software. The Abacus is the equivalent of an Apple IIe with 80-column and CP/M cards.

Colby Computer takes a different route to portability. Instead of building an entire computer, Colby sells you a kit that consists of a portable case (with a built-in, 9-inch, amber monitor). You follow simple directions that tell you how to take your Apple II apart and reassemble it in the Colby case. Because the Apple IIe consists of only a few hardware modules, mechanically inclined Apple owners should be able to perform the conversion in less than one hour, according to Colby.

An oddball in the Apple look-alike arena is Quadram's Quadlink add-on board for the IBM Personal Computer. This accessory converts a normal IBM PC into an Apple imitator. You can use the converted machine as an Apple II Plus or an IBM PC, depending on the diskette with which you start the machine. Not all Apple II programs work on the Quadram board, however, so you should check to make sure that the ones you wish to use do work before purchasing this accessory. Also, some owners have expressed dissatisfaction with the limitations of the Quadlink board. Buying an IBM PC and the Quadram board is by far the most expensive method of purchasing an Apple imitator, but, then again, you end up with the two most popular personal computers, housed in one machine.

Chapter 2

HOW TO SHOP FOR AN APPLE

You might be tempted to decide that you want an Apple computer and simply go to your nearest computer store and buy one. That would be a mistake.

Most people who buy computers don't do enough fact-finding and soul-searching before they make their purchase. The result of such impulsive buying is that they end up spending more money than they should, get less than they want and end up unhappy with their acquisition. With a little forethought, you can avoid all these problems, and that's the subject of this chapter.

Software first, hardware second

Probably the first question you ought to ask yourself is one that most computer buyers overlook: "Why do I want a computer?"

When you think about it, there are only two reasons to purchase a personal computer — you want one or you need one. If you need a computer, it is often because you need to become more productive in a particular area. For instance, as more and more writers use word-processing software on computers to write, it becomes more difficult for authors who use typewriters to compete. Therefore, an author might wish to trade in his typewriter and buy a computer that can handle word processing.

It should be clear that you need to buy a computer because you have a task (or tasks) that you need to expedite or perform. Unfortunately, too many computer buyers don't acknowledge this simple fact, and they buy a computer that looks fancy, or that costs the least or that others recommend because it works for them. Don't let this happen to you — the result will be that you will spend a lot of money and still won't have what you need.

Computers require software to perform any task. If you are looking for a computer to perform a specific task, you should start by examining all of the available software that performs that given task. Once you've found the program that works to your satisfaction, you can automatically determine your hardware needs. For example:

You're looking for an Apple II computer to perform word processing. You examine some word-processing programs and decide that you really want to use one called WordsWorth. You and your dealer examine the WordsWorth manual and discover that it requires the 80-column option, 64K of memory, two disk drives and a printer connected to an Apple Parallel Interface card in expansion slot number 1. Voilà. Your hardware has been chosen for you! All you have to do is choose what kind of printer to buy (making sure that the WordsWorth manual mentions that the program can utilize that printer, of course). Note that you would be wasting money if you bought a color monitor, joystick, extra memory, a serial or non-Apple interface card or anything else not required by WordsWorth.

If you had chosen your hardware first, you might or might not have purchased the right accessories for use with the software that best fit your needs; you would have to compromise your needs or buy additional equipment.

If you just want to buy a computer (i.e., don't need a computer), you still want to consider the software side of things first. Why do you want a computer — to play games, to learn more about electronics and computing, to use the computer as an educational tool for your children? Make sure you acknowledge your reason for buying a computer before you decide on your purchase. Consider this example:

You decide you want a computer. Most of the people you work with own one, and you're interested in seeing if you can use it in conjunction with another of your hobbies, stamp collecting. Besides, you have children, and you think that exposing your children to computers as they grow up will be valuable. You go to the computer store and, after sampling a lot of different software, decide that a filing program called The Cabinet of Caligari might work fine for keeping track of your stamps and that you and your children might enjoy games and learn-to-program programs. Your hardware choice is easy: you need a color monitor or an option called an RF modulator if you wish to use your own color TV (to make best use of the games), a joystick (also for games) and one disk drive.

Again, the example points out that the hardware choices are suggested by the types of software you are going to use. Sometimes you'll have to make some compromises in the hardware options you select, possibly because of price, but even so, you should consider the software first, and then look for appropriate hardware.

We'd be remiss if we didn't point out that the Apple II computer, as good as it is, is not necessarily the best choice of equipment, depending on why you need or want the computer. This is another reason you should make your selection of software first — you may find that another brand of computer best meets your needs. This statement may sound like heresy to you in a book about Apple computers, but it is not; it is simply realistic advice that, unfortunately, is too often ignored by computer purchasers. (Note: This book is just one of a series by *InfoWorld* on microcomputers; you might want to look over some of the others before deciding on the software and hardware you need or want.)

On the other hand, one of the nicest things about the Apple II is that you aren't restricted to just one task or software function. Although the Apple II might not be the best choice for one particular function, the fact that you can use it for many different functions makes it a good choice for a general-purpose system.

Selecting a store

Apples are available from a variety of sources. More than 1000 computer stores across the country carry the Apple IIe computer. Large department stores, such as Macy's, also sell Apple computers. Mail order can be another source for Apple computers, although Apple's distribution contract with dealers prohibits them from selling through the mail. Those who sell Apple IIs through the mail acquire their computers through Apple dealers, not directly from Apple. The local paper's classified ads probably have several used Apple II computers listed for sale.

So where do you buy your Apple?

The answer depends on what type of computer user you currently are and the type of computer user you eventually want to be.

Computer stores can be a good place to begin your consumer research, especially if you are a computer novice. Some computer stores offer substantial support for newcomers to computing — many offer special Learn Computing seminars during the evening or will arrange private tutoring for your first few hours using the computer. You might want to purchase a few books or magazines to help you understand what's available. Computer stores also tend to offer a wide range of both software and accessories, and store employees will often spend the time to explain things so that you understand them.

The level of service you get will vary from store to store, though. Try to get recommendations about stores from sources you can trust. On the negative side, the best computer stores tend to have higher prices than other outlets (usually these stores use manufacturers' suggested retail prices). In addition, computer stores can't afford to carry everything, and you might find that stores in some areas offer you a limited number of choices. Don't let that scare you away. Not only should you expect more service and support for the price, but you should also be able to dicker a bit on the total if you purchase everything from one store.

Here's what you're looking for in a good computer store:

☐ Evening or weekend training sessions
☐ Knowledgeable, easy-to-understand salespeople
☐ Wide selection of accessories and software

An offshoot of computer stores, software stores, has grown up in many areas. Like a good computer store, a good software store offers training, knowledgeable clerks and a wide range of choices. You might want to visit a software store before choosing your computer. Ask the clerks to show you what software performs the functions you desire. Good stores provide good customer support in the form of complete sales information, advice on what system(s) might be best for you, training and answers to your questions during your early use of the computer and help when things go wrong or when you get "snowed" by computer jargon.

Department stores also tend to feature good in-store support. The primary advantage of buying at department stores in your search for the perfect system is convenience. Generally, they feature a limited selection, often prepackaged into a single unit, at a slight discount over the cost of the package's elements individually. You can usually purchase computers from a department store using the store's credit card, thus amortizing the purchase price over time. Department stores aren't the best place to go for a wide selection of computer products or extensive training, though.

Most Apple-related magazines feature many mail-order advertisements that offer enticing prices on popular equipment and software. The mail-order route does offer the best prices on both equipment and software, but it offers virtually no individual support. Mail-order buying requires that you know exactly what you need and how to set it up when it arrives (that includes such often-overlooked items as cables and ribbons). In addition, you run the risk of getting shelf-worn equipment (i.e., not the current model or revision).

On the other hand, local retailers usually cannot match mail-order prices. Make sure that you're aware of the exact purchase price of your item when you order by mail — many operations charge 3% extra if you use MasterCard or Visa to pay and add a shipping charge as high as 5% of the total order. One last point about mail order: Do it by mail, not by phone. Federal laws give you a greater degree of protection from fraudulent or deceptive practices if you mail in a written order as opposed to phoning in that same order.

Apple forbids dealers to sell its equipment through mail order because the company doesn't believe mail-order dealers can provide enough support. If you have problems with a dealer — mail order or local — let Apple know. Apple is conscientious about monitoring the level of service its dealers provide and correcting any problems that may occur. Most mail-order Apple sellers, by the way, are not authorized Apple dealers; they purchase extra computers from authorized Apple dealers. Even so, Apple monitors where the mail-order ma-chines came from and can help you find local service when you need it.

In summary, if you know what you're doing and price is important, buy through the mail. If you're new to computers and need individualized help to select the right software and equipment, visit a few local computer stores or department stores, and select the one that you think provides the best direct, easy-to-understand answers to your questions and carries the software and equipment you choose.

The little things you'll need, but weren't told about

One area of constant consternation to first-time computer users is the "necessary accessories." The usual scenario goes something like this:

You've spent four hours at the local dealer's going over your needs and have selected an Apple IIe starter system, an Apple printer and several software packages. The salesperson tells you the total comes to $2495 plus tax. You follow the salesperson to the cash register and get ready to write your check. As the clerk rings up the total, he or she asks a few important, yet seemingly innocuous, questions such as "Oh, and of course you'll want a box of diskettes?" When the total appears on the register, it is $2745 plus tax. What happened?

"What happened" is this: It's the old "batteries not included" game. When you buy an Apple computer and disk drive, Apple supplies the minimum software. If you're going to use your computer for any serious purpose, you'll find that you need at least one box of diskettes, more likely two or more. Then you need something to store the diskettes in. The printer may come minus ribbon and paper. You might want a dustcover to protect your investment. A special extension cord with several outlets all controlled by one switch is handy, and a couple of Apple-related magazines and books might help you learn about your new system.

These simple accessories all cost money, and the total cost of your system can escalate quickly if you are not careful. We suggest that you consider purchasing the following accessories when you buy your Apple (sometimes you can get a salesperson to throw some of these into the deal at no extra charge if you purchase a complete system).

Accessories for the basic Apple IIe:

- ☐ At least ten diskettes (one box) $25-60
- ☐ A diskette holder that stores up to 50 diskettes $15-40
- ☐ A joystick (or touchpad) $30-150
- ☐ A cooling fan $50-100
- ☐ A switch-controlled extension cord $25-100
- ☐ A book on the Apple for novices $10-20
- ☐ Two or three Apple-related magazines $5-10

Accessories to add if you buy a printer:

- ☐ A box of plain paper (2000 sheets) $30-60
- ☐ At least three ribbons or refills $12-30

☐ A printer stand $20-50 (Make sure that you get a cable to connect the printer to the Apple and that the Apple has the appropriate interface card!)

As you can see, acquiring these simple accessories involves a great deal of potential cost. If you consider them as part of the system from the very beginning, you won't be surprised when it comes time to pay the bill.

FIRST QUARTER SALES BY SALES REGION

Section Two

What You Can Do with Your Apple

In this section, we explore what you can use your Apple for.

In Chapter 3, we'll take a look at software that Apple provides, as well as some alternatives to Apple-supplied programs. The next chapter covers application software, the programs that make the machine really useful. You'll see what's available in business, home and educational software for your Apple.

Chapter 5 shows you how to beef up the inner working of your Apple — by adding extra memory, for example. Chapter 6 shows you how to hook printers, monitors, disk drives, modems and other external devices to your Apple.

Apple-Supplied Software and Some Alternatives
Application Software for the Apple
Accessories for Inside the Apple
The World Outside the Apple

Chapter 3

APPLE-SUPPLIED SOFTWARE AND SOME ALTERNATIVES

Some basic types of software will come with your Apple. Which programs you receive depends on which Apple options you select.

The word *software* refers to sets of instructions for the computer to follow. Without software, an Apple II makes an interesting, but very large, paperweight. With software, the Apple computer performs tasks that are designed to make you more proficient, to entertain you or to educate you.

Software generally is grouped according to function category. The categories we'll cover in this and the next chapter are:

- DOS (disk-operating system) — the instructions that allow the Apple II to communicate with its disk drive.
- BASIC (Beginner's All-purpose Symbolic Instruction Code) — a special set of instructions that allows you to program (instruct) the Apple to do certain tasks.
- Business applications — task-specific software that performs functions usually associated with business practices, such as word processing (letter writing), accounting and so on.
- Home applications — task-specific software that performs functions normally associated with home or family needs, such as entertainment, money management, education and so on.
- Utility applications — software that performs maintenance functions for the computer, such as diskette copying, organization of information and so on.

   While the internal construction of software programs may be mystifying to you, it is of little importance to most users, and we will not discuss how to program a computer in this book. Instead, we'll concentrate on the above-listed categories of software, each of which allows you to make the computer perform a specific and useful task.

DOS — the disk-operating system

We'll start our tour of Apple software with the disk-operating system, the instructions to the computer that allow it to store, retrieve and modify information stored on a disk drive.

   We'll refer to the disk-operating system by the acronym DOS throughout the rest of this book.

   Apple's DOS, which is supplied with the first Apple disk drive you purchase for your computer, is fairly easy to learn. An operating system such as DOS is always present when you use disk drives on the Apple, although sometimes the operating system is loaded automatically by the system and you don't notice the process taking place.

   If you want a list of the files on a particular diskette, for instance, you type CATALOG. To "run a program" (start the execution of its instructions), you type RUN PROGRAM NAME (where PROGRAM NAME is the name of the program as it is stored on the diskette). Most of the other commands are just as simple to understand and use.

   Apple DOS has evolved over the years. You may still find older versions around, but it is unlikely that you'll encounter anything except the current version, DOS 3.3. In addition, Apple introduced a new type of DOS, called ProDos, which is patterned after a more sophisticated disk-operating system originally designed for the Apple III computer. If you are using your Apple II for serious purposes (as opposed to using it simply for education or entertainment), you might want to ask your computer dealer about ProDos and the advantages it provides over DOS 3.3. Apple started shipping ProDos with disk drives early this year.

   Apple has provided ProDos to many software companies that market Apple software; ProDos is likely to be distributed with many business-software products, because its speed, efficiency and additional features make it suitable for business use. Casual users of the Apple II, on the other hand, are more likely to benefit from exploring one of the alternative DOS's described below, rather than purchasing ProDos. When you're considering the DOS phenomenon, there's a problem, though.

   Unfortunately, the various Apple DOS's are not interchangeable. Pick one and stick with it if you want to minimize the confusion of learning multiple sets of commands.

   Apple isn't the only company that provides a DOS for the Apple II computer. Other companies offer a variety of enhanced DOS's as alternatives to Apple's DOS 3.3. The most often cited benefit of these non-Apple DOS products is that they perform disk operations faster than Apple DOS performs them. Such products include:

Pronto-DOS *Beagle Brothers*
David-DOS *David Data*
Diversi-DOS 2-C *DSR*
SpeedDOS *Softkey Publishing*
PIG-DOS 2.0 *Big Pig Software*

Although they may add increased instructions (some let you rename the commands — you could change Apple's CATALOG command to FILELIST, for example), most alternative DOS products perform exactly the same functions as DOS 3.3.

Another interesting — and confusing — area regarding DOS is that many software companies supply their programs with a special version of DOS that makes it impossible for you to ask for a list of files, copy the diskette and so on. Most game programs for the Apple have their own version of DOS. The only function of that type of DOS is to load the program into memory and start following the program's instructions. Generally, you cannot do anything else with that disk that you might normally do with Apple DOS 3.3.

BASIC and programming languages

Next on our list of Apple-supplied software is BASIC (Beginners All-purpose Symbolic Instructional Code). BASIC is a programming language. By that we mean that it is software that allows you to write the instructions to create your own custom software.

The original Apple II came with a BASIC called Integer BASIC, so named because it could calculate only with integers (whole numbers) — no decimals or fractions were allowed. Integer BASIC was stored permanently within the computer, in a type of circuit called a ROM (read-only memory). Because it didn't have to calculate fractions and was extremely fast, Integer BASIC was good for writing simple programs and particularly good for writing games.

As Apple IIs acquired more memory capacity, Apple changed the standard BASIC from Integer BASIC to one called Applesoft BASIC, which allowed users to work with decimal numbers and featured many enhancements of Integer BASIC. Applesoft's enhancements made the Apple more suitable for programming sophisticated business functions. The change from Integer BASIC to Applesoft BASIC was one of the key differences between the original Apple II and the Apple II Plus (the other major change was the expansion of the maximum amount of memory to 64K).

If you buy an Apple IIe (or an older Apple II Plus with 64K of memory), both BASICs are available: Applesoft is stored in ROM within the machine; Integer BASIC is loaded by DOS into a portion of memory when you start up the computer.

What can BASIC do for you?

Some programs that you purchase for the Apple require Applesoft BASIC to be present in the computer; they use a portion (or all) of the instructions stored in the BASIC ROM. Remember also that using BASIC to write instructions to the computer is one way of customizing your computer for the exact tasks you want it to perform. More important, learning to program in BASIC teaches you a great deal about how a computer functions. It is likely that students entering college in the near future will have to be familiar with simple computer programming, using programming languages such as BASIC.

If you become a knowledgeable BASIC programmer and find BASIC's speed limiting, you may want to investigate BASIC compilers that are available for the Apple. A compiler is a program that takes the English-like statements (such as PRINT, GOTO and so on) that comprise a BASIC program and reduces them to instructions more suitable to the machine. Every time the Apple encounters a BASIC instruction, the computer must first interpret the instruction (translate the English-like instruction into instructions the machine understands); this process takes time. Once a program has been compiled, no translation is necessary; thus the program is faster and more efficient. Some popular BASIC compilers are:

TASC   *Microsoft*

FLASH!   *Laumer Research*

Integer BASIC Compiler   *Synergistic Software*

Speed Star   *Roger Wagner Publishing*

Expediter II   *Sierra On-Line, Inc.*

Applesoft Compiler   *Hayden Book*

Einstein Compiler   *Alison Software Corporation*

Computer languages other than BASIC are also available for the Apple II; these languages include the following (the last three are popular machine-language-development programs directed toward advanced programmers):

Apple Pascal *Apple Computer*
Pascal: a highly refined, structured, general purpose language preferred by educators for teaching computer programming.

Apple FORTRAN *Apple Computer*
FORTRAN (FORmula TRANslation): predecessor to BASIC; designed for complex mathematical calculations on larger computers.

Apple PILOT *Apple Computer*
PILOT: a language designed specifically to create interactive instructional programs; widely used in educational institutions.

Apple Logo *Apple Computer*
Logo *Krell Software*
Logo: a graphics-oriented language designed for first-time computer programmers, especially young children.

TransFORTH *Insoft*
FORTH-79 *MicroMotion*
Forth: a curious mixture of low- and high-level programming constructs that results in compact, fast programs; originally designed to operate computer-run telescopes and other scientific instruments.

ALD *Insoft*
Lisa *Sierra On-Line, Inc.*
ORCA/M *Hayden*
Assembly, or machine, language: a set of English-like mnemonics used to represent specific, low-level computer operations (such as adding two bytes of memory together).

Chapter 4

APPLICATION SOFTWARE FOR THE APPLE

The term *application software* refers to software that performs specific functions or applications. This is the area in which the Apple II excels, since an enormous range of software choices are available to you.

Business applications

One of the most important categories of software for the Apple II computer is business applications. Some computer-industry observers say that with the introduction in 1979 of VisiCalc, a number-processing program for the Apple II computer that allows users to enter complex formulas and relationships and recalculate results automatically when any number changes, personal computers finally became more than playthings — they were useful tools.

Several subcategories of business software exist, and the most important are:

☐ Word processing
☐ Data base
☐ Number processing and finance
☐ Accounting
☐ Graphics

Word processing is the process of entering, modifying and printing out text documents using a computer. Word-processing software on a computer offers significant advantages over using a typewriter:

- ☐ Easy correction of mistakes.
- ☐ Easy editing of text.
- ☐ No retyping of entire drafts; you merely change those items that need updating.
- ☐ Increased productivity when the same documents are to be sent to more than one person.
- ☐ Spelling correction (optional on some word-processing software). Even if the word processor you are using doesn't offer a spelling checker, fixing spelling errors is much easier.
- ☐ More professional-looking finished documents: you use no strikeovers or white-out correction fluid, and the computer automatically justifies the margins.

After the introduction of low-cost word-processing software for the Apple II, two types of word processing were available: simple to use and understand, moderately sophisticated; and more difficult to learn, extremely sophisticated programs.

In the low-cost word-processing arena, some of the most popular programs are:

Bank Street Writer   *Broderbund*
The Write Stuff   *Harper & Row*
HomeWord   *Sierra On-Line, Inc.*
Home Writer   *MicroLab*
Pen-Pal   *Howard Sams*

Each of these under-$100 programs can, in conjunction with a printer connected to your Apple II, perform the basic word-processing functions that will allow you to easily create and modify letters, reports and other short documents. All are easy to learn and use, even if you are not a touch typist. None of them requires any additional equipment or accessories other than a printer. Bank Street Writer, in particular, was designed to help children learn and use word processing and is therefore especially popular with families who own a computer in the Apple II family.

If you want to do more advanced word processing, both the expense of acquiring the package and the number of accessories necessary tend to climb. First, most serious word-processing users need an 80-column card and a monochrome monitor. The reason for these acquisitions is simple: the more characters that can be displayed on the screen at one time, the more efficient the word processing is. You can see twice as many characters on an 80-column display as you can on a normal Apple display.

Seeing more characters allows you to view the document exactly as it is going to print out. The added number of characters also permits you to see items in context while editing and lets you move pieces of text around from one place to another within a document more easily. Unfortunately, 80-column displays require a monochrome monitor (black-and-white or green screen), because color TVs and monitors cannot adequately resolve the display 80-column cards create.

The more expensive word-processing programs often use features found only on more expensive printers. An example of this is proportional spacing, a method of justifying text that involves varying the space in which each character appears (it looks a lot like typesetting — as in this book — as opposed to typewriter-created copy).

The ability to create mass mailings of form letters to everyone on a list of names and addresses is another feature of advanced word-processing programs. Last, most of the more expensive word-processing programs offer users a greater variety of ways to move around within text, and change, move or delete the displayed text.

Some of the more popular advanced word-processing programs for the Apple include:

PFS:Write (IIe only) *Software Publishing Corporation*

Pie:Writer *Hayden*

Apple Writer II or IIe *Apple Computer*

Letter Perfect *LJK Enterprises*

Magic Window II *Artsci*

ScreenWriter II *Sierra On-line, Inc.*

Super-Text *Muse Software*

Word Handler II *Silicon Valley Systems*

Zardax *Computer Solutions*

EasyWriter *Professional Information Unlimited*

Word Juggler IIe *Quark*

Curiously, one of the most popular and sophisticated word-processing programs for the Apple II was not designed to be used on the Apple. Called WordStar, the program was originally designed for computers that used a disk-operating system called CP/M. In order to use WordStar on the Apple II, you must purchase an additional accessory, called a Z80 Processor Card and should consider buying an 80-column card (see Chapter 6 for more information). The creator of WordStar, MicroPro International, offers WordStar together with a Z80 processor and 70-column card for a special price, but you could purchase each of the items separately.

One word of warning about using WordStar on the Apple: you actually use the CP/M operating system instead of DOS 3.3. Therefore, you have to learn another set of instructions for the computer, and you may find that you cannot pass information from the word-processing software to other software you use.

Additional word-processing programs you might consider include spelling checkers and optional data-base merging programs; the latter are used to take name-and-address lists and combine them with text documents to create form letters (some word processors have this feature built in).

Sensible Speller *Sensible Software*

Magic Words *Artsci*

Lexicheck IIe *Quark*

MegaSpell *Megahaus*

MailMerge* *MicroPro International*

SpellStar* *MicroPro International*

*works only in conjunction with WordStar

If you are seriously interested in word processing, here are the hardware accessories you might want to consider to enhance your use of the software that you select:

☐ 80-column card
☐ monochrome monitor
☐ letter-quality printer
☐ second disk drive for storing documents
☐ detachable keyboard

Data-base software might be best described as "filing software." By this we mean the action of filing something in some organized manner (as in file folders within a filing cabinet), then retrieving it and using it when needed.

Name-and-address files are easily computerized, for instance. You enter all the names and addresses you need to refer to into the computer (through the data-base program). Later, you can retrieve individual entries, create reports or listings of some or all of the entries or use the entries within another program — for example, in merging the name-and-address list with a document in order to create form letters.

Filing programs range in sophistication from simple list-handling programs to advanced packages designed to keep and relate complex business data. The simple filing programs include:

PFS:File *Software Publishing Corporation*

PFS:Report *Software Publishing Corporation*

Quick File IIe *Apple Computer*

Data Factory *MicroLab*

The more expensive data-base programs generally offer several different ways to sort or retrieve information, more advanced report abilities than low-cost data-base programs have and the ability to relate information in one data-base to that in another. Examples of the more elaborate data-base programs include the following popular products:

VisiFile *VisiCorp*

DB Master *Stoneware*

Information Master *High Technology*

InfoStar* *MicroPro International*

dBASE II* *Ashton-Tate*
requires CP/M card

Yet another type of data-base program is that of the informal data base. Such products allow you to "scribble" information into the computer and then retrieve it, organize it or display it. Usually the program accomplishes its tasks by using phrases you specify.

Examples of such products include:

Visidex *VisiCorp*
Datafax *Link Systems*

A related product combines many of the features of data-base management with those of word processing. Called an "idea processor" by its developer, this product is invaluable for organizing thoughts, outlines and other types of information. You use it before you begin to write your document:

ThinkTank *Living Videotext*

Accessories that you might wish to investigate if you intend to make heavy use of data-base software are:

☐ hard-disk drive for storing large data bases
☐ 132-column printer for printing complex reports

Number-processing and finance software was probably the first area in which the Apple II was used for business functions. The program that pioneered the concept of Apple-as-business-tool was VisiCalc (the name stands for Visible Calculator), a program in which you receive a blank worksheet that you fill with numbers and formulas. The formulas serve as fixed information. Change one number or formula, and, depending upon the formulas in use, the results are instantly recalculated. VisiCalc found quick acceptance from business people whose work involved budgeting, financial analysis, cost analysis, statistics and many other similar tasks.

Imitators of VisiCalc quickly appeared, as did programs that performed a particular numerical function such as tax planning or loan calculations.

Among the most popular number-oriented programs are:

VisiCalc *VisiCorp*
VisiCalc IV *VisiCorp*
MagiCalc *Artsci*
Multiplan *Microsoft*
Desk Top Plan *VisiCorp*

Other number-oriented programs for the Apple II are:

Tax Preparer *Howard Software*
TK!Solver *Software Arts*

You will almost certainly want an 80-column card and possibly an add-on memory card if you use number-processing software. You may have to purchase additional software utilities to make use of these hardware additions (e.g., a VisiCalc preboot diskette from Videx). Here's the hardware you want to consider if you're using number-oriented software:

- ☐ 80-column card
- ☐ additional memory card
- ☐ 132-column-capable printer

You can use a personal computer for business accounting, but doing so is not particularly wise because of the large mass-storage requirements and the speed at which the Apple II disk drives process information. Apple sold an accounting package called Apple Accounting but withdrew it from the market in favor of supporting its BPI Accounting System.

The five modules that normally make up a full accounting-software package are general ledger, accounts receivable, accounts payable, payroll and inventory. If only one of these functions is of primary interest to you, you should consider using one of the more advanced data-base programs; an Apple II can handle small inventories, in particular, with a sophisticated data base such as DB Master.

Available accounting programs for the Apple include:

Peachpak Accounting   *Peachtree Software*

Hard Disk Accounting   *Great Plains Software*

General Ledger, Accounts Payable, Accounts Receivable, Payroll   *Broderbund*

Payroll Manager   *MicroLab*

The General Manager   *Sierra On-Line, Inc.*

BPI Accounting System   *Apple Computer*

Accounting Plus II   *Software Dimensions*

Accessories to consider if you are interested in handling accounting tasks with an Apple II include:

- ☐ hard-disk drive
- ☐ 132-column printer
- ☐ monochrome monitor

Graphics is the last area we mentioned in which many business applications are available for the Apple II. By *graphics software* we mean software that we can use to create, modify and display bar charts, pie charts, line graphs, bar graphs and scatterplots. Features to look for in graphics programs include the type of graphics allowed (bar, pie, scatter and so on), the number of data points you can enter, the ability to label indices and title the graph and such advanced features as data- or curve-smoothing and automatic scaling. Some graphics programs provide quasi-three-dimensional graphics and are well suited for comparative figures. The better graphics programs allow you to get the data to display from a calc-type or data-base-type program and offer a range of choices when it comes to printers or plotters that you can use.

You can use the Apple II for other types of serious graphics applications such as architectural drawing, engineering (computer-aided design) and commercial art design. The Apple II's graphic resolution (280 horizontal by 192 vertical dots displayed) severely limits such uses, however, especially if you are using color graphics. The Apple III, Lisa or Macintosh might be better choices for such detailed graphic work.

Among the most popular graphics programs for the Apple II are:

PFS:Graph   *Software Publishing Corporation*
VisiPlot   *VisiCorp*
VisiTrend   *VisiCorp*
Apple Plot   *Apple Computer*
Apple Business Graphics   *Apple Computer*
Versaplot   *Malibu Softcorp*
The Prime Plotter   *PrimeSoft*
Fontrix   *Data Transforms*
The Graphic Solution   *Accent Software*

If you plan to use a graphics program, you should also consider the following accessories:

□ graphics-capable printer
□ graphics plotter
□ color monitor

Before leaving the business-applications-software section, let's wrap things up by examining a unique application you might not have thought of using a computer for: time management. An Apple II can easily serve as an appointment scheduler or time-management device. Programs to handle these kinds of tasks include:

Time Manager   *Image Computer Products*
VisiSchedule   *VisiCorp*
Color Calendar   *Spectrum Software*

For those interested in scheduling projects, rather than or in addition to appointments, a program using many of the techniques found in business use of the critical-path method of project scheduling is available:

VisiSchedule   *VisiCorp*

Other such products may be available by the time you read this.

Last in our exploration of common types of business software is a look at so-called integrated software packages. By integrated, the creator usually means that the single program is capable of performing several different business tasks, such as word processing, calculations and data-base management.

The first Apple program to fit the bill was Incredible Jack, from Business Solutions. Incredible Jack is primarily a word processor, but it also features built-in calculation abilities similar to those of VisiCalc (although more restrictive) and data-base abilities as well. Using this single product, users can quickly put together reports and other documents that combine words, numbers and data.

One of the most interesting integrated programs is Jane, from Arktronics. Patterned after the advanced (and state-of-the-art) software Apple developed for the Lisa computer, this simple program uses pictures to indicate available functions (a small typewriter, calculator and file cabinet appear on the screen, representing word processing, number processing and data-base management, respectively). You use a supplied "mouse" to move a pointer on the screen to the picture of what you want to do and then press a button on the mouse. (A mouse is a small device that fits in the palm of your hand. You slide it across a flat surface, such as your desk; the movement of the mouse on the desk is translated into movement of a pointer on the Apple's screen.)

Because of its use of simple pictures (sometimes called "icons"), Jane is extremely easy to learn to use. The action of pointing to something is much easier for newcomers to computing to learn than is the typing of specific program names.

Apple, too, has introduced an integrated software package; it runs only on the Apple IIe. Called AppleWorks, the program combines word processing, number processing and data-base management. AppleWorks is not as easy to use as Jane, but AppleWorks does allow you to use data files you've created with Quick File and VisiCalc, a nice touch that experienced users of the computer will appreciate.

You might consider adding a timekeeping (clock) card to your Apple if you use time-management software.

Other business-oriented software for the Apple II includes:

First Class Mail *Continental Software*
Money Decisions *Eagle Software Publishing*
Executive Briefing System *Lotus Development Corporation*
VersaForm *Applied Software Technology*

Home software

Using an Apple II in the home opens up several areas of software for your consideration, primarily home-management and budgeting, educational and entertainment software.

In the home-management/budgeting category fall personal-finance programs, such as those that keep a computerized check register. Generally, however, such programs can do much more than merely keeping track of your checks. The better personal-finance programs keep track of tax-deductible expenses, expenditures by category and expenditures against budget; and they even perform a trend analysis to tell you which expenses are going up and which are going down. Some programs present graphic depictions of your expenditures, allowing you to see the relationships between your expense categories. Even better, some actually print out checks based upon your input — all you have to do is sign the check, stick it in an envelope addressed to your creditor and post it. Programs of this type include:

Dollars and Sense *Monogram*
Home Accountant *Continental Software*
Money Street *Computer Tax Service*
Personal Finance Manager *Apple Computer*

A related software category is investment or portfolio management. In this category we find:

Investment Evaluator *Dow Jones Software*
The Tax Manager *MicroLab*
The Market Technician *Datamost*
Teleminder *Teleware*
Stock Portfolio System *Smith Micro Software*

Other home-management software packages include everything from specialized data-base programs designed for home use to computerized cookbooks:

Micro Cookbook *Virtual Combinatics*
Nutritionist *N-2*
Family Roots *Quinsept*
Health-Aide *Knossos*
Personal Inventory *8th Dimension Enterprises*

Educational software

A second major category within home software is educational software. More and more parents are buying computers so that their children will have the advantage of being "computer literate" — the concept of being aware of computers and familiar with how to use them.

Educational software ranges across a diverse set of topics and target age groups. Software for preschoolers includes such computerized goodies as alphabet books, coloring books, shape-recognition builders and elementary math and reading primers. Some preschool software programs simply tell the child a story, usually asking the child to interact with the computer in some way. Other educational programs take alternative approaches to teaching children, such as "fun" practice and skill-development sessions. Such offerings include:

Mother Goose Rhymes *George Earl*

Stickybear Series *Xerox Education Publications*

Bop, Numbers *ABC*

Snooper Troops *Spinnaker*

Face Maker *Spinnaker*

Delta Drawing *Spinnaker*

Juggle's Rainbow *The Learning Company*

Bumble Games *The Learning Company*

Rocky's Boots *The Learning Company*

Kids on Keys *Spinnaker*

Alphabet Zoo *Spinnaker*

Story Machine *Spinnaker*

Ernie's Quiz *Apple Computer*

Early Games *Music Counterpoint Software*

More advanced educational software generally is designed to teach specific ideas, facts or skills. Offerings include everything from teaching touch-typing (MasterType) to teaching math skills (Math Blaster!) Many of the better educational software programs employ game or entertainment elements to motivate learners. Some of the more popular educational programs include:

MasterType *Scarborough*

Math Blaster! *Davidson & Associates*

Word Attack *Davidson & Associates*

Speed Reader *Davidson & Associates*

Algebra Arcade *Wadsworth Electronic Publishing*

Compu-Math *Peachtree/Eduware*

Compu-Read *Peachtree/Eduware*

Mastering the SAT *CBS Software*

English SAT #1-3 *MicroLab*

Typing Tutor II *Microsoft*

Punctuation Skills — Commas *Milton Bradley*

Ratios and Proportions *Milton Bradley*

(Plato) Elementary Algebra *Control Data Publishing*

Frog Jump *Scott Foresman*

Space Journey *Scott Foresman*

Spellicopter *DesignWare*

Wizard of Words *Computer Advanced Ideas*

An education-related category of software is that of training software. This type of software usually consists of a tutorial on how to use another piece of software or equipment. Some popular training programs are:

The VisiCalc Program *CDEX*
How to Use Your Apple IIe *CDEX*
DB Master Version 4 *CDEX*
BASIC Tutor *Supersoft*
VisiCalc *ATI*
Applesoft BASIC *ATI*
The Apple II *Muse*

The most popular category of home software, however, is that of entertainment programs. We can put most entertainment software into one of these categories:

□ arcade (dexterity)
□ adventure (role-playing, problem-solving abilities required)
□ thinking (problem-solving abilities required)
□ arts (drawing, music emphasis)
□ simulation (knowledge of simulated subject needed)

Most entertainment-software packages cost less than $100, with the majority listing for slightly less than $40 a program. Most entertainment software makes use of the Apple II's color-graphics capabilities, and much of it (especially the arcade and arts categories) makes use of a joystick, game paddle or touchpad.

In the arcade category, as you might expect, most of the entries are copies or close relatives of games that first appeared in video arcades. You'll find hundreds of shoot-'em-up, run-the-maze and climb-the-ladders games available for the Apple II. Among the most popular arcade games are:

Microsoft Decathlon *Microsoft*
Hard Hat Mack *Electronic Arts*
ABM *Muse*
Choplifter *Broderbund*
Microwave *Cavalier*
Raster Blaster *Electronic Arts*
Seafox *Broderbund*
Drik *Broderbund*
AE *Broderbund*
Serpentine *Broderbund*
Snack Attack *Datamost*
Gorgon *Sirius*

Zaxxon *Datamost*

Sneakers *Sirius*

Lode Runner *Broderbund*

Minit Man *Penguin Software*

Miner 2049er *MicroLab*

New arcade programs appear frequently, so check out the selection at your local computer or software store for the latest hits.

Computerized adventures derive in part from a popular board game called Dungeons and Dragons. This role-playing fantasy led first to a computer game called, simply, Adventure and then later to all sorts of derivative types. Most adventures are purely text-oriented and require high levels of problem-solving skills; others are graphics-oriented and less reliant upon text for planting hints, suggesting alternatives and so on. The most popular adventures include:

Zork I, II and II *Infocom*

Deadline *Infocom*

Starcross *Infocom*

Planetfall *Infocom*

Suspended *Infocom*

The Quest *Penguin Software*

Cyborg *Sentient Software*

Death in the Caribbean *MicroLab*

Wizardry *Sir-tech Software, Inc.*

Wizard and the Princess *Sierra On-Line, Inc.*

The Prisoner I, II *Peachtree/Eduware*

Another type of adventure or skill game plays more like an arcade game than the early adventure games (i.e., requires dexterity skills as well as problem solving). Programs in this arena include:

Aztec *Datamost*

Castle Wolfenstein *Muse*

Third on our list of entertainment categories is thinking games — games such as Chess, Checkers and Othello. Most of the games in this category derive from popular board games. Some derive from television game shows and feature anything from Concentration-like matching problems to word- and pattern-recognition games, with game-display boards. Still others use card games or casino games as their basis. Among the most popular of these thinking games are:

Odin *Odesta*

Chess 7.0 *Odesta*

Pro Poker *Quality Software*

Black Jack Strategy *Soft Images*
Word Challenge *Proximity*
Microgammon II *Softape*
Singles Night at Molly's *Soft Images*
Think Ahead *Power Up*
Broadsides *Strategic Simulations*
Pensate *Penguin Software*
Pool 1.5 *IDSI*
Crossword Magic *L & S Computerware*
Sargon III *Hayden*

The fourth category includes drawing programs, music-playing programs and other graphics-oriented programs. This category includes:

Complete Graphics System *Penguin Software*
KoalaPad + KoalaPainter *Koala*
PowerPad + Micro Illustrator* *Chalk Board*
Music Construction Set *Electronic Arts*
Picturewriter *Scarborough*
Songwriter *Scarborough*

includes hardware: touchpad device

Next in the entertainment categories is simulation programs. Here we find stock-market and general-investment games, among others. The more popular of these games include:

Millionaire *Blue Chip Software*
Flight Simulator *Sublogic*
Baron *Blue Chip Software*
Tycoon *Blue Chip Software*
Beat the Street *MEA Software*
Oil Barons *Epyx/Automated Simulations*
Free Enterprise *SRA Software*

Still other entertainment software exists. You'll find programs such as Astro-Scope, which makes astrological predictions; picture-show programs such as Ceemac; and even a few adult programs, including an "adult adventure" called Softporn from Sierra On-Line, Inc. Another popular category is the "make it yourself" game category. Such programs allow you to create your own games and include:

Pinball Construction Set *Electronic Arts*
The Arcade Machine *Broderbund*
Maze Craze *Data Trek*

Shopping for entertainment programs can be almost as much fun as using them. Most of the larger software stores (and computer dealers) have a wide range of current Apple entertainment software, and most will let you try a program before you buy. Browse through the store's offerings and ask a salesperson to give you a demo of the programs that catch your interest.

If you use your Apple a lot for entertainment purposes, you should consider purchasing the following accessories:

☐ color monitor
☐ joystick, game paddles or touchpad

Other software

Despite the extensive coverage we've given to Apple II software so far, we still haven't covered the entire spectrum of offerings. In the category of "other" software we've lumped several disparate, yet important, types of software you might want to consider. The primary subcategories include programming aids, utilities and communications software.

Programming aids run the range from programming languages, such as Apple Pascal, to advanced tools that make programming your computer (in Applesoft BASIC) easier. Some of the more useful of the programming-tools software packages include:

Bag of Tricks   *Quality Software*
DOS BOSS   *Beagle Brothers*
DOS Tool Kit   *Apple Computer*
Apple Mechanic   *Beagle Brothers*

Next on our miscellaneous list comes utility software. Utility software is what some refer to as "housekeeping" software — programs that keep your computer's diskettes and memory clean and organized. Here we have programs that are designed to do anything from diagnosing hardware problems to copying diskettes more quickly and efficiently than Apple's COPYA program. The utility class of programs includes:

XPS-Diagnostic II   *XPS*
Disk Organizer   *Sensible Software*
Disk Recovery   *Sensible Software*
Super Disk Copy III   *Sensible Software*
Disk Copy II   *Central Point Software*
Utility City   *Beagle Brothers*

The last of our miscellaneous software categories is one that is growing in popularity, that of communications software. Communications software, in conjunction with a modem, allows your Apple II to "talk" with and interchange information with other computers, Apple or otherwise. Such programs allow you to connect with so-called electronic bulletin boards, maintained by computer hobbyists for the dissemination of information about and for their computer, and to large "information utilities" such as CompuServe and The Source. These services offer everything from airline-flight scheduling and reservation entry, to multiplayer games, to the latest news and stock reports. As our nation becomes more and more electronically oriented, more and more of our transactions — banking, retail sales and information seeking — will fall into the domain of computer communications. The Apple II won't be left out of this coming revolution.

Among the communications programs for the Apple II are:

ASCII Express   *United Software Industries*

Data Capture 4.0   *Southeastern Software*

Dow Jones Connector   *Dow Jones Software*

Hayes Terminal Program   *Hayes Microcomputer*

Micro/Courier   *Microcom*

Transend 2   *Transend Corporation*

VisiTerm   *VisiCorp*

Softerm   *Softronics*

By now you should realize that the range of things that an Apple II can do is extraordinarily large and all-encompassing. An Apple II with appropriate software can handle almost any task that you could assign to a computer.

Already, well over thousands of commercial programs exist for the Apple, and that number grows daily. People use Apples for everything from keeping track of their winery's latest harvest to keeping track of their favorite sports team's game and player statistics. An Apple II has flown in the Space Shuttle, helping astronauts perform experiments, and Apples have shown up onstage with professional musicians. Obviously, we've been able to touch on only the most obvious and visible types of software currently available for the Apple.

If there's something you want to do with your Apple and we haven't listed an appropriate software program for that task here, consult with your local software store, read the Apple-related magazines for new product releases and consider purchasing one of the complete software listings published periodically in book form.

Chapter 5

ACCESSORIES FOR INSIDE THE APPLE

Have you ever looked inside an Apple II computer?

You see an impressive array of little black IC (integrated circuit) chips that form the brains of the computer; but, more important, you notice a row of empty slots across the back of the machine.

Those empty slots have made the Apple II one of the most popular computers of all time; they allow you to customize the Apple's electronics.

The eight slots in an Apple II and II Plus are labeled 0 through 7; the Apple IIe has slots labeled 1 through 7, plus an additional slot forward and to the left labeled "auxiliary slot." Some of the slots within an Apple have special purposes. The following table shows the standard assignments of certain slots.

SLOT #	APPLE II/II PLUS	APPLE IIe
0	RAM or ROM only	no slot
1	(printer, serial)*	(printer, serial)*
2	(serial, printer)*	(serial, printer)*
3	(80-column or communications)*	(communications)*
4	not assigned	not assigned
5	(2nd disk controller)*	(2nd disk controller)*

6	disk controller	disk controller
7	(video enhancements)*	(video enhancements)*
AUX	no slot	RAM and/or 80-column

(*Items in parentheses indicate optional equipment in order of preference. You can place other options in these slots.)

You're allowed a fair amount of flexibility in how you fill these slots. Apple alone offers a dozen or more possibilities. To simplify your task of understanding and selecting the right options, we'll deal with the options by functional categories. Before we go into these functional categories, however, you need a little more general understanding of what goes into the slots and why the various devices go there.

The Apple IIe comes as a basic computer. With the addition of a monitor or TV and the appropriate cable, you have a functioning computer. Such a computer is limited, however, since it has no practical method of permanently storing information (most Apple owners don't use the cassette interface because of its slowness in retrieving information) or turning out information in printed form.

To provide these additional functions, Apple designed its computer so that you can insert accessory electronics, usually referred to as "add-on" or "add-in" boards (or cards), into the eight expansion slots. Each add-on board usually performs one specific function, sometimes connecting to other devices, such as a disk drive or printer.

Almost all Apple IIe's are sold today in what is known as a "starter package." The starter package contains what Apple thinks are the bare essentials of a functional computer:

- ☐ Apple IIe computer
- ☐ Apple II monitor
- ☐ Apple Disk Drive II and add-on controller card
- ☐ 80-column display add-on card (sometimes)
- ☐ DOS 3.3

The Apple IIe starter package you buy today already has a disk-controller card in slot 6 and, possibly, an 80-column card inserted in the special slot in the IIe labeled "auxiliary."

Apple II and II Plus computers were sold in similar packages and usually came with a disk-controller card in slot 6 and, possibly, an extra 16K of RAM installed in slot 0. Thus, most Apple owners started out with six accessory slots that were empty.

Let's look at how you can fill those six slots.

Interface to the world

The term *interface*, in our parlance, means to connect — in the appropriate way — the Apple II to another device, such as a printer. Two major types of interface cards exist, parallel interface cards and serial interface cards, both named for the method by which they transfer information to and from the Apple.

Parallel interfaces send one character of information — eight bits (single units) of data — at a time, in other words, all eight bits of information in the character are sent in parallel to the receiving device, be it computer or printer. Serial interfaces send one of the eight bits at a time, sequentially, until all eight bits of a character have been sent. The differences between the two types, for the most part, are negligible as far as novice computer users are concerned. Most printer manufacturers favor parallel communications methods because of the lower cost of creating them; serial communications are appropriate when the distance between the computer and the device to which it is connected is long (greater than 20 feet).

If you are buying a printer, you'll need an interface card to go with it; otherwise, the Apple will have no way of communicating with the printer. First, select the printer you want; then note what type of interface it requires. That'll tell you what kind of interface card to purchase for your Apple. More often than not, printers are connected to an Apple through parallel interfaces, but it's best to make sure what kind of interface the printer you want uses before you buy an interface card.

Popular interface cards include:

Parallel Interface *Apple Computer*
Serial Interface *Apple Computer*
Pkaso *Interactive Structures*
Transcore *Quadram*
P/S Buffer Card *Prometheus*
Grappler+ *Orange Micro*

Most Apple software assumes that the printer interface card resides in slot 1. Some software programs allow you to modify this assumption. For the purposes of remaining as compatible with the rest of the world as possible, however, slot 1 is where your printer-interface card should reside.

A special type of interface card, called a modem card, is also available for the Apple. Modems are special serial-interface-like devices that translate computer information into signals that can travel via regular telephone cables to another computer. You can simply buy a modem and connect it to an Apple serial interface card, but you can also purchase an interface card that has a modem built into it. Such modem cards generally offer a wide range of features, including automatic dialing and answering, the ability to hang on to the phone connection you've made with another computer while you do something else with the computer and more. Among the most popular of these modem cards are:

Micromodem II *Hayes Microcomputer*
Modem II *Multi-Tech*
Multi-Modem II *Multi-Tech*
Networker *Zoom Telephonics*
Apple-Cat II, 212 *Novation*

Thanks for the memory

Another type of card that you can add to Apple computer is an additional memory card, either RAM (random-access, or changeable, memory) or ROM (read-only, or unchangeable, memory). This type of add-on card is most popular with Apple II and II Plus owners, because their computers offer less memory than the Apple IIe.

Apple II and II Plus owners can add 16K of RAM (and thus build their computer up to the memory size of the Apple IIe — 64K) by purchasing a RAM card and placing it in slot 0. Among the most popular of these cards are:

RAMCard *Microsoft*
16K Memory *Apple Computer*
AddRAM *ALS*
Macromem1 *Macrotech Computer Products*
RAMEX 16 *Omega Microware*

You can expand your Apple beyond 64K with several newer add-on boards. To make full use of these 32K, 64K and 128K add-on boards requires special software, sometimes supplied with the card, so be sure to ask what software is compatible with add-on cards before purchasing them. The 128K board is especially useful if you use VisiCalc and have large spreadsheets you need to manipulate. Here are some of the large memory add-on cards:

Legend 128K *Legend*
Multicore *Quadram*
RAMEX 128 *Omega Microware*
Flashcard *Synetix*
RAMDISK 128, 320 *Axlon*
Macromem3 *Macrotech Computer Products*

Apple IIe owners can expand their computer's memory from 64K to 128K by purchasing a special version of the 80-column card that goes in the auxiliary slot. Not all programs can make use of this extra memory, although, with the additional 64K in place, you can double the Apple's basic graphic resolution and add to the available colors that the Apple can display in high-resolution graphics. Some of the 80-column cards you can use for this purpose are:

64K 80-column card   *Apple Computer*
Vision128   *Action-Research Northwest*
192K Neptune   *Titan Technologies*
128K Memory Master   *Applied Engineering*

More character(s) for your Apple

Yet another type of add-on card is the video-display card. The Apple II normally displays up to 24 lines of 40 characters each. This display size is adequate for many purposes but is generally regarded as inadequate for business use of a computer, where displays of 24 lines of 80 characters are expected.

You can easily correct the Apple's display deficiency by purchasing an optional video-display card. All of the cards listed below go into slot 3, where the Apple II software checks to see if you have a special 80-column option. Apple II and II Plus owners have a wide range of cards to choose from, including:

VideoTerm   *Videx*
Sup'R'Term   *M & R Enterprises*
Smarterm II   *ALS*
Vision 80   *Vista*

In addition to the 24 × 80 display cards, you can even find a card for the Apple II that can display up to 40 lines of 132 characters each, almost a full written page of information:

UltraTerm   *Videx*

For the Apple IIe, you need a different kind of video-display card to expand the display to 24 lines of 80 characters each. You must plug the Apple IIe 80-column card into the auxiliary slot. (See the listing for add-on memory cards for additional cards that provide 80-column capability for the Apple IIe.)

Give your Apple a multiple personality

Apple computers come with a central processor (the heart of the computer — all information goes through this device) called the 6502 chip. Other systems use other processors, but the software that works with them cannot work with the 6502. If you want to use software developed for another processor, you have to purchase a special coprocessor card for your Apple.

For example, CP/M is a popular operating system that works only with 8080 and Z80 processors. We've already cited WordStar as being a professional, popular word-processing program that works only with CP/M. To use

WordStar on the Apple, you first have to purchase a processor card that uses a Z80 and a copy of CP/M. Many such cards exist, including:

SoftCard II/IIe *Microsoft*

z-Card II *ALS*

CP/M Card *ALS*

Z80 Plus *Applied Engineering*

Appli-card* *PCPI/MicroPro*

comes with WordStar

Purchasing a card with a Z80 processor and the CP/M operating system opens up a new world of software for your Apple, primarily in the business-application area. But that's not the only new world that you can investigate. Processor cards exist for the 6809 (processor used by the Radio Shack Color Computer), 68000 (processor of the Apple Lisa and Macintosh), 8088 (processor of the IBM Personal Computer) and others.

Each of these processor cards has its advantages and disadvantages, but we'd be remiss if we didn't point out that they are usually purchased either by hobbyists who just want to experiment with them or by people who have a specific need that only a certain add-on processor card can satisfy. For instance, people who own an IBM PC might want to get an 8088 processor card (the same processor as in the IBM) for their Apple so that they can develop programs for both computers simultaneously.

Other add-on processor cards for the Apple include:

Accelerator II (faster 6502) *Titan Technologies*

Stellation II (6809) *Stellation*

Saybrook (68000) *Analytical Engines*

PDQ II (68000) *Enhancement Tech*

QPAK-68 (68000) *Qwerty*

In the spring of 1984, Apple began supporting a special add-on called the Rana 8086/2, manufactured by Rana Systems. You use this unique device in place of the normal Apple disk drives. If you put an Apple II diskette into the drive and start the system, your Apple II acts like an Apple II. If you put an MS-DOS (the operating system used by the IBM PC and PC compatibles) diskette in the drive, a special processor inside the add-on drives is activated, and you have an IBM PC-work-alike computer. Up to 512K RAM and an advanced video-display processor are included in the Rana 8086/2. The drives hold up to 320K of information, in Apple or MS-DOS format. Included with the processor is the MS-DOS 2.0 operating system, Microsoft Graphics (GW) BASIC, Apple ProDos and DOS 3.3, and a special MS-DOS enhancement called Windows.

The Rana 8086/2 turns the Apple II into quite a different computer without sacrificing Apple II abilities.

Exotic add-ons for your Apple

We've just examined the most popular add-on cards for the Apple II, but we haven't begun to explore all the possibilities. Add-on cards are available for the Apple that you can use for:

- ☐ voice input/output or music synthesis (sound cards)
- ☐ time measurement (clock cards)
- ☐ high-quality color (RGB cards)
- ☐ programmers' aids (EPROM cards)
- ☐ scientific and lab use (monitoring/sensing cards)
- ☐ testing (oscilloscope cards)
- ☐ mass storage (hard-disk-controller cards)
- ☐ experimentation (wire-wrap, prototyping cards)

Some of these exotica are:

Music Card *Mountain Hardware*

Super Music Synthesizer *Applied Engineering*

Mockingboard *Sweet Micro Systems*

Echo Speech Synthesizer *Sweet Micro Systems*

Ditherizer II *Computer Station*

Thunderclock+ *Thunderware*

Voice Input Module *The Voice Connection*

Timemaster *Applied Engineering*

We're not done examining Apple accessories. The next chapter looks at the things you can add to the outside of the Apple II.

Chapter 6

THE WORLD OUTSIDE THE APPLE

Now that we've looked at what can go inside the various versions of the Apple II computer to customize its performance, it's time to look at what you can connect externally to the Apple.

Although the Apple II case contains the basic computer, you need a few extra devices to create a complete computer system. You'll want a monitor of some sort so that you can see what the Apple is doing, a disk drive or two to store important information permanently, perhaps a printer to create paper output from your computer and possibly some other types of equipment, as well.

Monitors

First on your acquisition list should be a monitor for the Apple. You can use any one of four basic types of monitors with the Apple:

☐ monochrome (e.g., black-and-white, black-and-green) monitor
☐ color monitor
☐ RGB color monitor
☐ television set

Of these options, the most tempting is the television set; after all, most homes have at least one. To use a television set with the Apple, you must purchase a special option called an RF modulator. The RF modulator takes the Apple's regular video-display signal and converts it into the type of signal television sets usually receive from an antenna.

There are several problems in using an RF modulator connected to a television set. First, a television set cannot resolve a picture as well through an antenna connection as it can if it is directly connected to the display circuitry (as is the case with monitors — a monitor is basically a television without a station tuner or antenna section). Second, since the RF modulator is actually performing the task of a television station (outputting a signal to an antenna), it tends to broadcast the Apple's display indiscriminately to any nearby antenna, even if it isn't directly connected to the RF modulator.

Most RF modulators send their signals on either channel 3 or 4; some older modulators used channel 33. To use a modulator, first connect it to the computer, then connect the modulator to your television and tune in the appropriate channel. You may have to do some experimenting with the channel tuning, contrast, brightness, focus and color settings of the television in order to get the best picture.

Although televisions are the lowest-cost option (because you usually use an already purchased TV), they are also the lowest-quality option. You can expect to pay $50 to $100 for a modulator. One caution: You shouldn't use television sets with 80-column cards in the Apple; the 80-column cards just put out too much information for the television to resolve, and the result is a blurry, fuzzy, unreadable display.

Apple provides a low-cost monochrome monitor in most of the starter specials a dealer may offer you. Monochrome monitors come in a variety of sizes, styles and colors. The most popular monochrome monitors show either white characters on a black background, or green characters on either a black or dark-green background (sometimes called a "green screen"). Another alternative features amber characters on a black background. The green and amber options are popular because they reduce contrast without reducing readability, meaning that you can stare longer at the display without experiencing eye strain. Monochrome monitors are especially good in conjunction with 80-column display cards.

Monochrome monitors hook up directly to the Apple II's video-output jack. Make sure you get the right cable for the monitor, because different manufacturers use different types of connectors.

A good-quality monochrome monitor costs from $100 to more than $200. Among the most popular monochrome monitors are:

Monitor II   *Apple Computer*
Monitor III   *Apple Computer*
ZVM 121   *Heath/Zenith*
300G, 300A   *Amdek*

Unfortunately, monochrome monitors don't show off one of the Apple II's niftier features: color-graphic displays. If color display is important to you, two options for high-quality color display are available.

The first option is simply a standard color monitor. Such monitors are more costly than their monochrome cousins, but you can generally purchase one for about the cost of a high-quality television set. Again, composite color monitors attach directly to the Apple II's video output.

A disadvantage of using composite color monitors is that they, like color televisions, are not normally capable of totally resolving the output of an 80-column display. Some people purchase both a monochrome and color monitor and connect both to their Apple so that they can then have the best of both worlds.

One of the most popular color monitors is the Amdek Color I, which comes from Amdek.

The last display option is also the costliest: RGB color monitors. An RGB monitor is a special breed of display designed for high-resolution, high-quality output. On the Apple II, you'll also need an RGB interface card (usually sold with the monitor) that plugs into slot 7.

RGB monitors are costly (going for $500 and up), but they feature finely detailed displays that are capable of resolving the output of an 80-column card. Some RGB interface cards allow you to pick a background and text color to replace the Apple's normal black-and-white text output. The most popular RGB monitors are:

Quadchrome   *Quadram*
RGB-I, RGB-III   *Taxan*
Color II   *Amdek*
HX-12   *Princeton Graphics*

Disk drives

You'll also want to consider getting one or more disk drives for your Apple II. The Apple starter kits sold by most dealers include a single disk drive and the interface card necessary to control it. Undoubtedly, you'll find that you'll soon need more than a single disk drive.

Originally, Apple users stored information on cassette tapes. Since the disk drive appeared in 1979, more than 98% of Apple II users switched from tape storage to disk storage. Almost no software is now available on tape, and virtually all Apple II users ignore the cassette-tape abilities of the computer, because working with tapes is so cumbersome and time-consuming compared to working with disks.

The Apple disk drives use standard, 5¼-inch floppy diskettes, storing about 143,000 characters of information on each diskette. You can purchase diskettes for as little as $3 each, so a disk drive provides a low-cost method of permanently storing a lot of information. Most serious Apple II users end up with 50 to 100 diskettes. Also, you should keep in mind that almost all Apple II software of any consequence is distributed on diskette.

Apple sells its own floppy-disk drive, called the Disk II. The first drive you purchase comes with a disk-controller card that plugs into slot 6 inside the Apple and a cable to connect that card and the actual disk drive. The second drive you purchase does not require the controller card (and is thus less expensive). Its cable plugs into the card supplied with the first drive.

You'll find that a two-drive Apple system is preferable over a one-drive system, as it makes copying faster and more efficient, aids in keeping program diskettes separate from data diskettes and makes twice as much information available at one time, without requiring you to change diskettes. Most business software requires two drives. You can add more than two drives to an Apple by using additional controller cards; this practice, however, can prove quite cumbersome.

Other companies also make drives for the Apple II. Unfortunately, not all drives are created alike. The important technical specifications of the Apple Disk II are:

- □ 35 tracks of information
- □ single-sided drive
- □ capable of half-tracking (in between actual tracks)
- □ stores 143K per diskette
- □ Apple recording method (called GCR — stands for Group Coded Recording)
- □ 256 bytes per sector; 16 sectors per track
- □ 300 revolutions per minute

The specifications of drives available from other firms vary considerably. A few mimic the Apple II characteristics exactly. Others offer 40 tracks or double-sided storage, or don't allow half-tracking. Let's examine what these variations mean.

If a drive has 40 tracks or double-sided abilities, you may not be able to use these additional features with standard Apple DOS 3.3. The manufacturer must provide an alternative DOS (or a program that modifies your existing DOS). You probably won't be able to interchange diskettes made with a nonstandard drive with your friends who have Apple drives. You may need to purchase a different disk controller along with the drive in order to use it. Many copy-protected programs will not work correctly with these drives.

But being nonstandard isn't all bad. Usually, you get much more data storage space with these drives — as much as 400K, three times what Apple offers. In addition, you'll probably find that these alternative drives are faster and quieter than Apple's. Some are even less expensive.

Half-tracking capabilities allow the Apple Disk II to read information that is slightly offset from its normal position; half-tracking is a feature often found in copy-protected software (most notably games). If a drive you purchase doesn't have half-tracking, it is likely that most copy-protected software will not work with that drive.

In short, don't expect a disk drive from another manufacturer to be exactly the same as Apple's. Make sure that the seller guarantees (in writing) that the alternative drive's specifications match Apple's. Find out about the alternative drive's specifications before you purchase it (try out the software you anticipate buying).

Among the most popular add-on drives for the Apple are:

C111, C112 *Concorde Peripheral*
A2, A82 *Micro-Sci*
Elite One, Two, Three *Rana Systems*
Micro Drive *Titan Data Systems*

A second type of disk drive for the Apple II is called a hard- or fixed-disk drive, so named because it stores information on a hard, fixed-in-place, coated metal platter instead of on a floppy diskette. The advantages of hard-disk drives are that they are fast, store enormous amounts of information (as much as 200 times what an Apple diskette normally stores) and allow file sizes larger than an Apple diskette with patches to DOS, and some can be shared by several Apples. The disadvantages are that they are expensive (generally, you'll pay more than $1500 for a complete unit) and cannot run all Apple software.

Furthermore, it is not convenient to back up (archive) important information stored on them. A hard-disk drive is almost a necessity for companies that need to share information (as through a computer network) or anyone who constantly uses large files (e.g., long name-and-address lists or other data bases that will quickly eat up disk space).

Hard-disk drives for the Apple are available from several companies, including:

Corvus (5,10 or 20 megabytes, capable of networking)
Mountain Computer (5, 10, 15 or 20 megabytes)
Corona Data Systems (Starfire 5, Starfire 10)

In addition, Apple has announced a hard-disk option for the Apple II called the ProFile. This add-on drive stores up to 5 megabytes of data and operates faster than the floppy-disk drives do.

Printers and plotters

Another add-on most Apple users purchase is some sort of printer.

A printer is a device that takes information from a computer and prints it out as copy on a page. It would take a whole book to describe the differences among printers and how to make an intelligent choice from all the possibilities. We'll try to present a summary of your choices through the use of several simple tables, which follow.

The first choice you must make is the type of printer to buy. By *type*, we mean the method by which the printer creates copy. Here's a quick summary of the differences:

TYPE	COST	QUALITY	GRAPHICS	REMARKS
dot matrix	low-medium	low-medium	yes (option)	quick, loud, standard interface card
thermal	low	low	yes	quiet, special interface card
letter quality	medium-high	high	limited	loud, standard interface card, special software
typewriter	medium	medium	no	slow, loud, special interface card
ink jet	medium-high	high	yes	quick, quiet, standard interface card, special software

Dot-matrix printers create their output by hammering a group of small pins against the ribbon, whose ink is transferred to the paper. If there are enough pins and they are grouped together close enough, printer quality can be quite good. Thermal printers use special paper and create copy by selectively heating portions of the paper where characters are to appear. When the paper cools, you see the characters

Letter-quality printers work much like typewriters. They strike a character on a printhead or ball against the ribbon to transfer the image. Characters are fully formed and of high quality. Letter-quality printers generally cost more than typewriters because the printers are designed for quick, constant use. Not all typewriters can work with a computer — they require a separate interface box outside the typewriter. Most typewriters used as printers are slower and less reliable than dedicated letter-quality printers. They make up for decreased speed and reliability by being less expensive.

Ink-jet printers are the newest technology. They work by spraying ink on the paper to create copy. They are quiet and fairly fast and produce moderate- to high-quality copy.

A large majority of Apple users purchase dot-matrix printers that are capable of graphics printing. The cost of such printers is low, and, if you shop carefully, you can generally find a printer that achieves decent printer quality, even for business correspondence, where you want your letters to "look professional."

Even among examples of one type of printer, the features that are available range from virtually none to dozens of useful and not-so-useful functions. Starting on the following page is a table to help you understand the various features that are available.

FEATURE	COST	USEFUL ON APPLE	REMARKS
friction-feed	—	yes	uses regular paper
tractor-feed	low	yes	uses continuous paper
print speed	—	—	the higher the better
alternate fonts	low	yes	look for correspondence-quality fonts
132-column print	low	yes	needed for some business applications
graphics	low-medium	yes	some offer color; needs special software
proportional spacing	medium	questionable	quasi-typesetting look
logic-seeking	low-medium	—	prints faster if present
bidirectional	low	—	prints faster if present
interface type	—	parallel best	serial second best

Of these features, most Apple owners opt for graphics, tractor- and friction-feed and a parallel-interface type. The most popular printers for use with the Apple include:

Imagewriter   *Apple*
Gemini-10x   *Star-Micronics*
630   *Diablo*
FX-80, RX-80, MX-80   *Epson*
Microline 92, 93, 84   *Okidata*
Gorilla/Banana   *Leading Edge Products*

Be forewarned that you can easily spend more on a printer than you did on your Apple II. Printer prices range from a little over $200 to as much as $3000.

A plotter is a special type of printing device that actually draws on the paper, sometimes in more than one color. Advanced graphics programs allow the use of a plotter instead of a printer. In general, a plotter creates graphs faster, using straight lines instead of dots, and with slightly better detail than most graphic printers. Popular plotters for the Apple include:

Color Plotter   *Apple Computer*
HP7470A   *Hewlett-Packard*
Strobe   *Strobe*
Sweet-P   *Enter*
Amplot-II   *Amdek*

Modems

In the software section, we mentioned that communications are a popular Apple II function. To have your computer communicate with another computer, you normally need a special piece of hardware called a modem (it stands for modulator demodulator — the name comes from the technique that performs the communication).

Modems allow you to connect your Apple II to your telephone line and then use the telephone line to connect your Apple II electronically to another computer — either another Apple, another personal computer (like the IBM PC) or a larger computer such as an IBM mainframe. For example, Dow Jones offers a large-computer investment data base that you can call up with your Apple II.

When you've connected it, you can use your modem-equipped Apple to find out about stock prices, news about companies whose stock you're interested in and many other investment-related activities. Some investment-software programs allow you to update your portfolio's values automatically while your computer is connected to Dow Jones.

Other information utilities available via modem include CompuServe, The Source and Knowledge Index. Each of these information utilities offers a wide variety of services — everything from programming to airline schedules to stock-market information to complex data-base queries in a variety of industries and markets.

Being connected to Knowledge Index via modem is a lot like having a university library available via phone. CompuServe and The Source both offer entertainment functions, as well, with everything from movie reviews to "chatting" with others connected to the computer.

Special-interest functions, including Apple II and III interest groups, are available through The Source and CompuServe.

All commercial services charge a start-up fee; thereafter, they charge by the hour or data base used. The larger services have local telephone access in most areas of the continental U.S., so you won't end up with high long-distance phone bills.

Noncommercial (free) bulletin boards also exist across the country. They're called bulletin boards because most of them operate primarily as message services. Some of these are Apple-oriented; others are more general in nature. Your local computer dealer might be able to direct you to several local bulletin boards.

Now that you know what to use it for, let's look at the modem itself. Modems communicate at either 300 or 1200 baud (bits per second; that translates to about 30 or 120 characters per second). The most common speed is 300 baud — 1200 baud is not as widely used yet, and you cannot use it reliably in some parts of the country because of noise on the telephone lines. Find out about the lines in your area.

Two types of modems are available for the Apple: internal and external. An internal modem consists of a card that fits inside the Apple; you simply plug your modular phone jack into the interface card instead of the phone. External modems require that you have a serial interface card inside your Apple. You connect a cable from the serial interface to the modem, then plug your modular phone jack into the modem instead of your phone. Several of these devices are available. Among popular external modems for the Apple card are:

Apple Modem   *Apple*
Smartmodem 300   *Hayes Microcomputer*
Smartmodem 1200   *Hayes Microcomputer*
Cat, D-Cat, J-Cat, Smart-Cat   *Novation*
Pro-modem 1200   *Prometheus*

Drawing devices

The color graphics on the Apple II have attracted a great deal of attention to the activity of drawing with a computer, both for fun and for specific serious applications, such as executive presentations (in place of slides) or drafting. In response to this attention, several types of drawing devices have cropped up.

Apple was the first company to offer a drawing device for the Apple II; it's called the Apple Graphics Tablet. The Graphics Tablet consists of a flat, board-like device about 16 inches square. A special interface card that comes with the Graphics Tablet goes inside the computer in one of the slots. Connected to it is a special pen, which you use to draw on the board. A program translates the location of pen pressure on the board into a location on the screen.

You can also point the pen at special locations on the board to change the color or method you're currently drawing with. You can choose other options such as saving your picture to a diskette. Tablets other than Apple's exist for the Apple II, but they are not necessarily always widely available.

A less expensive alternative to the Graphics Tablet is a light pen. Instead of pointing this device at a special board, you point the pen at the Apple II's screen display. Thus, there is a direct correspondence between your actions (moving the pen) and the display. The light pen, like the Graphics Tablet, may come with a special interface card, or, in some cases, it may simply plug into the Apple's game I/O (input/output) plug. One of the most popular light pens for the Apple II is the Gibson light pen (LPS II).

Even less expensive, yet still providing exceptional drawing capabilities, is a touchpad, such as the KoalaPad. The touchpad plugs into the Apple's game I/O plug. You draw with it by moving your finger or a supplied special pencil around on the touchpad. The Koala touchpad comes with special drawing software and is compact enough to store on top of one of the disk drives.

A touch tablet for the Apple II that is similar to the KoalaPad is the PowerPad from Chalk Board, Inc., which features a larger working area and lower price than the KoalaPad. A more expensive drawing tablet similar to the Apple Graphics Tablet is available from Houston Instrument and is excellent where precise coordinate location is a must.

A less expensive method of drawing with an Apple II is to use game joysticks or paddles and to purchase software that allows you to draw with them. This is also the least precise method of drawing using the Apple; you should only consider using it for recreational purposes. Many graphics programs allow you to use the cursor keys on the Apple keyboard for input; these programs are excellent when you require pixel-by-pixel (graphic dot by graphic dot) manipulation.

The latest drawing device available for the Apple is the AppleMouse II. This device fits easily in your palm. You slide it over a flat surface, such as your desk, to move the drawing pointer on your screen. This device is acceptable for drawing freehand, but not for tracing, as you can't see the surface beneath your hand and the mouse. As this book went to press, Apple had demonstrated, but not yet released, its Mouse. By the time you read this, both the Mouse and its accompanying program, MousePaint, should be available.

Sound

The basic Apple II is capable of making a wide range of sounds; but the quality of the sound is not equal to that of professional instruments.

You can turn your Apple into a professional-sounding instrument in any of several ways, however. First, you can purchase a music-synthesis interface card or adapter. Most of these come with software that allows you to create new music and play the music back through your stereo system, which is connected to the interface card with a cable. Popular music cards include those manufactured by:

ALF Products
Mountain Hardware
Sweet Micro Systems

Some professional musicians — Neil Young, Herbie Hancock and Todd Rundgren, for example — use Apple II computers in their acts. They use one of three professional synthesizer options for the Apple:

Simply Music   *Syntauri*
alphaSyntauri   *Syntauri*
Soundchaser   *Passport Designs*

Each of these synthesizers comes with add-on interface cards and a piano-like keyboard. The range of sounds these systems are capable of producing is quite impressive, especially considering that the synthesizers add only $1000-$2000 to the Apple II's cost.

Both companies provide software (some of it optional) to do everything from automatically playing the music you create to printing out the notated music via graphics printer. You can also use multiple voices and manipulate sounds electronically.

Keyboards

The original Apple IIs (and II Plus's) keyboard was not particularly well suited to the needs of touch-typists or serious business users of the computer. No lowercase letters were available without internal modification, keys did not repeat even if you held them down (you had to press a special REPT key to do this), some standard computer symbols were missing and had to be entered in an unusual manner and special-function keys were lacking.

The Apple IIe keyboard eliminated some, but did not get rid of all these faults. Add-on keyboards replace or work in conjunction with the Apple II's keyboard.

Numeric keypads, for example, provide you with a convenient way to enter numbers into the Apple. Some of the popular numeric keypads or special-function keyboards are:

Numeric keypad   *Apple Computer*

Tender   *Track House*

Keywiz VIP   *Creative Computer*

Full, detachable keyboards are also available. These keyboards replace the Apple II keyboard, usually offering a full set of keys and symbols. They also allow you to enter "shorthand" versions of names or functions by pressing a single key (pressing the Delete Word key instead of holding down the Control key and pressing another key).

Such keyboards are available from:

EPS keyboard   *Executive Peripheral*

Keytec   *Keytec*

Lowercase enhancements

You can add lowercase characters and other enhancements to older Apples by purchasing the appropriate hardware. (This hardware can require soldering or moderate electronics skills; your attachment of it voids the warranty on the Apple.) These include:

Enhancer II   *Videx*

Lowercase Plus   *Lazer Systems*

Game equipment

Last on our list of equipment to consider for your Apple II comes game equipment. We refer to joysticks, game paddles or other devices used primarily for making the playing of games more convenient than is possible when you use the keyboard.

Apple used to provide a set of game paddles with the Apple II and II Plus. A set of game paddles consists of two separate controllers, each with a single button and a knob that turns. Turning the knob controls one function within a game, such as moving a spaceship back and forth across the bottom of the screen. Paddles are handy for most shoot-'em-up games. Popular paddles are made by Apple and Hayes.

Joysticks are more popular than paddles; especially now that Apple games have become more complex, you have more directions or things to control than a single paddle can handle. Joysticks come in a variety of types, with differences in the position of the firing button(s), the method in which the joystick moves and the size of the mechanism. Look for one that is comfortable when you hold it in your hand.

Most serious game players prefer joysticks that self-center (that is, return to the center of the screen if you let go of the handle). Joysticks available for the Apple include:

Apple Joystick   *Apple*
Mach III   *Hayes*
Premium Joystick   *KRAFT*
Starfighter   *SUNCOM*

The game I/O plug on the Apple II and II Plus is inside the computer and consists of an IC socket; the Apple IIe also has an external connector for game I/O. If you have a IIe, you should look for paddles or joysticks that use the external connector, because it is sturdier and more convenient to use than the internal one.

Other

One other item of external hardware is the cooling fan. If you've added a significant number of goodies to your Apple, it will get hot inside when you run it for a while. If it gets too hot, the computer may work erratically or not at all. Heat also tends to decrease the life of the computer's components. So a cooling fan is a fairly important consideration for an Apple owner. As a result of this situation, external fans are popular add-ons for Apple users. Some of the fans available include:

Cool+Time   *Tencal*
System Saver   *Kensington Microware*

We certainly haven't covered all the hardware options available for the Apple II, only the most popular ones. Check out the advertisements in Apple-oriented magazines to find out what other types of equipment you can add to your Apple.

Section Three

Keeping Your Apple Up

How do you keep your Apple healthy and happy? What do you do if something goes wrong? Chapter 7 will give you the answers.

In addition to information about maintenance, this section provides, in Chapter 8, additional sources of information on Apple computers.

Maintenance: Sources of Information
Other Sources of Information about the Apple

MAINTENANCE: SOURCES OF INFORMATION

Once you have an Apple, you'll want to keep it healthy.

The Apple II comes with a 90-day warranty that covers parts and labor. Apple's dealer-servicing policy works on a "swap" basis: if your Apple has a bad part, the dealer immediately swaps that part with a reconditioned one, returns your Apple to you and returns the defective part to Apple for replacement or reconditioning. That means that, with normal Apple servicing, you shouldn't be without your machine for too long (usually a day or two, at most dealers).

You can extend the basic warranty by purchasing an optional Extended Warranty Plan from your Apple dealer, sometimes called Apple Care. This moderately priced policy extends the basic warranty for 12 months. If your Apple is beyond the original warranty period when you enroll in the Extended Warranty Plan, the dealer must first check out the machine (usually for about $50) to make sure it has no hidden defects that might later need attention.

Apple requires dealers to buy a basic parts kit and a set of diagnostic software and manuals. Therefore, all Apple dealers are usually well equipped to isolate computer maladies quickly. If you're curious or want to do initial checks yourself, you can buy several software programs that run through a series of quick checks on your computer (memory test, diskette test and so on). These programs usually cost less than $100. You can purchase them from most dealers or software stores.

The part that most often fails on an Apple II is the on/off switch. Unfortunately, dealers cannot simply replace the switch. Instead, they must replace the entire power supply, since the power switch is built into this module. If your power switch fails when your machine is out of warranty, you are not looking at a $2 part and hour's labor, but at a much more expensive part, plus labor. If you use your Apple constantly or for business purposes, it makes sense to purchase the Extended Warranty Plan.

Other parts of the Apple that develop problems more often than the rest of the computer are the keyboard and the disk drives. The electronics within the Apple rarely develop problems under normal use. Theoretically, the nonmechanical parts within an Apple II should last at least ten years and possibly throughout your lifetime.

You can do a few things to extend the life of your computer. Because you know which parts are most likely to develop problems, you should concentrate your efforts on these few things:

Leave your power switch in the "on" position and use a power strip or external power switch to turn the computer on and off.

Don't bang on the keys, and keep the keyboard clean. Don't drop liquids or objects into the keyboard. Vacuum the keyboard periodically if it gets dusty or dirty. Keep animals off the keyboard!

Don't force diskettes into the drive — instead, slide them in gently. Use premium-grade diskettes instead of low-cost specials, as the premium grades tend to be less abrasive to the disk-drive heads. Use a disk-head-cleaning kit on each drive once every six months or so. Keep the drive doors closed when they're not in use. Put a junk diskette in the drive if you have to move or transport it (to keep the head from coming into hard contact with the pressure pad if it's jolted). Never remove a cable or interface card while the power is on. Unplug the Apple before removing or reconnecting an item.

Normal maintenance of your Apple is simple and fast. Keep the case closed and clean. Use a mild, liquid detergent to clean the case, but do not spray or pour it on the case (wet a rag with the detergent and use that). Keep your diskettes in a closed, protective container. Do not move the Apple around. If you must move it, open it up (with the power off) and make sure no cards or connections have come loose.

Once a month, open up the lid of the case and gently push down on all socketed IC chips (have your dealer show you how to do this). If you move your Apple a lot or it experiences vast temperature changes, the chips tend to creep out of their sockets, reducing their electrical contact area.

Once a year, open up the lid to the Apple case and gently remove each interface card. Use a new pencil eraser and rub it across the contacts in the tongue of the interface card to clean them (don't do it over the open Apple!). Replace each card in its original position.

If your dealer doesn't offer to show you how everything connects, ask him to. Make sure you have a list of where each card and cable attaches, just in case you ever need to take the cards or cables off the computer and put them back later. Be extremely gentle with cables, especially those that plug into the game I/O plug, as you can break off the connections by trying to force a connection or by hastily grabbing the cable and yanking at it to remove it.

What to do when the computer won't work

Rarely, your Apple may refuse to function correctly or even to turn on. Follow this list of procedures:

1. Check to make sure the Apple and monitor are plugged in.
2. Check the contrast and brightness turners on the monitor. You could be receiving the display, but not be able to see it because one of the knobs has been accidentally misadjusted.
3. Check to see that all cables are still connected in their usual fashion.
4. Check to make sure you are using the right diskette.
5. Leave the computer off for a few minutes, and try again.
6. Check the requirements of the software you are using to make sure that you have all the necessary hardware.
7. Call your dealer and describe your problem.

Some of the things on the list seem obvious, but you'd be surprised at how often they identify the cause of the problem. The Apple is such a reliable computer that, more often than not, any problem is caused by human, not computer, error.

One last caution: If you ever see smoke billowing from your Apple, or see sparks coming from your computer, turn if off immediately and do not attempt to use the computer again until your dealer has thoroughly checked it out. Failure to do so can result in catastrophic damage to the computer, or worse yet, electrical shock or fire.

Chapter 8

OTHER SOURCES OF INFORMATION ABOUT THE APPLE

This book is a buyers' and users' guide. We've given you a general idea of what is available for the Apple and, in Part II, we provide in-depth reviews of popular software and hardware options. Even so, there is more to learn about the Apple, so here are some of the ways you can learn more.

Books

First on our list of other sources comes books about the Apple. One of the best-selling books about the Apple is:

The Apple II User's Guide, Poole, et al. (Osborne/McGraw-Hill, 1983)

This book covers much the same information as do the Apple manuals, but does so in a more integrated, organized and compact fashion. Other general books about the Apple include:

Kids and the Apple, Carlson (Datamost, 1981)
The Apple Connection, Coffron (Sybex, 1982)
The Creative Apple, Pelczarski and Tate (Creative Computing Press, 1983)
The Apple User's Encyclopedia, Phillips, et al. (The Book Company, 1984)
Primer for the Apple II/IIe, Pirisino (Brady, 1983)
Understanding the Apple II, Sather (Quality Software, 1983)
Apple Software 1984, Wells et al. (The Book Company, 1983)

Books on how to program the Apple abound. To learn about programming the Apple in BASIC, take a look at the list of books that follows.

Programming the Apple: A Structured Approach, Campbell and Zimmerman (Brady, 1982)

Programming Tips and Techniques for the Apple II/IIe, Campbell (Brady, 1984)

Basic Apple BASIC, Coan (Hayden, 1982)

BASIC for the Apple II: Programming and Applications, Goldstein (Brady, 1982)

Applesoft BASIC Made Easy, Hafler (Brady, 1983)

Intermediate-Level Apple II Handbook, Heiserman (Howard Sams, 1983)

Polishing Your Apple, Honig (Howard Sams, 1982)

I Speak BASIC to My Apple, Jones (Hayden, 1982)

BASIC Exercises for the Apple, Lamoitier (Sybex, 1982)

Apple Files, Miller (Reward Books, 1982)

Apple BASIC for Business, Parker and Stewart (Reston, 1984)

Some Common BASIC Programs, Poole (Osborne/McGraw-Hill, 1979)

Business Applications for the Apple II/IIe, Zimmerman et al. (Brady, 1984)

or in other languages, such as Pascal or Logo:

Apple Logo: Activities for Exploring Turtle Graphics, Bailey (Brady, 1984)

UCSD Pascal for the Apple II/IIe, Day (Brady, 1984)

Pascal Programming for the Apple, Lewis (Reward Books, 1981)

Apple Pascal, a Hands-on Approach, Luehrmann and Peckham (McGraw-Hill, 1982)

Turtlesteps: An Introduction to Apple Logo, Sharp (Brady, 1984)

or even in assembly language:

Using 6502 Assembly Language, Hyde (Datamost, 1981)

Apple Machine Language, Inman and Inman (Reward Books, 1983)

Graphically Speaking, Pelczarski (Softalk Publishing, 1984)

Apple Graphics and Arcade Game Design, Stanton (The Book Company, 1982)

Assembly Lines, Wagner (Softalk Publishing, 1982)

Additional books that relate to the Apple are:

The VisiCalc Book, Beil (Reston, 1984)

The Custom Apple, Hofacker and Floegel (IJG, 1982)

Enhancing Your Apple II, Lancaster (Howard Sams, 1984)

Hundreds of books on the Apple II already exist, with more being published every day. If you don't want to be overwhelmed when you go looking for a book on the Apple, it is a good idea to know the type of book you want.

Magazines and users' groups

Apple-oriented magazines also provide lots of information about the Apple II computer. Among the most popular Apple magazines are:

InCider
A+
Nibble
Softalk (Apple)
Call-A.P.P.L.E.
Peelings
Apple Orchard

InCider, Nibble, Apple Orchard and *Call-A.P.P.L.E.* tend to have a lot of programming examples and articles that probe the inner reaches of the machine. *A+, Peelings* and *Softalk* provide more reviews and overviews. Other magazines that often run articles of interest to Apple owners include:

InfoWorld
Popular Computing
Personal Computing
Personal Software

Yet another source of information about the Apple is local users' groups. Users' groups get together, usually once a month. The members of these groups tend to be enthusiastic and knowledgeable, and you're likely to pick up all kinds of helpful hints.

Most users' groups have newsletters or magazines, offer free software to members and have special-interest groups for those interested only in certain uses of the Apple. Because of the large numbers of Apple computers, you should be able to find a users' group near where you live. Your local Apple dealer should know of the local users' group. If not, write to the International Apple CORE, which is located at 908 George Street, Santa Clara, California 95050.

That completes our overview of the Apple II family. There's a lot of information in the overview, so you may want to go back over all or parts of it, or you may want to go right on to Part 2 of this guide, the product reviews.

Part 2

REVIEWS

InfoWorld *instituted its product-review process at the magazine's birth in early 1980. Since then,* InfoWorld *software and hardware reviews have gained a reputation as accurate, objective evaluations of microcomputer products. Products are evaluated by independent reviewers, who work closely with* InfoWorld. *A list of reviewers who wrote the product evaluations in this book follows these guidelines. To permit easy comparison of products, all product reviews follow a similar format. The format is based on a Report Card, which we print with each review.*

To help you understand our evaluation process, we're summarizing the criteria our reviewers use to evaluate products. We apply a different set of guidelines to software and hardware products, but our overall goal is to enable our readers to make informed decisions about buying hardware and software products.

The products reviewed in this book represent a sampling of the myriad products available for the Apple.

Software-review guidelines

In reviewing software products, our reviewers consider the following areas:

Features.   *Reviewers describe what the product does and how it does it. They consider factual information about the product, then provide the information readers need to decide whether the product is appropriate to the task they have in mind.*

Performance.   *Here, reviewers assess how well a product performs its intended task. They determine who the intended user of the product is, what his or her needs are and how well the products fulfills those needs. Reviewers also measure the manufacturer's claims for the product against its actual performance. A product should perform its intended tasks in a reasonable amount of time, and reviewers assess the product's relative speed.*

Ease of use.   *Ease of use comprises three categories: ease of installation, ease of learning and ease of operation.*

Ease of installation deals with the degree of difficulty a user will encounter setting up a program for the first time.

Ease of learning examines the degree of difficulty inexperienced users of the program will encounter when they employ the product.

Ease of operation explores the general level of complexity involved in continued use of the product.

Reviewers consider these three categories to give an overall rating to the product in the Ease of Use category.

Error handling. *Any good program should be able to routinely handle incorrect input and other mistakes without damaging data or causing undue difficulty. Anytime a user tries to make an irrevocable change, for example, the program should ask for confirmation of the change. In addition, the program should be set up to prevent or minimize loss of data in the event of a power failure or the failure of some piece of hardware Reviewers assess how well the program prevents and deals with errors.*

Documentation. *Documentation for computer products has a reputation for being awful. Reviewers rate documentation based on its conciseness, clarity and readability. The primary consideration of a product manual's usefulness is whether it is written so that anyone can understand it. If appropriate, reviewers also evaluate the existence and effectiveness of a product's "on-line" documentation (information the program provides on the computer's screen). In any case, if you have to be a technician to comprehend the document, its value is minimal.*

Support. *Although this area does not receive a grade, reviewers note in the review what customers can expect for support from the company.*

You'll notice that we have grouped the products reviewed into general categories. Some products may appropriately fit into other categories, but we've tried to put each product into its most relevant area.

Hardware-review guidelines

In reviewing peripherals, our reviewers consider the following areas:

Features. *Same as software.*

Setup. *Some equipment is more difficult than other equipment to set up. In any case, reviewers discuss what users have to do to set the product up for use. They evaluate the clarity of setup instructions and tell readers whether all the components for setup are present.*

Ease of use. *In this category, reviewers evaluate two categories of use. Are the controls on the product easy to learn and use? Is the product easy to use in sustained operation?*

Performance. *This is the primary evaluation category reviewers consider. Reviewers perform standard measurements of products (printer speed tests, for example), and they evaluate how well the product performs its intended use in the following categories:*

> *Abuse testing — what happens, for example, if you leave the product on for 48 straight hours?*
>
> *Environment testing — how well does the product work in its intended environment?*
>
> *Specification testing — if a manufacturer claims its printer produces 100 characters per second, does the printer really work this fast?*
>
> *Overall usefulness — does the product perform well continuously?*

Documentation. *Same as software.*

Serviceability. *Hardware will not function correctly forever. Reviewers assess the "after-the-sale support system" the manufacturer has developed or built into the product. Reviewers consider such factors as warranties and service contracts in this category.*

Grades. *Reviewers use the following grades to rate products in the categories listed above:*

Excellent. *The product clearly excels and has no deficiences that affect use.*

Good. *The product has no significant shortcomings and should prove capable in day-to-day use.*

Fair. *The product has some significant shortcomings, but these can be circumvented, or they affect only some specialized use of the product.*

Poor. *The product cannot be recommended in this category because it has serious shortcomings.*

List of reviewers

Russ Adams
Henry F. Beechhold
Ed Bernstein
June Brevdy
Timothy A. Daneliuk
Frank J. Derfler, Jr.
William A. Feinberg
Saul D. Feldman
Cynthia E. Field
Freff
Gregory R. Glau
Doug & Denise Green
Amanda Hixson
Thom Hogan
Rik Jadrnicek
Larry G. Leslie
Patti Littlefield
John V. Lombardi
Janet E. Meizel
Tom Neudecker
Marty Petersen
Joel Pitt
Mark Renne
Phillip Robinson
David Sevres
Donald S. Teiser
Karen A. Weiss

WORDS

The programs reviewed in this category work with words. They let you process, arrange, rearrange and organize words...something you could never do with a typewriter.

REVIEW

WordStar

The introduction of WordStar in June 1979 effectively ended the debate about whether a word-processing program for a microcomputer could meet the needs of professional writers and typists. Features such as screen formatting, block and line moves, block merges from files, automatic hyphenation, print pausing and global search and replace were no longer strictly the province of dedicated word processors.

WordStar is generally acknowledged as the most comprehensive word-processing software available for micros running the CP/M operating system.

WordStar supports all of the standard cursor movements and editing features. You can move the cursor by character, by word or by line, or move it to the beginning or the end of a file, a screen or a line. By using the Quick command, you can issue repeating cursor movements. For example, the cursor can step through a file, word by word.

WordStar's ability to manipulate blocks of text was the editing feature we liked best. Many word-processing programs can only copy or move blocks of text within the current file. To insert blocks of text from disk files with some of these programs requires that you make the disk file, delete unwanted portions of the file and then move the block from disk to memory. Other programs require that the blocks be chained together during formatting.

WordStar provides a series of block markers that you can place in the text to indicate the start and end of the text to be manipulated. Once you have marked the block, you can copy and move it within the file or write it to the disk. You can have blocks stored on disk read into the file you are editing.

REVIEWS

InfoWorld
Report Card

WordStar

	Poor	Fair	Good	Excellent
Performance	☐	☐	☐	■
Documentation	☐	☐	■	☐
Ease of Use	☐	■	☐	☐
Error Handling	☐	☐	■	☐

Summary
WordStar is MicroPro's popular word-processing program. You have to learn many control-key commands to use the program, but its complexity is matched by its power.

System Requirements
☐ *Z80 processor card for the Apple II series*
☐ *CP/M 2.2*
☐ *64K RAM*
☐ *One or more disk drives*
☐ *Printer recommended*
☐ *WordStar program disk and system installation program*
☐ *Bundled with either the StarCard Z80 processor card or with MicroPro's "Professional" Package — a spelling-checker and mail-merge program*

Suggested list price: $495; WordStar Professional, $695

MicroPro International Corporation
33 San Pablo Avenue
San Rafael, CA 94903
(415) 499-1200

Finally, you can move and copy blocks, as well as save edited files to disk as either text, binary programs or basic programs.

You must pay for WordStar's power, however, by having to learn a multitude of control-key commands. These commands are especially prevalent in the process of text formatting. WordStar provides you with on-screen command lists and short Help files.

The command lists are divided into four user-selected levels. At the lowest level, the Help screen only appears when you request it. Each of the successive levels' command lists is displayed whenever you are editing text, and each displays additional help. At the highest level, approximately the top half of the screen is devoted to Help displays.

We liked the Help files displayed when editing; we also liked the ability to adjust the amount of Help list shown, from "none" to "all." MicroPro also supplies a set of helpful, stick-on keytops upon which the control-key commands are printed.

Features supported by WordStar (depending on which printer you use) include: underscore (characters only or continuous), doublestrike characters, boldface or shadow print, strike out (typing characters one on top of another), ribbon-color selection, print pause to change daisy-wheels, subscripts and superscripts, margin controls and much more.

As a text editor, WordStar is outstanding. As a text formatter, it rivals dedicated word processors. Even with all of the Help screens, key tabs and extensive documentation, however, WordStar could, we believe, overwhelm many users.

Professional writers or typists who master the program will find its performance outstanding. The program

supports several of the available 80-column cards for the Apple II series, as well as many letter-quality and dot-matrix printers.

By using provided utilities, you can configure the program to work with those terminals and printers not directly supported by using provided utilities. We suggest that novice users purchase the program from a local dealer who will configure the system and provide support.

Plan to spend about 14 hours to complete all three levels of the tutorial, and expect to refer to the reference manual or any of the many independently written WordStar instruction books. You also need to have a general understanding of the CP/M operating system.

Those in favor of dedicated word processors point out that WordStar's use of control-key commands is a major drawback. The argument is that it is awkward to type two keys at the same time, and that function keys perform better. It would take another whole keyboard just to house the function keys WordStar needs. We found that touch-typists adapted to the use of multiple keystrokes faster than to the use of function keys that required them to move their fingers off the general keyboard. Typists we queried considered use of the control-key commands to be equivalent to use of the shift key for uppercase characters. WordStar follows this dictum. The program gives you complete control; it does not attempt to trap illogical but legitimate commands. Fortunately, you can correct most inadvertent errors. A command to cancel the previous command (perhaps when you have issued it in error) would be a desirable feature.

To exit from the Edit mode, you must move the present file to disk or confirm your decision to exit without updating the file. If the file is sent to the disk, WordStar saves the previous version with a filename extension of .BAK (for *backup*). Should you lose power while editing, the work file in memory is lost, but the file and backup remain on the disk. You have available a command to update the disk file periodically while editing. If you press the Reset key while using WordStar, the system reboots, leaving you in CP/M and losing any input since the last update.

The documentation for WordStar is adequate. The reference manual, training tutorials and installation manual are well written. The text is easy to read; at the same time, it is specific. It alerts you to possible errors, which are identified with icons warning you to "remember," "keep this in mind" or "use caution."

A three-ring binder holds the documentation, which is divided into sections with tabs. Each section is indexed and has a table of contents.

WordStar is sold both by local dealers and through mail-order houses. User support is supplied by MicroPro, but when its technical services lines are busy, you are advised to contact the local store where you purchased the program.

Because the WordStar series of programs is not copy-protected, MicroPro, like many other software houses, attempts to screen out users of pirated copies by requiring that users identify themselves and provide the serial number of their copy before they get assistance.

We found that WordStar lived up to its billing and the praises it has received from thousands of users. It is powerful and complex. We found that it performed well, making easy such tasks as formatting tables — which is difficult for most programs to handle.

We question whether home computerists need the additional features for routine correspondence and, if not, whether the cost of the program and the time required to master the commands make it a worthwhile investment. For professional writers or users in offices, we recommend the package. In these cases, users often need to design unusual text formats. Also, in office situations, systems based on different microprocessors are frequently in use. Because WordStar runs on virtually all of the CP/M machines, it allows users the luxury of having only one program to learn.

WordStar is expensive, but MicroPro's decision to bundle the program with its spelling-checker/mail-merge and indexing programs (for $695) or with a CP/M processor card for the Apple makes the cost reasonable. StarCard, the CP/M card included in the package, is manufactured by Personal Computer Peripherals, Inc. (PCPI), and is sold elsewhere for $375 as the Appli-Card. This card features a fast 6 MHz Z80B processor with 64K of on-board RAM. The card comes with release 2.2 of CP/M and several utilities from Digital Research. We found two of these programs to be most helpful. DOSRDSK allows you to use the 64K of RAM on the card as a "pseudodisk" for the Apple's 6502 processor under DOS 3.3. ADOSXFER allows you to transfer programs from CP/M to Apple DOS, or vice versa. You can transfer text, binary, Applesoft or Integer BASIC.

The ability to transfer between operating systems means that you can use your Apple communications programs to transmit and capture both CP/M and DOS 3.3 files with one program. The card also provides a video driver that simulates a 70-character display in high-resolution graphics, for those who don't have an 80-column card.

On the other hand, programs written for the Microsoft CP/M Card may not run on the Appli-Card because they rely upon the Apple for certain graphics and cursor routines that the Appli-Card performs. The StarCard/Appli-Card comes with an installation manual and a copy of Murtha and Waite's excellent guide, the *CP/M Primer*. The package lacks a good reference manual for advanced programmers.

WordStar is an excellent word-processing program for extensive and complex tasks. Because of the cost and time required to learn the system, we recommend Apple users carefully evaluate their needs prior to selecting WordStar.

—*Tom Neudecker*

REVIEW

ThinkTank

ThinkTank, by Dave Winer and Jonathan LLewellyn of Living Videotext, is a complex program that uses an outline format to help you organize your thoughts and ideas quickly. Called an "idea processor," the product produces "electronic outlines."

For this review, we used an Apple IIe, which provides uppercase and lowercase letters, and an 80-column screen display. Novice computer users can use ThinkTank, but some experience with word processing and knowledge of the Pascal operating system are helpful.

ThinkTank requires two disk drives because the program disk is often in use, and the data disk is constantly updated. You usually store only one outline file on each disk, so you can expand an outline as needed. If you have a hard-disk system, though, you can choose the size of the outlines and place several on one disk. Systems with floppy disks can also use the hard-disk versions, and you can again predetermine the size of the outlines.

Once you get ThinkTank running, your screen becomes an arena for your ideas. The upper area, occupying most of the screen, is called the text area; it displays your outlines. The bottom four lines represent the command area, which displays the various instructions for manipulating your outline.

The text area displays your outline on the screen in the form of main headlines and indented, minor headlines. The different headlines represent a more detailed outline, with subheadings and paragraphs located beneath the main headings. Headlines that have a plus sign (+) in front of them indicate that there is more information located beneath that heading.

You can see or expand any headline on the text area or collapse any detailed text to its main headings. Each paragraph or block of text under a headline can have a maximum of 2048 characters. A large bar cursor highlights the main headlines so that you can easily find where you are in a complex outline. Your outline might not fit on the screen all at once, but you can scroll through it using the bar cursor.

Several command menus allow you to manipulate your text. The main commands include Expand, Collapse,

New, Move, Delete, Edit, Keyword, Window, Port, Files and Extra. Many of these commands have submenus, which give you additional control and power.

In addition to the main command menu is a secondary command menu, which you can access through the Extra command. This menu contains commands for Copy, Alpha, Promote, Merge, Date, Utilities and Special.

The Special command takes you to the Specialist Command menu. These commands allow you to use ThinkTank with other programs and commands. For example, you can format, copy and list contents of a floppy disk. Advanced users can add their own commands to the Specialist Command menu.

ThinkTank uses the Port command to print an outline, transfer information from one outline to another, back up outlines or send outlines to another ThinkTank user. Three different styles are available: structured, which moves the text files; plain, which is used for outlines that will be edited with a Pascal-compatible word processor; and formatted, which is used for printed copies.

The formatted style provides 16 different settings, including line spacing, margins, headers, footers or a table of contents, complete with page numbers. You can send your outline to a text file and edit it with your favorite word processor for extra control.

Pascal users will delight in the program's ability to use the Pascal operating system. Apple DOS users need not fear, since ThinkTank contains all the necessary utility files in its DiskManager option so that with a few simple keystrokes you can initialize and copy disks.

You must format either your floppy disks or hard disk with the Pascal operating system. Once you have formatted these disks, you can then use them with any other Pascal program.

Your dealer should configure your hard disks. ThinkTank has separate commands for the Apple II series and Apple III computers.

This program does not pretend to be a word processor. In fact, it is more than a word processor, as opposed to being a substitute for one. With it, you can begin writing in outline form and switch to paragraph form whenever you choose.

Although ThinkTank is an idea processor, it does not do your thinking for you. You must have some idea of the main headings and subheadings that you intend to use. It is easy to add information, but moving paragraphs is a bit more difficult. For example, we were unable to add a subheading to a paragraph that had already been created under a main heading. Familiarity with the program will reduce such problems.

You must also keep in mind that paragraph length is limited. Once the allotted space is used up, you cannot add even one more character.

Do not expect ThinkTank to clarify all of your disjointed thoughts with the touch of a key, and expect to spend some time learning how to use it. This program, however, rewards your efforts with better-than-average flexibility and control over your text.

The editing features make text revisions fast and easy. You can go directly to the headline or paragraph that needs editing without having to scroll through a long document. On the Apple IIe, the Delete and up- and down-arrow keys help to make the editing easier.

We could do nothing to make the program crash. If you press a wrong key or try to perform a task that ThinkTank

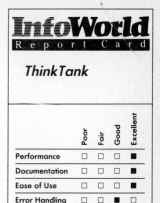

InfoWorld
Report Card

ThinkTank

	Poor	Fair	Good	Excellent
Performance	☐	☐	☐	■
Documentation	☐	☐	☐	■
Ease of Use	☐	☐	☐	■
Error Handling	☐	☐	■	☐

Summary
ThinkTank is a complex idea processor that uses an outline format to help you organize your thoughts quickly. Although novices can use this program, some experience with word processing and knowledge of Pascal are helpful.

System Requirements
☐ *Apple II, II Plus, IIe, III*
☐ *DOS 3.3*
☐ *64K RAM (II and II Plus); 96K RAM (III)*
☐ *Two or more disk drives; or hard disk with Pascal operating system*
☐ *Monitor; 80-column text card for file*

Suggested price list: $150

Living Videotext, Inc.
1000 Elwell Court
Palo Alto, CA 94303
(415) 964-6300

can't perform, an error message appears on the screen.

It is difficult for you to lose your data, unless there is a power failure. You are prompted to save each paragraph and headline, and you cannot leave a paragraph until you have saved it. The authors also caution users, several times, to back up all outlines, both on disk and on paper. The error messages are easy to understand, and they are all clarified in the program's manual.

The ThinkTank manual is a complete, easy-to-read document of 228 pages. It is so well organized that you do not have to read the entire manual before using the program. Included with the manual is a one-page reference card that summarizes how the program is organized.

The program manual is divided into two parts. Part I introduces you to the program, explains the system requirements, provides a tutorial with a sample outline and gives useful suggestions for using the program. Part I also includes a glossary of terms, an introduction to the Pascal operating system, information on disk management, technical notes about hard-disk drives and an ASCII conversion table.

Part II is an alphabetized reference guide that includes all ThinkTank commands, a list of error messages and an index. It also contains a list of figures and tables, along with their page numbers.

Since ThinkTank is not copy-protected, you are encouraged to make backup copies for your own use. The author welcomes your input and suggestions and can be contacted by phone.

ThinkTank is one step ahead of an ordinary word processor and is part of the new generation of software that fully develops microcomputers' capabilities.
—*Doug and Denise Green*

REVIEW

Bank Street Writer

Pity the poor Apple II home user. He knows microcomputers can make wonderful word processors, but he's also overwhelmed by the time, money and know-how required to make a choice among the multitude of programs available — not to mention the time needed to learn to use one. Besides, he's been told the Apple has shortcomings as a word processor.

Enter the Bank Street Writer. For a relatively small investment, it provides nearly everything most households need to write letters, draft reports and even do homework. It's also a simple-to-learn, remarkably well-documented little gem of a program that may spell an untimely death for many a typewriter.

It comes on a double-sided disk that includes a complete on-screen tutorial. Virtually identical versions for Atari and Commodore 64 home computers are available; an enhanced version for the IBM PC and PCjr is also on the market.

The program supports either parallel or serial printers.

One great bargain the Bank Street Writer offers is a "cure" for one of the major drawbacks of using an Apple II or II Plus as a word processor. The drawback is the lack of lowercase letters, and the cure lies in the program's use of the Apple's graphic abilities to "draw" uppercase and lowercase letters on the screen. Other hardware and software packages for Apple accomplish the same thing, but most cost far more than the Bank Street Writer.

The program makes no attempt to cure the other major drawback of Apple word processing on off-the-shelf Apples — the display has only 40 columns. That lack acknowledged, Bank Street Writer offers many other features.

The Bank Street Writer is fully compatible with the Apple IIe. It takes advantage of the IIe's special keys, such as the up and down arrows for cursor movement, but otherwise operates in the same way as on the Apple II and II Plus.

The program is geared for users who have never operated a word-processing system or even a computer.

Such users might want to begin by reviewing the manual, but those who have used word processors before can probably start right in.

The program reduces all word-processing activity to one of three modes — Write, Edit or Transfer. After you boot the disk, the screen displays a text "window" with room for 18 lines of type, each 38 characters long.

Meanwhile, at the top of the screen, above the outlined text window, appears the menu that corresponds to the Write mode. The program reminds users that they can use the left and right arrows to erase text. It also reminds Apple II or II Plus users that pressing Shift-N once capitalizes the next letter typed. Pressing Shift-N twice is the same as pressing the Shift Lock key, and you get all capital letters. (Apple IIe owners can simply use the Shift key, as with a typewriter.)

At this point, the Bank Street Writer operates as a word-processing program.

Words that extend beyond the right margin of the text are automatically "wrapped" onto the next line. The text automatically scrolls up eight lines when you reach the bottom line of the text window. When text memory is exhausted, a warning sounds — but more on that later.

The next stop for most writers is the Edit mode, which you enter by pressing the Escape key once. The text window remains the same, but the menu above it changes to provide a new set of options for altering text or moving the cursor. Simplicity — if not always speed — remains the key. At this point you can erase or move text. The process is slower than in other systems, but — conveniently and reassuringly for inexperienced users — you can always recover from inadvertent erasures or moves by using the Unerase or Moveback menu option in the Edit mode, either of which puts you right back where you started.

In the Edit mode, you can use a search-and-replace function to find certain words or phrases in the text and replace them with others.

The third mode provides transfer operations — in short, anything involving communicating with the disk drive or the printer. As in the Edit mode, you use the left- and right-arrow keys to choose among the options. The disk options allow you to save files to the disk, complete with a password for security; retrieve them from the disk; and delete or rename them. You can also initialize a new disk.

The two printing options are Draft, which prints the text just as it appears in the 38-character, single-spaced text window, and Final, which asks a series of questions regarding how you want the printed version to look. You can double- or triple-space. You can also change your margins from 40 to 80 and put headers at tops of pages.

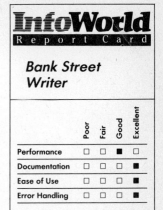

Summary
Bank Street Writer is an easy-to-use word processor that runs on Apple computers. All operations are divided among three modes. Clear menus and uppercase/lowercase character-sketching ability are two of its best features.

System Requirements
☐ _Apple II, II Plus, IIe_
☐ _48K RAM_
☐ _One or two disk drives_
☐ _Dot-matrix or letter-quality printer_

Suggested list price: $69.95

Broderbund Software
17 Paul Drive
San Rafael, CA 94903
_(415) 479-1170_

We particularly liked the feature of the Final option that lets you see where each page of printed text will break and allows you to change that point.

Finally, the Transfer mode offers a Clear option to erase current memory and a Quit option to exit from the program altogether. Both options warn you of the danger that the text in memory will be lost and offer you a chance to cancel the command.

In addition to the three modes, the Bank Street Writer offers a well-thought-out utility program. By pressing the Escape key while booting the disk, you load the special Utility program. It allows you to alter many aspects of the main program.

These aspects include the type of cursor (blinking or underline), how many disk drives are in the system and default formats for printing documents.

The Utility program can also convert standard text files, such as those of Apple Writer or other word-processing programs, into the binary code the Bank Street Writer understands. It also converts Bank Street Writer files to text files. Be warned, however, that the conversion processes are extremely slow.

In their successful effort to keep the program completely straightforward, the Bank Street Writer's designers have sacrificed some features common to most word-processing programs. This program does not provide you with the ability to choose different types of justification, to hyphenate or to embed commands — such as those for boldface or underline in the text. You can, however, center individual lines.

The program is designed to operate with either one or two disk drives. Therefore, the entire program is loaded into memory when you start so that you can replace the program disk with a data disk, and the program takes up a large portion of memory. As a result, it limits each file to about 1300 words in a 48K system or 3200 words with a 16K RAM card or Apple Language Card.

You can check the space available at any time by pressing Control-S while in the Write mode. Once you exceed 1300 words, the response time for certain functions slows down markedly. (The program apparently considers every six spaces a word.)

In general, the program performs admirably, as well as the manufacturer claims. The division of all operations into the three modes, along with the corresponding menus, makes learning to operate it extremely simple.

The only serious drawback lies in its lack of speed. In particular, switching modes and erasing or moving blocks of text is slow and a bit awkward.

The program is designed so users are unlikely to make many errors. When you commit an error such as trying to retrieve more text from the disk than current memory allows or using the print commands without a printer hookup, you're always given an explanation of the problem you've created and a chance to recover.

Nothing short of a power failure is likely to cause you to lose memory. Even pressing Reset is not fatal.

We suggest one caution, however. As memory begins to fill and response time begins to suffer, the right and left arrows can be tricky to use for deleting text. If, for instance, you are near the right edge of the text window and you repeatedly use the right arrow to delete several words, a problem can develop.

The key, in effect, can outtype the display. Letters get deleted faster than the display indicates. Then, when you release the key, suddenly another 10 (or 30) letters disappear from the screen.

The system offers safeguards against most catastrophes. It protects you from inadvertently quitting the program or clearing memory without saving to disk. There's also a warning if you try to save a file under a name that already exists.

You get two approaches to documentation with the Bank Street Writer, both excellent. One is the on-screen tutorial, available on the flip-side of the double-sided program disk.

The other is a 35-page manual that is among the best pieces of documentation we've seen for inexperienced computer users. Without being condescending, it carefully describes everything from putting the disk into the drive to setting printing defaults. A combined glossary and index describes all functions.

The package comes with two identical copy-protected disks, one as a backup. Broderbund simply says it "fully guarantees" the program, and it will replace any physically undamaged disk at no charge. Damaged disks can be replaced for $5. No time limit is stated.

The Bank Street Writer doesn't offer all the features of higher-priced word-processing packages for Apple. With its simple commands, clear documentation and true uppercase and lowercase abilities, however, it is a pleasure to use and an excellent choice for word processing on a home computer.
—*Ed Bernstein*

REVIEW

Super-Text

Muse's Super-Text Professional and Super-Text Home/Office are the most recent versions of one of the oldest and most popular word-processing systems for the Apple II family of computers. Like the original Super-Text II, both of these new packages separate the editing and formatting stages of word processing. Each has a full screen editor with a complete complement of cursor-movement controls and a variety of powerful editing commands, and a print module that can format your text in accordance with embedded format commands.

To use Super-Text Professional you must have an 80-column card for your Apple, an Apple IIe, or an Apple II or II Plus with a lowercase adapter. You'll need an 80-column card to take advantage of two important features of the professional version. With an 80-column card you can set Super-Text to display text formatted so that it lies between a prescribed left and right margin while you edit it and help messages on the screen.

The 80-column cards Super-Text Professional works with are the Videx Videoterm, the ALS Smarterm and the Full-View 80. You can use the program with the special 80-column card for the IIe, and it will take advantage of the full RAM on a IIe with 128K.

Super-Text Home/Office uses the Apple's high-resolution screen display to display text using software character fonts. You can choose to have it display text in either 40, 56 or 70 columns. It displays text in uppercase and lowercase without any additional hardware. It even has a special design mode, which

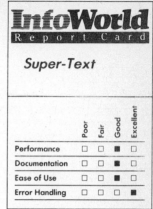

InfoWorld
Report Card

Super-Text

	Poor	Fair	Good	Excellent
Performance	☐	☐	■	☐
Documentation	☐	☐	■	☐
Ease of Use	☐	☐	■	☐
Error Handling	☐	☐	☐	■

Summary
These new versions of Super-Text offer some important improvements to one of the better Apple II word processors. Both are good tools for composing new text. They offer a fine assortment of editing and formatting capabilities.

System Requirements
☐ *Professional: Apple II or Apple IIe, II Plus with lowercase or 80-column*
☐ *Home/Office: Apple II, II Plus, IIe*
☐ *Both: 48K RAM, one disk drive*

Suggested list price: SuperText Professional, $175; Home/Office, $125

Muse Software
347 N. Charles Street
Baltimore, MD 21201
(301) 659-7212

permits you to design your own high-resolution character sets.

The editors in both programs operate in three distinct modes: Cursor, Add and Change. You use the Add mode for original entry of text, at either the end of the text buffer or into the middle of the active text buffer. While in the Add mode, the computer keyboard functions essentially as a typewriter keyboard. Depressing a letter key will place that letter into the current text position and advance the cursor, while pressing the left-arrow key erases the last letter typed into the text.

You can define a special string of up to 30 characters to be entered into the text buffer each time you use the : key while in the Add mode. This feature, the so-called The key, is retained and improved from the original Super-Text II package. It can be valuable in saving keystrokes when you use a string repeatedly in a particular text.

In the Change mode, text typed at the computer keyboard replaces the text currently displayed at the cursor position. A useful feature from the original Super-Text II, which is retained in both packages, is an audible key click in the Change mode to remind you that you are typing over text that's already in the text buffer.

Finally, in the Cursor mode you can access the various cursor-movement commands, as well as a host of other editing and utility features. (Some of the cursor commands are also available in the Change mode.) Both Super-Text versions have a full complement of cursor movement and scrolling commands; you can use single keystrokes to move the cursor in single steps, and Escape sequences to provide express moves to the top, extreme left or right or bottom of the screen, or the beginning or end of the text buffer.

In the Cursor mode, you can use the J key to jump the cursor to the point of the most recent four changes in the text — the first J jumps to the most recent, the second to the next most recent and so on. Other single-key commands scroll the screen a line or page at a time.

Both packages have an excellent global Search-and-Replace command, which you can use within the current text buffer or across a linked set of text files. With both commands you can request a search for a string you explicitly specify, or you can call directly for a search for either the string at the current cursor position or the target string of the most recent previous search.

Search strings can include wild cards of two distinct types, and you can use a single search command to look for one of several distinct strings. When the Replace command is invoked, you can elect to have all occurrences of a given string replaced automatically, or you can cause the program to query each replacement opportunity individually.

A novel feature of the Replace command provides a count of the number of strings actually replaced, and a clever variant usage of the Replace command allows you to use it to count the number of occurrences of any given string within the text. Counting the number of spaces within the text gives an approximation of the number of words in the text.

Both Super-Text packages permit you to mark a block of text. You can then copy, move or delete the block you've marked. You can also save a marked block to a file, and, if the file already exists, you can choose to have Super-Text append the block to the file or replace the file entirely.

Super-Text allows you to save all or any part of the file you're editing under any name you choose at the time you save it. This ability contrasts with other word processors, which force you to select the output file name at the time you start editing. You can merge files up to the capacity of the text buffer, too.

You can perform a variety of other disk operations without leaving Super-Text, including deleting files from storage disks and initializing new storage disks. When you wish to perform a disk operation, Super-Text displays a neatly formatted listing of your storage-disk directory and prominently displays the amount of free space currently available on the disk.

You embed format commands in the body of your text to specify the way in which you'd like it to appear when Super-Text prints it. You can specify the placement of the left and right text margins, the number of lines on a page, and justified or ragged-text margin. You can change these print specifications repeatedly within a single document.

You can direct Super-Text to number pages, with either absolute or chapter-relative numbering. You can choose the position of the page at which the number is printed. You can even ask Super-Text to print multiple header and footer lines on every page or on alternate pages.

With both versions of Super-Text, you can preview the formatted output on the screen before you actually have the output sent to your printer. In the Preview mode, a line across the screen indicates page breaks. You can interrupt previews at any time to scroll back to the previously displayed page.

The professional version of Super-Text divides the CRT screen into two independent windows within which to view the text you're editing. With the split screen you can edit one part of a text while you view another

noncontiguous part simultaneously. You can also take advantage of a less useful math mode in the Super-Text Professional that embeds a calculator feature and of some supportive numerical format controls; the latter make it easier to produce reports with columns of numbers. Neither feature is available in Super-Text Home/Office.

You can save the files you create with either of these word-processing packages as either text or binary files on standard Apple DOS 3.2 disks. Files produced by earlier versions of Super-Text can only be sorted on specially initialized disks.

On the whole, both new versions of Super-Text perform well. They respond quickly to cursor-movement commands and scroll pages rapidly. You can save and load files in binary format to and from the disk quickly. The global search-and-replace commands are processed at an adequate, but by no means blinding, speed.

The original Super-Text II was often unable to process input and update the screen rapidly enough to keep up with expert typists. When you entered text rapidly (especially at the top of a crowded screen), Super-Text II would occasionally drop characters you typed. The new versions of Super-Text both use a type-ahead buffer to avoid this. The screen display still lags behind input from time to time, and this can be disconcerting if you chance to glance up at the screen.

The three character fonts in the Home/Office version are all quite readable, although the 70-column font clearly requires a monitor rather than a TV set. Super-Text generally responds to commands more quickly when you use the 40- or 56-column display than it does when you use the 70-column display.

Having three fonts to chose from is a handy feature because you can take advantage of the greater amount of text visible with a 70-column display when that's important to you, and you can use the more easily readable 40-column display when your eyes are tired or you don't have a high-resolution display device.

We found one minor bug in the way Super-Text Professional handled embedded format commands — it added an extra line feed when the last character before a new paragraph fell on the right text margin. But the print program generally worked wonderfully. Super-Text does not support proportional spacing.

Muse Software uses a modified version of the Apple 13-sector DOS 3.2 on its disks. Although Muse makes its disks bootable on machines equipped for the 16-sector DOS 3.3 — which helps make life easier for most Apple owners — Muse storage disks are limited to 13 sectors, rather than the 16 sectors that are possible with DOS 3.3. Thus the majority of Apple owners who are equipped to use 16-sector disks must needlessly lose 18% of their potential disk capacity.

Super-Text offers a powerful assortment of features, and it takes some effort to learn to take advantage of all of them. On the whole, though, given its power, it is relatively easy to use. The cursor-movement keys approximate the four points of a compass, and the various command keys are generally well chosen for their mnemonic value.

Muse has obviously put considerable effort into simplifying some of the harder-to-use features of the original program. For example, you are now guided by menus when you want to assign special printer characters. A variety of commands from the original have been simplified, as well; commands that required the use of the Control key in the original version now often don't.

Neither Super-Text Professional nor the Home/Office version allows you to alter the default character mode in which it boots. If you use an 80-column card, for example, you must explicitly enable it each time you load Super-Text; similarly, if you typically want to use the Home/Office version in its 70-column mode you must explicitly elect to do so after it boots in its default 56-column mode. This feature can be disconcerting if you're using the professional version and own an 80-column card, but do not have a lowercase adapter on your Apple. You'll be forced to read screens full of virtual gibberish (lowercase characters displayed on an uppercase-only screen) as you blindly navigate your way through Super-Text en route to enabling your 80-column card. It's unfortunate that Muse did not provide a method for permanently reconfiguring the disk for the preferred operating mode.

Both packages come with complete, clear and well-written documentation, but neither includes a set of tutorial lessons, as do many competing packages. The manuals have complete tables of contents, and divider tabs — not provided in the manual for the original version — help you locate chapters. Unfortunately, neither manual includes an index.

On the whole, the program handles errors well. Any time you attempt to do anything damaging, the program asks for confirmation. Both versions display the amount of space available on a storage disk whenever you try to save or load a file and allow you to initialize new data disks without leaving the program. This helps you to avoid the disastrous possibility that you might be unable to save a file you have been editing.

The new versions of Super-Text offer some important improvements to one of the better Apple II word processors. Both are good tools for composing new text. They offer a fine assortment of editing and formatting capabilities.

—Joel Pitt

REVIEW

PFS:

There are four basic programs in the PFS: series. The original program of the series, PFS:File (when it was introduced in 1980 it was called Personal Filing System), is a form-oriented information system that allows users to design forms on the screen (called "pages"), fill them with information and retrieve the information by complex selection criteria. The program allows the forms to be printed only in a "labels" style format and not in a more useful "column" or "tabular" format. This lead Software Publishing to introduce a program that lets you specify how you want the information created by PFS:File to be reported in tabular format — PFS:Report. PFS:Graph allows you to create line graphs, bar graphs and pie charts, either automatically from the same data files used by PFS:File and PFS:Report, or from data entered on the keyboard. In addition, PFS:Graph allows you to create graphics from VisiCalc files. PFS:Write is a word processor that not only creates text files, but also calls for information from the PFS:File, PFS:Report and PFS:Graph. With the PFS: package you can write a letter, memo or report and include data from a

PFS: data file and include a pie chart or bar graph previously generated by PFS:Graph. The series is now topped off with a new set of applications modules collectively called PFS:Solutions. Rather than struggle with designing forms, users can purchase an applications module that will run on PFS:File or PFS:Report immediately. These applications modules cost only $20 each. They include forms to handle your checking account; organize your home budget; manage your hardware/ software collection (disk library); tally your personal or business assets; do invoices, ledgers, payrolls and mailing lists; and keep track of your stock portfolios, appointments schedules and expense accounts.

Once you learn how to use PFS:File, which is not too difficult, you already know how to use the other programs because the philosophy of operation is the same. The same keystrokes accomplish the same functions in all of the programs. However, in order to achieve compatibility in a series of programs released over a period of four years, PFS: has had to continue some questionable functions. "Pressing 'Control-C' to continue" is an example of this. Whenever you enter something, the natural inclination is to press Return. Control-C often means "bail out," "quit" or "abort." The PFS: logic was to use Control-C (and in some cases the Tab key) to mean "continue." The Tab key is right next to the Escape key, which deletes everything you've entered.

Another flaw is the dearth of editing functions for designing a PFS:File form. If you want to reposition an entire phrase, you must erase what you have by typing over it and then retyping the

Summary
The folks at Software Publishing, creators of PFS:File, Report, Graph, Write and Solutions, have been "integrating" programs for years, and getting better at it all the time. Generally, the elements of the PFS: series do their jobs admirably. PFS:File is a file manager, not a data-base-management system, and cannot handle lengthy or complex information. The most significant drawback of the PFS: package is the rather idiosyncratic philosophy of operation that Software Publishing carried over from its first offering, PFS:File.

System Requirements
☐ *Apple II Plus, IIe*
☐ *DOS 3.3*
☐ *64K RAM*
☐ *One or two drives*
☐ *Optional printer, Plotter*
☐ *Optional 80-column card*
☐ *(Also available for IBM PC)*

Suggested list price: $125 for each program; $20 for PFS:Solutions

Software Publishing Corporation 1901 Landings Drive Mountain View, CA 94043 (415) 962-8910

phrase. The series is easy to use, though.

The programs are menu-driven, and you seldom have trouble figuring out what to do next. We particularly liked the way PFS:Write uses a technique that is good for people who know how to operate a typewriter but don't know what word processing is all about. When you are in PFS:Write's text-entry mode, the screen looks just like a sheet of paper. Along the bottom is a ruler that is clearly marked so you can see what horizontal position you are in. When you set and clear tabs, "T" marks on the ruler appropriately appear or disappear. A line indicator lets you know what line you are on. You know just how your page is going to be printed so you can avoid "widows" and "orphans," the first line of a new paragraph at the bottom of a page, and the last line of a paragraph at the top of a new page.

PFS:File, the heart of the series, is a file-management program, not a data-base-management program. File management refers to a single file. A data-base-management system can have more than one file.

For example, in a file-management system, each record in an inventory file might contain an item name, its description, part number, manufacturer and manufacturer's address and phone number. If you had 500 items from the same manufacturer, you would have to carry the manufacturer's address and phone number once for each record, or 500 times.

With a data-base-management system, however, you could establish one file for the item, part number and manufacturer. In another file you could have each manufacturer's address and phone number, and in a third file you could have item descriptions. You could extract the product description and the manufacturer's address and phone

number from the appropriate files as needed.

PFS:File can only work with one file at a time. It cannot relate information between files. Moreover, you can only put one file on one disk. A PFS:File can hold up to 1000 (32,000 on a hard disk) simple forms (or records). The actual number depends on how many pages are in the form, how many items are in each page and how much data you enter in each item. Given a total data storage capacity of 128K per disk, and allowing for some necessary internal file usage by the program (14 bytes out of each page and 5 bytes for each item), an average mailing-label program consisting of name, address, city, state, ZIP code and possibly phone number would occupy about 1000 forms per file.

Since PFS:File was first introduced, some significant improvements have been made in it. Now you can change form designs even after you have entered data. You can sort printouts by any item on the form instead of just the first or key item. You can selectively copy or merge files even if their form designs differ. You can print multiple copies and save up to eight print specifications for each file for repeat usage. A meter keeps you posted on how much disk space is left.

The PFS:Report program was developed to alleviate the printing deficiencies of PFS:File. The PFS:Report program can produce up to nine vertical columns of information. These columns can contain either information from the records or calculations derived from numerical information contained within one or more fields. Files larger than the computer's memory can be sorted because the sorting is accomplished by a "sortwork" disk. You cannot send special printer codes to the printer during printing, however. Appendix D in the PFS:Report manual shows you how you can write a special BASIC program that sends the appropriate codes to the printer before printing.

The main features of PFS:Graph are that you can define three types of graphs: line graph, bar graph and pie chart. You can enter data from the keyboard or from PFS:File data disks or VisiCalc files. Up to four different bars or lines can appear on the same graph as long as their vertical and horizontal axes are similar. The program is flexible in allowing you to create labeling, grid lines, shading and so forth. You can create color charts on the screen, and with a plotter you can get those colors on paper.

You cannot include graphics in your text file if you have a Grappler, Grappler+ or Pkaso printer interface card. While you can call for bold printing in text, you cannot use bold printing in the header, or underline the header. Only left and right justification are available; full justification is not. In this sense the PFS:Write program behaves more like a typewriter than a word processor.

All of the PFS:Programs are good at handling errors. It is a pleasure to see appendices in the documentation that list all of the error messages and what they mean. The documentation is all good. The only application program we tried was called "Employee." It keeps track of employee statistics and has predefined reports that, without any programming, make a list of employees' birthdays in order by date, and even include the name of the employees' supervisor. You can report employee participation in the benefits program of your company, as well as make a list of the work and home phone numbers of each employee, including department

extensions. You can also print salary reports. You can edit any of these programs and customize them to your own specifications.

In summary, we have mixed emotions about the PFS: series. It has survived the test of time and has been on the best-seller lists. The programs deserve many of the accolades they have received because they have filled a vital need. There are many satisfied users, making good use of these programs. It is not a perfect system (though nothing is), but its flaws are perpetuating. Each new program in the series must carry the imperfections of its predecessors in order to preserve compatibility. In this new era of icon menus and mouse technology, it is like looking at the past instead of the future.
—_Marty Petersen_

REVIEW

Screenwriter II

Screenwriter II, a low-priced word processor for the Apple II family of computers, offers a rich assortment of features. It includes a full-screen editor that uses the Apple's high-resolution-graphics capability to display text in uppercase and lowercase characters, a mail-merge capability and printer spooling.

Screenwriter II runs with minimal hardware — it requires only one disk drive and 48K of RAM — but it can take advantage of additional hardware. Indeed, some of its features require more hardware: You can only use the

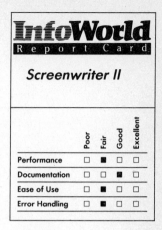

InfoWorld
Report Card

Screenwriter II

	Poor	Fair	Good	Excellent
Performance	☐	■	☐	☐
Documentation	☐	☐	■	☐
Ease of Use	☐	■	☐	☐
Error Handling	☐	■	☐	☐

Summary
Screenwriter II is a low-priced word processor that gives excellent value for the money. It offers a long list of useful features for editing and printing text. Although Screenwriter's documentation is good, learning how to operate the complex package takes time.

System Requirements
☐ _Apple II, II Plus, IIe_
☐ _48K RAM_
☐ _One disk drive_

Suggested list price: $129.95

_Sierra On-Line, Inc.
Sierra On-Line Bldg.
Coarsegold, CA 93614
(209) 683-6858_

printer spooling, for example, if your Apple has two disk drives.

You can tailor Screenwriter II's display to your equipment and needs. Its screen editor offers you a choice of two different character sets: one displays 70 columns of text on a screen line; the other displays only 40 columns across the screen — its larger characters are suitable for display on a TV if you don't have a monitor. You can even use Screenwriter II with an Apple IIe 80-column display.

Like many other word processors, Screenwriter apportions its functions between two subprograms: a full-screen Editor, with which you create and edit text, and a print program called Runoff, which formats text according to your embedded commands and directs the resulting ouput to your printer.

When you boot Screenwriter II, an initial menu offers you three alternatives: you can use its full-screen Editor, you can use its Runoff program to print existing text, or you can view or alter the program's default operating configuration. If your Apple has 64K or more of RAM, the editing and runoff subprograms can be coresident, and you can switch between them without reloading either program from the disk.

Screenwriter's Edit program is powerful, but it has an unusual and complex design. You may find it somewhat difficult to master. The Editor operates in two modes: a Command mode and a Direct Edit/ Entry mode. The Editor displays the text you're editing on the upper 20 lines of the Apple II monitor screen and uses the bottom four lines for a command entry/message area.

When you're in the Command mode, the text you type appears on a command line at the bottom of the display screen,

and Screenwriter responds to your command when you press the Return key. In the Direct Edit/Entry mode, you type directly into the text buffer at a position marked by a cursor that is visible in the text area. The Direct Edit/ Entry mode operates in two distinct submodes: Insert mode, in which the text you type is inserted into the text buffer at the cursor position and advances the text ahead of it, and a Change mode, in which the text you type overwrites and replaces the text at the current cursor position.

The variety of Editor functions is impressive. You can move the cursor through your text in many different ways: left or right, up or down, a word at a time, a page at a time and so on. Screenwriter searches forward or backward for strings that you specify, and if you wish, replaces them with alternate strings. You can even use wild-card characters in your search strings, and you can use block operations to rearrange text.

The Editor also provides a variety of unusual functions. While in Command mode, you enter # to get a count of all the words in the file you're editing; you enter = for a count of the characters in your text. Also, you can obtain any Apple DOS command from the Command mode. You can even assign strings of characters to individual, infrequently used keys in order to facilitate entry of frequently used words or phrases.

You can use some editor functions in both main Editor modes; others are available in only one. For example, many cursor-movement commands can work in either mode. The key entries required for a given movement differ between modes although they're generally similar. To move the text cursor to the beginning of the text buffer while you're in the Command mode, for example, you type the letter B on the command line and then press the Return key. If you are in either of the Direct Entry modes, on the other hand, you type a Control-B.

Some of Screenwriter's cursor controls are awkward. Many word processors assign related functions to groups of keys that are located near each other; their proximity and relationships help you remember their functions. Screenwriter II, however, uses words associated with the key letters. Thus, the A key advances the cursor down one line on the screen (in the Command mode, the Control-A combination does the same in Edit/ Entry mode); the J key jumps the cursor to the next line. Some functions require two keystroke sequences, and, although the sequences are logical (e.g., pressing Escape Control-A reverses the advance and moves the cursor up a line), they're difficult to use.

The awkwardness of Screenwriter's cursor commands is offset somewhat by one of its special features: you can use a joystick to control the cursor's position.

Screenwriter II's Runoff program is as rich in special features as its Editing program. You use embedded format commands to specify how you want your printout to appear. You can set and reset margins throughout the text, center or justify the text at the margins you select and control pagination. Runoff even incrementally justifies your text if you have an appropriate printer.

In addition, you can set conditional page breaks, specify up to four header or footer lines on each page, request underlined or boldfaced printed text and specify automatic hyphenation.

And there is more! Screenwriter handles footnotes and automatically indexes documents as it prints them. Finally, Screenwriter's mail-merge facility lets you produce customized form letters and even permits you to conditionally include text in your output.

Screenwriter is a complex package, but it contains no bugs. You may encounter some performance problems when you use the Editor, however.

When you enter text in Insert mode, Screenwriter does a large amount of processing to continually update the graphics-screen display. As a result, the screen display can lag behind your keyboard input. Screenwriter captures your input in a keyboard input buffer and generally does not lose characters. When you use the 70-column display and type text at the top of the screen, you can type so far ahead of Screenwriter that it drops characters you've typed.

Another performance problem occurs when you edit large files. The large size of the Screenwriter II program limits the room for text in the RAM edit buffer to less than 6K, about three double-spaced pages on a 64K Apple II.

Screenwriter II uses your floppy disk as a memory device to let you edit large files. It does so transparently, transferring text between its memory buffer and its disk scratch file as needed. But these disk transfers are slow, and the speed at which Screenwriter II responds to your commands is affected adversely.

The Screenwriter II manual introduces you to the program's features gradually. Its three major sections are entitled "The MiniWriter," "The Creative Writer" and "The Complete Writer."

The manual has a table of contents and a complete index generated by Screenwriter. The package includes four reference cards. The manual is well written and provides good examples. Still, Screenwriter is not an easy package to learn to use.

Summary
Word Juggler IIe is an editor/formatter word-processing program that runs on the Apple IIe. This sophisticated, memory-based word processor uses the ProDos operating system. Its use is somewhat limited, though; you should check to be sure it will work with your system's setup.

Word Juggler IIe

InfoWorld Report Card

	Poor	Fair	Good	Excellent
Performance	☐	☐	■	☐
Documentation	☐	☐	■	☐
Ease of Use	☐	☐	■	☐
Error Handling	☐	☐	☐	■

System Requirements
☐ Apple IIe
☐ ProDos 1.0 (included on disk)
☐ 128K RAM
☐ Two disk drives
☐ Printer: 80-column card recommended

Suggested list price: $189 (indicates Lexicheck spelling checker)

*Quark, Inc.
2525 West Evans, Suite 220
Denver, CO 80219
(303) 934-2211*

On the whole, Screenwriter II is an excellent value. It is not without faults, but they're largely the result of the package's ambitious goals. The Editor's performance decreases somewhat when you edit large files, but the package offers an outstanding formatting capability and performs well when you edit smaller documents.
—*Joel Pitt*

REVIEW

Word Juggler IIe

Although you'd think there'd be scant demand for another Apple word-processing program, especially one that runs only on the IIe and not other Apple II machines, the Word Juggler IIe from Quark has enough interesting features to be worth a closer look. (A version of Word Juggler for the Apple III is also available.)

This program belongs in the editor/formatter class of word-processing programs; that is, you begin by entering and editing text, inserting codes and symbols that will tell the formatting part of the program how the text should be printed. Then, once the words are in the correct order, say what you want to say and have appropriate paragraph divisions, the formatter takes over and prints out the document with justified margins, proper spacing, boldfacing, underlining, superscripts and subscripts and additional print enhancements. Other word-processing systems combine these functions so that you can see how the printed page will look on your editing screen.

Word Juggler's performance is quite good in both categories of editing and formatting — with some qualifications.

Entering and editing text is essentially painless. The program responds quickly to a wide range of commands that cut, paste, move, copy, save, recall and merge bits and pieces of documents to produce a final text that is just the way you want it. The range of editing features offered by the program is as extensive as those available in all but the most complex editors and should prove more than sufficient for all but the most demanding word-processing tasks.

The program is constructed with the Apple IIe keyboard in mind. Where that keyboard is deficient, Quark supplies special keycaps with editing-function labels.

Moreover, the package comes with a small plug-in board that enables all the key combinations the program expects; the board comes with installation tools and instructions. A special template across the top of the Apple keyboard completes this complement of visual aids. The additions are helpful and make learning and using this program easy.

Word Juggler IIe is a direct descendent of an Apple III word-processing program; this background explains its sophistication and, especially, its use of the ProDos operating system. Yes, that's right, this Apple IIe program does not run under DOS 3.3 but under the ProDos operating system.

The disks (original and backup) come with enough of the operating system to run the program, and the files created under Word Juggler IIe are incompatible with Apple II DOS 3.3, although the system has utilities to read in text files from the old operating system and Apple Pascal files as well.

Word Juggler works best with a reasonably robust Apple IIe, one having an 80-column card, 128K and two drives. Unfortunately, because of the limitations inherent in the Apple disk drives, no more than approximately 60 pages of double-spaced text can reside on a disk. Furthermore, Word Juggler has a limit of 785 lines of text, or about 30 double-spaced pages, for each individual document you choose to edit.

The good news about this memory-based word-processing strategy is that both the editor and the formatter are fast. Movement about the file; insertions, deletions and moves; and formatting zip right along.

The program handles that moment of truth — when you run out of space — with grace and charm, allowing a calm, orderly exit to disk.

The formatting routine performs practically all the major functions you might expect, including justification using microspaces: ragged-left and -right margins; spacing; and print enhancements such as boldface, underline or overstrike. In addition, the formatting routine has a facility for character replacement and printer-control strings.

The Character Replacement feature permits you to define one character entered on the screen as another character at print time. This is useful for inserting special characters that may have one special meaning for your keyboard or the word-processing program and another for your printer.

Printer-control strings are sequences of characters that need to be sent to the printer to implement some printing aspect such as compressed print, color, paper changes or the like. These printer-control strings go to the printer without affecting the text at all.

Word Juggler's Preview feature displays the document in "normal" display. Only underlining, boldfacing, superscripting and subscripting are shown in inverse video. Footers and headers, along with page numbers, appear on the screen as well.

An unusual Typewriter mode turns the Word Juggler editor into an electric typewriter, sending everything you type directly to the printer, including backspaces, negative line feeds and many other controls supported by your printer. You can use this feature to create short memos that are not worth the trouble of working through formatting routines.

Among the many features of this package are a side range of facilities to make possible the assembly of documents, the creation of form letters and the processing of variables. Although the program is a good word-processing system, its real strength lies in its multiple and complex commands that allow you to insert information derived from one or another auxiliary file into a file. The use of variables that you can call, insert or change in accordance with a variety of criteria and conditional tests makes this a powerful document-processing system, one that is suitable for complex mailing-list or form-letter applications.

Any application that needed to use all these features, however, would probably require more disk storage space for files and data than is available on the anemic Apple II disk drives. The program would probably operate best in a hard-disk environment — with five or ten megabytes of space for lists available for complex selecting chores that were worth the time to automate.

The program copes with data files created under ProDos as well as those generated by PFS:File or Quickfile. In addition, you can use Word Juggler to convert DOS 3.3 text files to ProDos files. The program can write standard ASCII text files under ProDos for use by other programs that do not contain any special control codes for formatting.

Quark also produces a competent speller called Lexicheck IIe as a companion to Word Juggler IIe. This program does its job quickly and efficiently. It permits you to construct special dictionaries and has admirable speed in checking and correcting documents, partly thanks to the program design that keeps the entire text in memory. Lexicheck only works on files created with Word Juggler IIe.

What are the disadvantages of this program? Well, unless you are converted to ProDos or have few DOS 3.3 programs and files, the nonstandard but authentically Apple operating system may be an annoyance. But ProDos does permit you to use multiple directories and other more sophisticated operations, so Word Juggler IIe may well be a major word-processing contender in the ProDos environment.

The program's limitations on file size, as well as its editor/formatter structure, may present a problem in some applications. The program comes with a good manual, clear explanations and several printer-setup tables. Not all printers are listed, and although the manual has detailed information on how to create your own printer-setup tables, the task is best left to professionals or skilled Word Juggler users.

Be sure you try this program on your printer/interface-card combination. Word Juggler comes prepared to cope with only a few configurations. The Apple Serial Card with a Diablo 1650 printer worked for most tasks, but failed to underline or boldface properly and wouldn't print bidirectionally. This combination works fine with most other Apple II word-processing programs. When we contacted Quark about this problem, a Quark technical consultant offered to resolve this printer problem if we would send complete printer information and interface-card data to him. Unfortunately, the disks are copy-protected, but backups are available for a small fee.

In short, this is a good product — reliable, powerful, generally easy to use and predictable. It has an advanced operating system. You can use it to best advantage in applications employing hard disks to process complex lists and form letters. Word Juggler comes ready to work with many popular interface cards and printers.

—*John V. Lombardi*

REVIEW

Apple Writer II

Apple Writer II is a word-processing package for the Apple IIe that you will not outgrow, whether you use it in school, at home or at work. Help files and the unusually clear manual mean that even novice computer users will have little difficulty preparing simple documents at first and more complex texts later.

The Apple Writer II package includes both a master and a backup diskette. As the manufacturer suggests, you should use the master and store the backup in a safe place.

The master diskette contains a series of help files to which you can refer at any time by simultaneously depressing the Open Apple and ? keys. The Help menu that appears offers you a choice of on-screen descriptions of such Apple

Writer II features as commands, cursor movements, tabs; and saving and loading files and embedding commands to customize the printing of your documents. Because such information on the diskette is essential for inexperienced users, the ideal system configuration includes two disk drives. This setup lets you keep the master diskette in drive 1 and a diskette for saving and loading files in drive 2. If your system includes only one drive, you have to remove your file diskette and replace it with the master diskette whenever you need help with commands and procedures. An alternative to disk switching, however, is keeping the Apple Writer II manual handy.

Apple Writer II provides a 40-column display, but if you have an Apple 80-column text card in the AUX.CONNECTOR slot inside your computer, the monitor gives you a "what-you-see-is-what-you-get" 80-column display and your text-editing tasks are simplified.

This word-processing software offers the usual uppercase and lowercase letters. As with any text editor, you can delete, move or insert text. The program offers automatic wordwrap at the end of each typewritten line, so you only need a carriage return to end a paragraph.

These abilities are standard for most word-processing software, but Apple Writer II offers other features that help you create professional-looking memos, letters and reports. These additional capabilities include a Find/Replace option for substituting one word or phrase for another. You might take advantage of this feature, for instance, to find out if you overused a particular phrase.

A real timesaver is Apple Writer II's glossary-forming function, with which you can create a file of up to 99 definitions (words or phrases) that the

program inserts into your document wherever you indicate by designator codes.

Apple Writer II is suitable for formatting and printing both personal and professional documents. Not only can you change tabs easily, but you can also save routinely used tab settings in a file for future recall. You can embed commands for underscoring text, printing subscripts and superscripts, and even automatically formatting footnotes within your text. A Print/Program command menu allows you to format your document in terms of margin settings, line spacing, page numbering, text justifying and page-length setting. A special file on the master diskette offers additional printer options such as variable pitch.

Apple Writer II can perform well, even if you've first learned only the few following commands. Pressing Control-N clears the screen for a new document. Pressing the Delete key erases characters. Editing is easy since you control the cursor with the four directional (arrow) keys. Pressing Control-S saves your document; Control-P brings you to the Print/Program command menu. You can accept the default values if you wish and press NP (new print) to begin the printing process.

Eventually, most users will want to take advantage of other Apple Writer II features. For rapid editing, you can use directional keys or control characters to move the cursor word by word instead of character by character, up or down 12 lines at a time, to the beginning of the document or to the end of the document.

Instead of individual characters, you can delete words or paragraphs. Words

Summary
The Apple Writer II word-processing package from Apple Computer provides standard text-editing abilities, along with such advanced features as Find/Replace and a glossary-forming function. The on-screen assistance and documentation get high marks.

System Requirements
- [ ] *Apple IIe*
- [ ] *DOS 3.3*
- [ ] *64K RAM*
- [ ] *One or two disk drives*
- [ ] *80-column text card suggested*

Suggested list price: $195

*Apple Computer
20525 Mariani Avenue
Cupertino, CA 95014
(408) 996-1010*

or paragraphs you have eliminated with control characters go into buffers (temporary areas), so you can retrieve them later. You can also "cut and paste" (move text to new locations) easily. You don't have to memorize commands and procedures for the advanced features of Apple Writer II, because you can easily check them in the manual's index.

Finally exiting from Apple Writer II is easy. Before allowing you to quit, the program reminds you that you may not have saved your latest document and asks you if you really want to quit. This reminder is just one indication of Apple Writer's safety valves. At other points in the program, you can cancel incorrect commands by pressing the Return key. The program ignores incorrect inputs.

The documentation consists of the 208-page Apple Writer II manual and the 147-page WPL (Word-Processing Language) booklet, which is a programming manual you can use as an adjunct to Apple Writer II to customize reports, write individualized form letters, do arithmetic calculations and create your own menus.

The Apple Writer II manual is well organized and clearly written. Its layout is so easy to follow that the "uninitiated" may be tempted to think that all manuals are as well put together. Those of us who have lost our way in the documentation maze from time to time know an outstanding handbook when we find one. This is it.

This manual makes *no* assumptions. Novice microcomputer users receive clear explanations or are referred to an appendix — appendix A, for instance, is an introductory tutorial that takes about 1½ hours — or another Apple manual. The manual urges experienced users to skip a section and move on to another area that may be less familiar.

The format of this 7½×9-inch, spiral-bound manual, in addition to being well planned, is aesthetically pleasing. Important features and notes are highlighted in color: gray boxes contain extra tidbits of information; blue triangles serve as warning signals, indicating problems that you may encounter. The manual is noticeably lacking in errors of omission. The package could benefit, however, from the addition of a laminated quick-reference card or, better yet, a keyboard template.

A program as well conceived and well documented as Apple Writer II will probably not cause you any serious problems. The software comes with a 90-day limited warranty. After this period, if you've returned the software license agreement in the package to Apple Computer, Inc., the company will replace any defective diskette without charge.

Apple's copyright policy is clearly stated in the software license agreement. Since you receive a backup diskette, you may not make copies of Apple Writer II. In addition, you may use Apple Writer II "only in connection with a single computer." A user report form in the package encourages you to report problems or suggest changes to improve the software.

Apple Writer II is a versatile word-processing package that offers text-writing and text-editing functions, as well as various advanced features. The fundamental commands of the program are easy to learn, and you can look up more advanced commands in the clearly written, well-organized manual.

—*Cynthia E. Field*

REVIEW

Magic Window II

Magic Window II is a much-improved version of a venerable Apple II word-processing program. The program is designed to simulate a typewriter, and it uses a "magic window" that moves across an imaginary page.

Magic Window is a "what you see is what you get" word-processing program. The screen image shows page breaks, headers or footers, page numbers and any other characters that will appear on the final printout.

In its earlier version, the program was less than satisfactory because it used a 40-column display — you couldn't see an entire line at one time, — which made proofreading difficult. The new version of Magic Window II eliminates this problem.

The program can now take advantage of an 80-column board to provide a reasonable width for the magic window, or it can use the Apple's high-resolution Graphics mode to generate its own 70-column display. The latter display is not as satisfactory as 80 column, but most competing programs offer similar text displays. In either case, Magic Window II can handle text lines as wide as 160 characters, although you must shift the screen window once or more to view lines of this length.

Magic Window contains many of the editing features you would expect in an Apple word-processing program, although it is not a full-screen editor. You cannot move the cursor by word nor can you backspace to the previous line. Magic Window can scroll your text from the top or bottom of the file, either a line at a time or in half-screen blocks, and can go forward or backward any number of pages.

When you want to insert or delete text, you have some limitations. The editor is always in the Typeover mode, and to insert, you either open up a new line, split an old line, or insert a blank character and then type the new character. You can delete by line, character or cursor to the end of a line, but not by word. You can split and join lines anywhere in the text. If your inserted text exceeds the current line length, the display wraps around to open up a new line for more text.

An interesting feature of Magic Window permits you to copy the character above the cursor: you can create tables with repetitive labels or similar text. You can save and recover deleted lines from a memory stack, which can hold up to 16 lines. You can also use this stack for cut-and-paste operations. If you push more than 16 lines onto the stack, the program deletes the first lines from the stack to make room for the last ones you enter.

The program can justify and reformat text, but in a rather clumsy fashion. If you make changes in your text that leave gaps in lines, you must close them with the Glue command, which reconnects line fragments. You can glue one line or paragraph at a time. If you glue one paragraph at a time, you must separate the paragraphs by a single blank line for single-spaced text and four blank lines for double-spaced text. If you don't, the Glue command removes all your carefully constructed paragraph indents. You can justify text one line or paragraph at a time to provide left, right or complete justification. This routine does not move words among lines to reformat a paragraph. Instead, it reformats text on a line-by-line basis, so you do need to glue your lines first.

InfoWorld Report Card

Magic Window II

	Poor	Fair	Good	Excellent
Performance	☐	☐	■	☐
Documentation	☐	☐	■	☐
Ease of Use	☐	☐	■	☐
Error Handling	☐	■	☐	☐

Summary
In its new version, the word-processing program Magic Window II can use either a 70- or 80-column screen display. The program is easy to use and performs competently if you use it to produce short or medium-size documents. For the production of long or complicated documents, it is slow and less effective.

System Requirements
☐ *Apple II, II Plus*
☐ *DOS 3.3*
☐ *48K RAM (64K desirable)*
☐ *One disk drive*
☐ *Printer (optional)*
☐ *80-column display board (optional)*
☐ *Keyboard enhancer/lowercase adapter (optional)*
☐ *Shift-key modification (optional)*

Suggested list price: $149.95

Artsci
5547 Satsuma Avenue
North Hollywood, CA 91601
(818) 985-2922

Magic Window can print all your text or a range of pages. To indicate the range, you specify the start page and the number of pages you want to print. You can print a duplicate of the formatted file to disk, and you can list files that you want printed in sequence. Magic Window also supports single-sheet or continuous-feed paper.

The program works with a large number of printers and printer-interface cards. Its printing subsystem supports micro-space justification for printers such as the Diablo (an undocumented feature), and it does a fine job with superscripts, subscripts, underlining and boldface. You can enter any special printer-control characters into the file, and the line formatter handles these with ease, ignoring nonprinting characters.

Magic Window's filer subsystem handles the details of storing, retrieving and managing the word-processing files the program uses. The program can read from and write to both formatted and unformatted files. Formatted files contain format information such as tabs, page size and other information that you have set from within the editor, as well as your text. It is best to use this file for edited documents. An unformatted file is a standard ASCII text file which only contains material that you type. You can use this file for source-code and program files, as well as data that you want to insert into other documents.

The program handles document-merge reasonably well, although you might have trouble assembling complicated documents. Magic Window's Search and Replace and Find functions work as you would expect.

Since this is an in-memory word-processing program, it works reasonably fast, although production of long documents can be slow.

Your system's memory size (48K or 64K) determines the possible size of your document in memory. If you are using the 70-column mode instead of an 80-column board, your document size is reduced because the screen routines take up memory space. Maximum document size approximates 26K (or 16 double-spaced pages), and the screen shows you the number of free sectors in memory, possibly to ease comparison with disk space. The program issues repeated loud warnings when the memory is full, and, if you ignore them, you can overrun the memory and crash the program.

Magic Window is a useful word-processing program. Many functions are menu-driven, documentation is good, and the range of features is adequate. Although the editor is not as elegant as some others on the market, it is competent, easy to use and reasonably fast. You can use it effectively to produce short- to medium-size documents and letters that do not require extensive editing or complex formatting.

—*John V. Lombardi*

REVIEW

PIE:Writer

PIE:Writer is a comprehensive word-processing program that combines many editing and formatting features. You use the operations mode to enter text. You can save files as Text, or as

Binary, with nonprinting formatting commands that control your printer.

The cursor keys move the cursor up, down, left and right in single steps. This arrangement on the Apple II Plus uses the Control key. You can also move the cursor to the top or bottom of the screen page, the beginning or end of the file, the start or end of a line, or to the next word right or left. The program's Search commands move the cursor to any specified phrase, either forward or backward in the file.

You can easily delete words or lines, and the remaining text reclaims the freed space. You can copy blocks of text (in increments of lines) or move them within the file. PIE:Writer's Search and Replace commands can find and change strings either singly or all at the same time.

PIE:Writer's command level provides most Apple DOS commands, such as Init, Catalog and Rename. In many cases, you can use abbreviations to make these commands, thus saving yourself keystrokes. You can obtain a word or line count of the file in memory. You can also connect a file in memory to a disk file or vice versa.

You can send a disk file to the printer, video screen or a device in a motherboard slot. This feature, and the ability to format and save text files on disk, means you can use PIE:Writer with a modem as a basic terminal program to transfer files between computers.

The program can merge strings from a file, such as a mailing list, into another file to create a customized form letter (mail-merge).

Using the Apple's Exec command, you can create macros: single commands that perform a series of routine commands. PIE:Writer includes a macro to automatically back up a file. The disk file is renamed with a .BAK

extension, and then the current memory file is saved to the disk with the original name.

PIE:Writer's Formatter interprets special commands you place in the file to structure final output. The program places these commands on a separate line preceding the text they manipulate. Commands include centering, line adjustment, line spacing, headers and footers, automatic page numbering, page breaks, boldface and underlining (if your printer supports them), and others.

The Formatter also controls the printer routines. It can format and print, write to disk or display the final version on the screen. You can print selected pages, as well as make up to 99 copies of the selected text.

PIE:Writer tries to follow any formatting command. The program disregards commands it does not support and proceeds to format the text. The program does not format the text on the screen as does WordStar — you must leave the Editor to view formatted text on the screen or to transfer it to the printer. Nor does the program allow you to mark text blocks that begin within a line or end within a line to copy or move. The text-printing routines are more flexible than WordStar's, though, and the Editor and Formatter commands are easier to learn.

Furthermore, PIE:Writer is written in open code (both basic and machine level). This open coding allows you to modify the program for special uses. Like most other word processors, PIE:Writer does not work with printers capable of micro-spaced proportional printing.

All of PIE:Writer fits in memory. This allows it to move text quickly (without disk probes). This version of

InfoWorld
Report Card

PIE:Writer

	Poor	Fair	Good	Excellent
Performance	☐	☐	☐	■
Documentation	☐	☐	☐	■
Ease of Use	☐	☐	■	☐
Error Handling	☐	☐	☐	■

Summary
PIE:Writer is a comprehensive word-processing program with which you can format and edit text. Editing commands are easy to learn, but formatting commands take longer to master. The program has more functions than most other word-processing programs for the Apple, making the time spent learning it worthwhile.

System Requirements
☐ *Apple II, II Plus, IIe*
☐ *DOS 3.3*
☐ *48K RAM minimum*
☐ *One or more disk drives*

Suggested list price: $149.95

Hayden Software
600 Suffolk Street
Lowell, MA 01854
(800) 343-1218
(617) 937-0200 (in MA)

PIE:Writer, however, is designed for computers with a maximum of 64K RAM; thus the program has buffer space for text only up to this limit. Today it is common for Apple IIe's and many Pluses to have extra memory.

The allocated buffer holds about 15 pages of text. If your documents are larger, you must split them into modules you can chain together during formatting. This procedure makes editing larger documents more difficult, but it also allows file lengths up to your available disk storage.

Although PIE:Writer's commands are easy to use, the program's extra functions and abilities require practice and learning to master. The time you spend (about an hour of hands-on study) learning to use the editor is worthwhile because you can use it to write programs. Formatting commands are more difficult to learn, and several hours are required to master the program.

Once learned, the system is easy to use and powerful. Your ability to embed control and escape commands, to program the printer, is useful, as is the ability to write formatted files to disk rather than to the printer.

PIE:Writer's documentation is well written and indexed. The disk utility supplied with the program makes learning the editor easy. The documentation is organized more as a reference manual than tutorial, but it is complete.

Hayden Software provides telephone support to registered users.

PIE:Writer is a comprehensive word processor that exceeds the abilities of most other such programs for the Apple and can perform a variety of formatting tasks.

Once mastered, the program commands are easy to use. The Editor is straightforward — both novice and advanced users will quickly be able to edit files — but beginners will find the Formatter more difficult. As you spend time with the program, though, you learn shortcuts and more fully appreciate PIE:Writer's power.

—*Tom Neudecker*

NUMBERS

The programs in this category help take the headache out of dealing with numbers. For example, they prepare taxes, calculate spreadsheets and formulate schedules.

REVIEW

VisiCalc Advanced

VisiCalc, the granddaddy of electronic spreadsheets, was first introduced in 1979. VisiCorp has since improved the product. The result of several efforts is VisiCalc Advanced Version, which operates only on an Apple IIe with 128K bytes of memory, an 80-column card and two disk drives. A printer is helpful if you want to print out your spreadsheets.

One of the most notable improvements in the program is the inclusion of on-screen help. At any time during operation, you can type ? and get information related to what you're doing at the moment. You can then ask for more detailed information or return to your worksheet.

It is still familiar in appearance, though. The new version still uses numbers to identify rows and letters to designate columns. You move the cursor from cell to cell by pressing the four arrow keys. You can also go directly to a cell by typing its coordinates.

The cells in the advanced version behave differently, however. You can now modify them with a large range of so-called attributes. Cells, locked to a fixed width in the original version of VisiCalc, now can be widened or narrowed at will, so that items such as 12 for a payment number and 43939208372 for an account number can go into adjacent columns. You can set cell width, as any of the other attributes, individually, or you can choose one width for all cells. Text stored in cells for the purpose of labeling columns can now be left-justified, right-justified or centered within the cell itself. You can dress up your worksheet so it has a more attractive appearance. You can also

REVIEWS

InfoWorld
Report Card

VisiCalc Advanced

	Poor	Fair	Good	Excellent
Performance	☐	☐	■	☐
Documentation	☐	☐	☐	■
Ease of Use	☐	☐	■	☐
Error Handling	☐	☐	☐	■

Summary
VisiCalc Advanced may look pricey for a spreadsheet, but it may be worth it. A good improvement over the original product, it now includes more calculation capability, more flexibility in defining your worksheet and a help facility. It's an all-around good product.

System Requirements
☐ *Apple IIe*
☐ *DOS 3.3*
☐ *128K RAM*
☐ *Two disk drives*
☐ *80-column text card*
☐ *Printer optional*

Suggested list price: $400

VisiCorp
2895 Zanker Road
San Jose, CA 95134
(408) 946-9000

"hide" the contents of cells from view, if, for example, the data are of an internal nature that you don't necessarily want to display on the finished worksheet. The hidden data may also be sensitive information you want to keep confidential. You can also tag cells so you won't inadvertently erase or alter them.

VisiCalc Advanced Version gives you a wide variety of options when it comes to printing your worksheet. Don't worry about your spreadsheet being too wide for the printer to accommodate. The sheet can be as large as 63 columns wide by 255 rows deep, and the program can print the spreadsheet in sections you can later paste together. You can print out any worksheet or part of a worksheet as you define it. You can instruct the printer to break the worksheet into pages, number the pages and print with titles, and you can set the page length, width and margins.

By using the "expression" attribute during printing, you can show the formula of any cell or group of cells.

The other attributes help you on the screen. The Tab attribute speeds up data entry by allowing you to skip directly from one cell to the next cell you have identified with that attribute. The program sports a split-screen feature; you can divide the screen either horizontally or vertically, and you can operate on each section independently. The Format attribute lets you display numbers as integers, aligned to the left or right, as dollars and cents or in a graphic format. The graphic format uses asterisks to form a horizontal bar graph whose width is proportional to the value of the data.

Keystroke memory allows you to store a repetitive pattern or sequence of keystrokes and subsequently use a single key instead. You can define, erase or edit sequences that may contain any

number, formula, label or command up to 123 keystrokes in length. You can create up to 26 such sequences.

The ability of VisiCalc Advanced Version to perform calculations has improved over the original version. A date-and-time function lets you compare two dates. For those who want to do any financial work involving interest rates, present and future values of annuities or monthly payments, VisiCalc Advanced Version has functions that will calculate these factors.

The VisiCalc manual is good. Its small size makes it easy to prop up on a crowded desktop. Its hardcover loose-leaf format makes flipping through the pages easy. Both a complete glossary, which defines functions and phrases, and an index are combined in a single listing. The manual is tutorial where it needs to be, yet concise when acting as a reference manual. We wish more programs had the wall-size flowchart included here. It diagrams the interrelationship of all the keystrokes, commands and features.

A chart like this is necessary because of the complexity of VisiCalc. It is not the easiest program to learn. For instance, the command line is a series of letters. What you see on the screen is ABCDEFGIKMPRSTVW. You have to refer to the chart if you want to find out what those letters mean.

We do find some fault with the start-up instruction, though. The package contains two disks; the first disk is solely for loading and cannot be copied. The second is the program disk, which you can copy. You use the loader disk only once each session.

According to the loading instructions, you put the loader disk in drive 1, turn the power on and wait until the disk stops whirring. Then, according to the instructions, you remove the loader disk, insert the program disk and repeat the operation. But repeating the operation for the program disk won't work because when you reset the computer, you erase whatever the loader disk put into memory. What you're really supposed to do is put the loader disk into drive 1 and the program disk into drive 2 and *then* begin.

Customer support from VisiCorp products is good, The company maintains an 8 A.M. to 5 P.M. (Pacific time) hot line, (408) 942-6000, in addition to its regular corporate number. If you want to increase your expertise or productivity with VisiCalc Advanced Version, a subsidiary of VisiCorp called VisiPress publishes a book called *VisiCalc Advanced Version Worksheets for Business*, which contains models for expense accounts, calculating your net worth, estimating the cost of a job, evaluating and depreciating equipment and forecasting sales.

If you had to choose any single program as being the most useful and valuable in an unlimited variety of ways, you probably would choose VisiCalc. Some of the competition is providing the same features at a cost that makes VisiCalc look expensive. VisiCalc has some desirable features that other products don't. Multiplan, for instance, won't handle files in DIF (data-interchange format), nor will it do date-and-time arithmetic, nor calculate interest rates on loans (unless you specify the formula). VisiCalc is a good choice for spreadsheet work.

—*Marty Petersen*

REVIEW

Multiplan

It's no accident that Microsoft's Multiplan was voted the 1982 Software Product of the Year by *InfoWorld* magazine. Multiplan is a good electronic spreadsheet program that incorporates special functions to facilitate its use for financial models. It gives the pioneer of electronic spreadsheets, VisiCalc, a good run for its money.

Multiplan has the same spreadsheet capacity as VisiCalc — 256 rows by 63 columns. You can place a variety of information in each of its cells (a cell is the intersection of a row and column). For instance, if you are preparing your household budget, you can label the columns by month and label the rows with category names, such as Income, Food, Clothing, Rent, Insurance and Charge Accounts. You can then fill the cells with applicable numerical information, such as how much money you spent on food in March, or how much rent you paid in January.

You can put formulas, as well as numerical information, into cells. Column 13 (the column after December in our example), for instance, can have a formula that represents the total of the preceding 12 columns or a year-end summary. In the same manner, you can create cells that display monthly totals.

The advantage of an electronic spreadsheet is that, if you change one number on the spreadsheet, the program automatically updates all other cells that display information related to that number (such as the monthly and year-end totals in our example).

When you first boot Multiplan, your screen displays a blank grid of cells with a set of commands underneath. The

InfoWorld
R e p o r t   C a r d

Multiplan

	Poor	Fair	Good	Excellent
Performance	☐	☐	■	☐
Documentation	☐	☐	☐	■
Ease of Use	☐	☐	■	☐
Error Handling	☐	☐	☐	■

Summary
Multiplan is a useful electronic spreadsheet program that has many similarities with VisiCalc, the first electronic spreadsheet. Multiplan incorporates many special functions that make it useful for building financial models. It is as easy to use as a complex program of this sort can be, and it comes with excellent documentation.

System Requirements
☐ *Apple II, II Plus, IIe*
☐ *DOS 3.3*
☐ *48K, 64K or 128K RAM*
☐ *One or two disk drives*

Suggested list price: $275

Microsoft Corporation
10700 Northup Way
Bellevue, WA 98004
(206) 828-8080

cells are numbered across the top and down the left side. You can identify cell address or location by its coordinates, such as R3C5 for row 3, column 5. This notation differs from that of VisiCalc, which uses letters of the alphabet for columns and numbers for rows. Thus R3C5 in Multiplan would be E3 in a VisiCalc spreadsheet.

The command line that appears on the bottom of the screen, below the grid, lists the options you have. This command setup is another major difference between Multiplan and VisiCalc. When you use VisiCalc, you have to first type /, and the program then presents a series of letters at the top of the screen, each of which represents a command. You have to know what those letters represent, either by looking through the manual or, if you have the Advanced Version of VisiCalc, invoking on-screen Help.

Multiplan's commands are in plain English — the program uses words, such as Alpha, Blank, Copy and Delete. Although, at first glance, word commands seem easier to understand than letter commands, the word commands take as much time to learn. Also, although Multiplan's commands are English words, they still don't tell you how to achieve a desired result — you usually have to resort to the program's on-line Help feature.

Multiplan's on-line Help screens are good — wherever you are in the program, if you press ? you can get help in the specific area in which you're working. You can page through the program's entire 63 pages of Help, or you can call for Help by major categories. Although the Help screens are helpful, they can sometimes be ambiguous.

As you use Multiplan to create your own spreadsheets and design your own formulas, you begin to appreciate a major innovation of the program — your ability to name cells. Naming is different from labeling. For example, a cell labeled "Profit" is just a cell that contains text information, but a cell that contains data information — usually the result of a formula — can be named "Profit." You can also name cells containing sales data "Sales," and the cells containing cost information "Cost." The advantage of naming cells is that you can write a formula for profit — for example, Profit = Sales − Cost and place it in the desired cell. (When you use VisiCalc, you have to say F3=F1−F2.)

Working with large spreadsheets can be irritating if you have to scroll from one end of the spreadsheet to the other when you want to compare labels (usually on the extreme left side of the spreadsheet) with recent data (usually on the extreme right). When you use Multiplan, you can divide the screen up into as many as eight windows (VisiCalc offers you two) and you can even put borders around them. Thus you can permanently display your row labels along the left edge, your column headings along the top edge and use the rest of the screen area for cell manipulation.

Multiplan can work with not only one spreadsheet but can link up to eight spreadsheets at a time. This means, for example, that a national sales manager can devise a spreadsheet that can call for data from several regional spreadsheets and can then produce a grand summary. Multiplan can also do iterative calculations. As an example of an iterative calculation, suppose you earn $1000, and you want to pay your salesperson 10% of your *net* (not gross) profit. If you gave the salesperson $100, that would leave you with $900, but

$100 is not 10% of $900 (your net profit). The problem in trying to determine the exact amount of the commission is that each value depends on the other. This situation is known as a circular reference — the computer has to recalculate many times until you have a result as accurate as you want it to be.

Multiplan does not support DIF (data-interchange format), which is popular with VisiCalc users because it allows graphics and other programs to use your speadsheet data. Multiplan does, however, have its own variety of DIF, called SYLK (symbolic link). You can use SYLK to exchange information between Multi-Tool software tools and other application programs. Multi-Tool software is a new series of software designed to build custom Multiplan worksheets in minutes. Multiplan can convert DIF files into the SYLK format.

Multiplan displays, on the bottom of your worksheet, a "percentage of memory left" to advise you of memory usage.

No program as complex as Multiplan or VisiCalc is easy to learn to operate. Microsoft has learned a thing or two from VisiCalc's original procedures, however, and has improved them. One of these areas concerns replicating, or copying, groups of cells. When you replicate part of a spreadsheet using VisiCalc, you type a formula specifying the coordinates of the starting and ending cells to copy (the source range) and the coordinates to which you want to copy them (the target range). Using Multiplan, you can move the cursor to the locations you want to "pick" from and "put" to, and the replication process operates more smoothly and with less effort.

Multiplan offers more special functions than the original VisiCalc program. Multiplan can calculate the average value of a specified range of values. The program can also compute the standard deviation (useful for those who use the bell-shaped normalization curve) and can count the number of items in a list. If you want column or row totals, instead of entering "R2C7=R2C1+R2C2+ . . . " you can use the Sum function and merely type "R2C7=SUM (R2C1:R2C6)." Alternatively, you can put the cursor on the cell in which you want the total to appear, press =, type SUM and move the cursor to the cells you want to total (or enter the cells' names).

One of the most powerful functions in any program is its ability to perform IF...THEN...ELSE logic — and Multiplan is no exception. This logic, as well as AND, OR and NOT logic, is included in Multiplan's special functions.

With its Lookup function, Multiplan can tell you the cell address of any specified value in a table or can scan through data and pick out maximum and minimum values in a list of values. It can even calculate NPV, the net present value (amount of money) that you require now to produce a specified cash amount in the future, given some interest rate.

Multiplan comes in a clear plastic box that can form an easel to prop up the manual in an easy-reading position. The manual is the same small size as VisiCalc's and has the same high-quality features: hard-cover, three-ring binder, heavy paper, professional-grade printing and screen diagrams.

Two disks come with the program — a loader disk and a program disk. The loader disk is copy-protected in an unconventional way — Microsoft lets you make one, and only one, backup copy. You can make as many copies as you like of the program disk, however, which saves a lot of wear and tear on the disk.

Microsoft supports its customers with a hot line, (206) 828-8089, which is staffed by technicians.

Multiplan is a second-generation electronic-spreadsheet program. Microsoft built on the basic ideas of VisiCalc and has added a few innovations of its own to improve the product. (VisiCalc, however, has many of these same improvements in its new Advanced Version.) Each program has something the other does not have.

—*Marty Petersen*

REVIEW

Tax Preparer

Tax Preparer, the latest edition of HowardSoft software for the preparation of individual income-tax returns, provides you with a completed Form 1040 that is suitable for filing with the IRS. This program is a useful tool for professional tax preparers, as well as individuals who wish to automate the yearly chore of reporting their income and deductions to the federal government. Using Tax Preparer, you can print pages 1 and 2 of Form 1040 on preprinted forms, or you can print these pages on blank paper and align them on an acetate facsimile of the 1040. You can then copy the acetate and blank 1040 form together on a regular copier to yield a "printed" quality 1040.

Tax Preparer also prints all normally required supporting schedules in facsimile form. The program's facsimile supporting schedules do not much resemble those that you might be used

to seeing, but they do conform to current IRS guidelines for computer-generated forms.

Tax Preparer uses a regular 1040 format for the preparation of returns. That is, you start at the top of the page, fill out your name, social-security number and occupation. Working your way down the page, you fill in your filing status, exemptions and dependents and, eventually, salaries, interest, dividends and so on.

For items of income and deductions, the program produces supporting schedules through its Itemizer function. Tax Preparer's Itemizer, or I, feature is not to be confused with itemized deductions — the I feature is Tax Preparer's key to multiple supporting schedules. Here's how it works: If you want to prepare a tax return for a single taxpayer, a single entry in the salaries line of the 1040 mode may be enough. If, however, the taxpayer is married or has changed jobs during the year, you must summarize the wage income. Tax Preparer's I feature takes you to a supporting schedule where you enter the various amounts of salary income. The program then totals all the entries and properly includes them on page 1 of Form 1040. Using this procedure, you can go through a 1040 and prepare all necessary schedules.

For interest and dividends, Tax Preparer prepares a facsimile Schedule B for a supporting schedule. To prepare this schedule, you must be on the interest or dividend lines of the 1040. If you then use the I feature, Tax Preparer goes directly to the facsimile Schedule B for supporting input. If the Schedule B does not provide enough room to adequately summarize your interest and dividend income, another touch of the I feature will take you to a secondary supporting schedule. The same method works with items of deduction. Whether a professional or an individual is preparing the return, Tax Preparer efficiently aids in organizing, compiling and computing the data.

Tax Preparer can decrease the drudgery of tax-return preparation and can increase its mathematical accuracy. Often if you change one number on a tax return, you must then change many others. If you are preparing your return manually, a few changes can result in hours of additional calculations — and you run the risk of introducing arithmetical errors. With Tax Preparer, however, you can easily enter and recompute any changes in a matter of minutes.

For professional tax-preparers, the program offers a useful means for them to maintain a disk library and ease record-keeping by using storage disks. Additionally, Tax Preparer can print client billing and instruction letters. You can obtain California-state supplements to the software, and the program's manual indicates that other state supplements might soon be available.

Tax Preparer has limitations — most noticeable is its slowness. The program requires a fair amount of time to refresh itself (reorganize its memory space) between inputs. You can use additional memory to speed up the data input and computational time, but the cost of additional memory needs to be weighed against the program's additional performance.

The program's second limitation relates to its scope of technical coverage. For example, Tax Preparer cannot prepare schedules for moving-expense deductions or the foreign tax credit.

Tax Preparer isn't a good planning tool, but it doesn't claim to be tax-planning software. Tax-planning software allows you to analyze the effect of several variables over a series of years, but Tax Preparer can handle

only one year at a time. Since the tax laws change so frequently, good tax planning always involves consideration of which year is the most beneficial for you to receive certain items of income or to take certain deductions. Tax Preparer isn't set up to perform these functions (but then, tax-planning software doesn't prepare tax returns).

Tax Preparer is easy to use, if you read the program manual before you start using the program. The program's screen instructions are well organized and logical. You must be familiar with federal tax law to efficiently and correctly use Tax Preparer, though.

Tax Preparer is well set up to handle your input errors, because the software accepts few types of entries. If you enter an erroneous command, the program prompts you to correct it. Tax Preparer allows you to fix an error or to go forward in spite of an error message, through the use of options.

Tax Preparer's documentation comes in a 9×7-inch loose-leaf binder. Pouches hold the dual-sided software disk and a blank storage disk that you must initialize. The manual is readable and easy to follow. It has no index, but the table of contents is comprehensive.

The manual makes a good effort to explain the complexities of the federal income-tax law for individuals. It wisely suggests professional advice for novices. It also suggests you use various IRS publications if you want to learn more about the tax laws and want to know how to do computer-prepared tax returns. The tax-planning supplement to the documentation for 1983 suggests that you can use the 1982 software for 1983 projections; however, it underestimates the effect that the new Alternative Minimum Tax

InfoWorld
R e p o r t   C a r d

Tax Preparer

	Poor	Fair	Good	Excellent
Performance	☐	☐	■	☐
Documentation	☐	☐	☐	■
Ease of Use	☐	☐	■	☐
Error Handling	☐	☐	■	☐

Summary

Tax Preparer enables you to produce a computer-prepared, Form 1040 tax return that is suitable for filing with the IRS. It is useful to either professional tax-preparers who prepare hundreds of tax returns or individuals who wish to prepare their own returns. You should have some knowledge of income-tax law to use this product. The program's documentation is excellent.

System Requirements
☐ *Apple II, II Plus, III*
☐ *DOS 3.3*
☐ *48K RAM*
☐ *One disk drive*
☐ *Printer*

Suggested list price: $225

HowardSoft
8008 Girard Avenue, Suite 310
La Jolla, CA 92037
(619) 454-0121

(AMT) has on 1983 returns in certain situations.

Tax Preparer comes with a 90-day warranty. The program is not copy-protected, but you can only use copies for backup purposes. Yearly updates are essential, and HowardSoft provides them at a reduced cost. The company also provides registered users with program updates and improvements when applicable.

Tax Preparer is a useful tool for tax professionals and individuals who understand the income-tax laws as they apply to individuals. Professionals who are already using a computerized tax-preparation service should weigh the benefits that Tax Preparer can provide — for example, savings in cost and time.

—*David Sevres*

REVIEW

Practical Accountant

Practical Accountant is a single-entry bookkeeping system for the Apple II family that is flexible enough to handle small-business accounting needs. Softlink has put together a straightforward accounting system that will meet most of the needs of people who have small accounting problems. Farmers, retailers and managers could easily use this simple system.

Our judgment is that Practical Accountant does exactly what it is advertised to do. It is *not* a sophisticated accounting system to rival $3000 products. It does provide simple computer-aided accounting to small-business operations.

Practical Accountant handles both accounts payable and accounts receivable as well as cash-flow reports and forecasting. You may also use the program as a simple payroll system: it will print checks and give you a breakdown of individual expenses.

Like most accounting systems, Practical Accountant allows you to define your own chart of accounts. You can use up to 50 categories with 300 subcategories and 20 tax-type definitions. The system will handle a maximum of 634 transactions (either a check or a deposit) with two disk drives, which are the required minimum. That's roughly 52 transactions per month. If you add an additional disk drive, you can have 1130 more transactions. With four disk drives, you could have a total of 2800 checks or deposits. No special modifications are required to use the additional drives.

The use of an 80-column card is optional with the Apple IIe; you can't use it with an Apple II or Apple II Plus. Although the card is not required, it does allow you to view your reports before you send them to a printer. Without the card, you cannot view the entire report until you print it.

Reconciling your checkbook with a bank statement each month is easy with this program. You can have it search for checks written between two dates and indicate whether or not the bank has received them. Once you've done that for all your checks and deposits, you should have a total that agrees with the bank's total.

If you make a mistake entering a record into Practical Accountant, you can easily change it at any time. All totals and ledgers will automatically change when you edit the record.

The program generates different reports. You can call either short or extended reports that are listed by date, payee, accounts receivable, accounts payable, reconciled, unreconciled or any combination of the above. You can also obtain cash-flow reports by category, subcategory or tax types as you have defined them.

The performance of the program is average. The primary factor that slows it down is that it regularly stores your information while you are still working. The advantage of this slowness is that you lose a minimum amount of information in the event of a power failure or other problem with your computer's memory.

Practical Accountant uses menus to guide you through its operation and has a number of built-in Help options in case you get stuck. You receive complete examples and step-by-step instructions for preparing disks, entering information, getting reports and creating backup copies of your disks. There are no installation requirements, and all terms, including the word *menu,* are defined on the screen the first time they are used.

A complete novice should have no problem with Practical Accountant, since it assumes no expertise in accounting or computer science. The commands are easy to remember and the program takes advantage of the special keys on the Apple IIe.

The program deals with errors in the same spirit as its instructions do. If you enter an improbable date, you receive an error message, and can enter it again. If the question calls for a *Y* or *N* answer, those are the only letters the program will accept. The program also prevents you from giving an incorrect response to a menu prompt. In some cases, you can even ask for possible correct answers to the current question.

The documentation includes a spiral-bound, 213-page manual and a reference card covering the Apple II, II Plus and IIe computers. The manual has tutorial and reference sections. The tutorial section contains 11 chapters taking you step by step through the Practical Accountant system. This section begins explaining accounting systems, terms and concepts. The manual also has sample charts of accounts for small-business and farm applications. Every function and procedure is covered in this section.

The second section is a reference guide for all the commands for experienced users. All menus are represented in flowchart form with complete explanations. There are also instructions you can follow to change certain features of the program. This section is complete and should answer any questions you have. Both sections are written in clear, readable language, and all "mysterious" terms are defined before use.

Hardware and software requirements are also clearly defined in the reference section. The index is thorough and provides quick access to either section. In short, the style and organization of the documentation are excellent.

Customer support comes through dealers and directly from Softlink. Softlink has a toll-free number and provided quick, courteous and correct answers to our questions. You can make your own backup copies of both the diskettes containing the program and those containing your information. In fact, the publisher recommends you do this.

Overall, the program is good. It has the features needed for many accounting applications without the overhead of complicated accounting

InfoWorld
R e p o r t C a r d

Practical Accountant

	Poor	Fair	Good	Excellent
Performance	☐	☐	■	☐
Documentation	☐	☐	☐	■
Ease of Use	☐	☐	☐	■
Error Handling	☐	☐	■	☐

Summary
Practical Accountant gives Apple II owners a good single-entry accounting system. It is well suited to its audience of small-business owners, managers and others who don't need double-entry bookkeeping. Its documentation is well written, and the program gives first-time users clear explanations. We recommend it.

System Requirements
☐ *Apple II, II Plus, IIe*
☐ *64K RAM*
☐ *At least two, and can use as many as four, disk drives*
☐ *Printer and 80-column card (for IIe) recommended*

Suggested list price: $150

Softlink
3255-2 Scott Blvd.
Santa Clara, CA 95051
(408) 988-8011

REVIEWS

Summary
VisiSchedule is an excellent tool for planning and monitoring projects built from as many as 160 subordinate jobs. Its documentation is fine; its backup policy is open to criticism.

System Requirements
- ☐ *Apple II, II Plus or III*
- ☐ *Apple Pascal (run-time system supplied with program)*
- ☐ *48K RAM for Apple II or II Plus; 128K for Apple III*

Suggested list price: $300

VisiCorp
2895 Zanker Road
San Jose, CA 95134
(408) 946-9000

systems. It is not the answer to everyone's accounting problems, but it does cover small applications extremely well. The program takes the needs of novices seriously with its ease of use, clear explanations and enjoyable documentation. If you need a small, single-entry accounting system, we recommend Practical Accountant.
—*Mark Renne*

REVIEW

VisiSchedule

VisiSchedule from VisiCorp is a software package for the Apple II that you can effectively use as a tool for planning and monitoring projects built from as many as 160 subordinate activities.

VisiSchedule is a menu-driven program that provides commands for entering and editing project-schedule data along with manpower and cost data. The program develops project schedules from the data, which take into account the order in which the component activities of the project must be completed and respect stipulated earliest start dates for activities.

Project schedules are displayed in graphic form on your CRT as they are developed. If necessary, you can recall and review them.

You can print the schedule's graphic representation and a variety of other reports pertaining to your projects as well. You can save project data sets in disk files and recall the data for modification.

You can also transfer project-related data to DIF (data-interchange format) files for other application programs to use.

VisiSchedule analysis of a project starts with the entry of information associated with the project. In the usual sequence of events, the first information that you enter when planning a project with VisiSchedule is a description of the project as a whole.

Next you enter information about the skills required to perform the jobs, including salary levels.

For VisiSchedule to determine the project schedule, you have to provide it with the details of your working calendar and with a detailed list of the component activities and their relationships.

VisiSchedule refers to the component activities of a project as "jobs." It allows you to assign a description (of up to 30 characters) to each job of a project, and it expects you to specify a duration for each job as well.

In addition, for each job, VisiSchedule expects you to specify an earliest date on which the job can begin. You can also specify up to nine jobs that must be completed as a prerequisite to starting the given job.

Finally, VisiSchedule allows you to specify a deadline date for each job, the fixed cost associated with each job, and the manpower skill requirements for each job.

As you enter job-related data, VisiSchedule displays a graphic depiction of your schedule in the upper portion of the CRT. Calendar dates are printed across the top of the screen and day or week numbers (as appropriate) are displayed one line beneath them.

Descriptions of up to 17 jobs are displayed in columns 1 to 16 on the left side of the screen. The program uses lines, arrows and various special symbols beneath the calendar to show how it would schedule those jobs. Because of the limited size of the CRT display, you can only see a limited portion of the calendar at any one time.

VisiSchedule provides a variety of commands so that you can shift the display to change the group of jobs' schedules, which is important when you are dealing with more than 17. As you enter new jobs, the program revises your schedule and updates the schedule's graphic display.

You can use the schedule's graph to find out the earliest times at which jobs *may* start and the latest times at which jobs *must* start to prevent delaying the project's completion date. As jobs are completed, you can enter that data in VisiSchedule and change the graph accordingly. At any time, you can print the graph for consultation and review purposes.

You can direct VisiSchedule to display manpower requirements for any one job category or in total along with the schedule. You can direct the program to adjust the schedule of jobs (within the confines of their earliest and latest start dates) to level manpower requirements in any one skill category.

In addition to the printed schedule graph, VisiSchedule can also print three different types of text reports for a project: a "project description report," which gives the description, skill categories, working days and holidays, and various summary totals for a project; a "job description report," which provides summary details about each component project job; and a "tabular job report," which prints user-selected, job-related information in parallel columns of a report page. You can even determine the sorting order in which jobs are listed in the two latter reports.

When you need graphs requiring more than one horizontal page, VisiSchedule prints the graph on a series of pages you can tape together.

On the whole, VisiSchedule does what it's supposed to do accurately and well. Its schedule graphs are computed flawlessly, and the graphic schedule display is attractively designed within the limits of the standard ASCII character set.

Its schedule computations are performed at an entirely acceptable but not blinding speed. There are, however, other areas in which its speed may be of some concern. When the VisiSchedule display contains its maximum number of activities, it takes about six seconds to redraw that display each time it's changed or shifted.

In the course of entering and reviewing a schedule with a large number of activities spread over a reasonably long period of time, this delay is apt to occur a significant number of times (certainly at least once for each new job added to the schedule). These six-second delays can add up to a considerable waiting penalty in the course of a session.

This problem could be partly alleviated if you could shut off the display of the schedule graph when you entered job-related data. Unfortunately, VisiSchedule offers no way to do this. A similar problem occurs because VisiSchedule is written in Pascal. As a result, it reads the program disk after almost every command.

This disk-reading doesn't slow the program down more than a second or so each time. The number of commands you are likely to enter in the course of using this menu-driven program is high, though, so the cumulative time penalty that results from these one-second delays can be substantial.

All input to VisiSchedule is governed by menu commands.

VisiSchedule's menus are a model of fine human engineering, and, as menus, they are always easy to use. The menus are in the same format as most of VisiCorp's other "Visi" product menus. In certain situations, however, a menu-driven command structure can make input more difficult rather than easier for users. This is the case in one important aspect of VisiSchedule usage: data entry.

For example, to enter the name and duration of a single job, you must press the Return key twice for each item you enter.

With a question-and-answer dialogue, you could avoid pressing the Return key twice. A screen-entry method would save even more keystrokes. When you are entering data for a project that involves many jobs, the two or more Return keystrokes per entry detract significantly from VisiSchedule's ease of use.

VisiSchedule has a default technique that it applies when you add to jobs or insert new ones into a job schedule. This default is supposed to ease data entry, but often it makes job entries more difficult instead.

VisiSchedule assumes job prerequisites according to well-defined rules. You must redefine prerequisites when you don't want the assumed ones.

In addition, you may have a scheduling situation in which the assumptions were incorrect. In such situations, it is a nuisance to repeatedly override the assumptions. A command that could cancel the default assumption of prerequisites would facilitate entry of schedules.

The documentation for VisiSchedule is good. The package comes with a handsomely bound, attractively printed manual that is well written and complete. It leaves no stone unturned.

It includes a tutorial that leads first-time users through the use of the package and all of its features. It has a complete reference manual for experienced users, a table of contents, and a full index.

The manual's six appendices include one that provides a complete listing and explanation of all program- and system-error messages, one with instructions on interchanging VisiSchedule data with other applications and one containing a summary list of the program's capacity. Other appendices include a bibliography on scheduling and a helpful glossary of terms used in scheduling.

The appendix on exchanging files with other applications includes an overview of the data-interchange format (DIF) and listings of three sample Applesoft BASIC programs that read and write DIF files.

Unfortunately, there is no documentation describing the internal structure of VisiSchedule's own files or techniques that you might use to import data from other applications into VisiSchedule.

VisiSchedule's error handling is superb. It anticipates both the usual and some rather extraordinary user errors and intercepts them with an error message and report before any damage can occur.

It recognizes and returns meaningful error messages for a variety of hardware error conditions and general environmental errors such as damaged disks. The program keeps you from loading a new schedule into memory if doing so may inadvertently wipe out a project schedule that you have not yet saved.

Conversely, VisiSchedule reminds you that you have already saved a project-schedule file, if you try to save it again.

The error messages are short and generally meaningful. Numbers are assigned to the error messages — 75 in all — and you can consult the manual's appendix for more detailed explanations of any message.

VisiCorp provides a telephone hotline number for customers or dealers. We had no occasion to call for help, so we cannot evaluate the company's support in this respect.

VisiCorp's backup policy seems worthy of serious criticism. VisiSchedule is a copy-protected program. VisiCorp provides a 90-day warranty on the original diskette and will replace it free of charge if it's found to be defective within that period.

Diskettes that fail after 90 days but within the first year of use will be replaced for $20. Owners can purchase one backup copy of the program for the same fee.

These fees for backup and replacement copies are among the highest we've seen in the industry. Given the substantial, albeit justifiable, initial cost of VisiSchedule, and its high level of disk activity, these charges seem particularly ungracious.

—Joel Pitt

REVIEW

VersaForm

Simply put, VersaForm is an impressive information-handling system for the Apple IIe and II Plus. With this program you work with exact duplicates of any paperwork you now use for data storage and manipulation. Just as you now do on paper, you work with *forms* on your video screen; this feature lends itself to quick familiarization with the product. Best of all, there are no cryptic commands to learn and use.

You begin by designing your form. This is a surprisingly simple task: moving the cursor around the screen, you type in the names of what you want to keep track of and add ellipsis points to indicate field lengths. You store alphanumeric information in columns, and you can instruct the system to do whatever math you need between them. Columns can extend over multiple pages. Each form can include up to 50 data fields and track up to 4000 characters of information. The system can keep running totals and carry entries from one column to the next.

You also mark the fields you want VersaForm to automatically fill in (look up the price and description for item #KMG-6 and fill it in on the form). You then indicate where the program should use error-checking functions. For instance, if your inventory items must contain three letters, a dash and a numeral (such as KMG-6), you can tell VersaForm to accept only those entries that adhere to your format.

If an entry has to be numeric within a certain range of figures, you can specify this information, and VersaForm won't allow you to make a mistake.

Once you create your form, you select the number of forms you want to save on each data disk (300 is average). A manager can design a form for clerical entry and almost completely safeguard it. Because the program lets managers do the design work for forms and reports, they can reasonably expect that subsequent data entry will be correct.

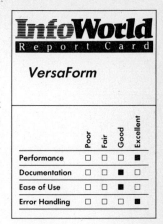

InfoWorld
R e p o r t   C a r d

VersaForm

	Poor	Fair	Good	Excellent
Performance	☐	☐	☐	■
Documentation	☐	☐	■	☐
Ease of Use	☐	☐	■	☐
Error Handling	☐	☐	☐	■

Summary
VersaForm is an intelligent data-management system. Since you can design your own data-entry formats and produce reports to your specifications, VersaForm may be the only file-handling system you need.

System Requirements
☐ *Apple II Plus, IIe*
☐ *Apple Pascal*
☐ *64K RAM*
☐ *Two disk drives*
☐ *80-column card (optional)*
☐ *Hard disk version available at extra cost on Apple II*
☐ *(Versions of VersaForm are available for the Apple III, and the IBM PC and compatible computers)*

Suggested list price: $389

Applied Software Technology
170 Knowles Drive
Los Gatos, CA 95030
(408) 370-2662

The thick manual teaches its material well, as does the special tutorial minimanual. The tutorial comes with its own disk that covers file creation and reports. Brief on-line Help is available as you use VersaForm.

The latest version of the system overcomes one of the major weaknesses of the original package: you can now change the fields on your forms after you've entered data into them. When you first design a form, it's easy to omit data or to underestimate the space you need for your information. VersaForm now allows you to adjust the fields and their locations on your forms. It even lets you change key items — fields on which the system searches — so it can locate data rapidly for you.

Although cumbersome, the process works. You can copy the form design on a new blank disk and make your changes. Then you ask VersaForm to transfer the original data (which remains intact, by the way, on its original disk) into the new forms on the new disk. All data with exactly the same field names will be moved. If your new form includes shortened fields, the program truncates the information. If you eliminate some of the original fields, they won't appear on the new form. In both cases, you are warned. The documentation also warns you if your new form has different checking or calculating instructions. Transferred data might not be correct according to your new rules.

The system lends itself to working with figures. To create an invoice, for example, the system looks up prices and item descriptions (from 99-item lists), does automatic-line extensions (3 filters at $1.50, total $4.50) and subtotals, adds sales tax at the rate you specify and displays a final total. It prints your new invoice and it files the data. Once you have stored data on the disk, you can ask VersaForm to search your files

and produce reports based on what it finds.

Since the system creates reports you design, you have the power to pull out both general information and specific data. Selection conditions include what you'd expect (less than, greater than, equal to and so on).

If, for instance, you worked in the wholesale-appliance business and kept customer sales and warranty records in VersaForm files, you could not only trace how many Lennox furnaces you sold during 1984, but also how many model number G14-Q3-80 units you sold to one specific customer during May 1984, what your gross profit was for these items and how many had warranty repair problems.

Your reports take advantage of a unique Report Work disk that stores the summary data for you. This program lets you create reports that contain more details than your Apple can hold in memory and serves as a storage file for your report data. VersaForm can search multiple disks, as long as the data is stored in the same format on each. It also allows you to create and save report specifications; when you are ready to go into the files and extract the data, you enter your exact selection conditions at that time.

The package includes an on-screen calculator with its own Help screen. You can enter control codes so that your printer will use emphasized print or 132-character lines. You can browse through your files, moving forward or backward, as you wish. The system keeps an index for each item, based on its key, to help you find a particular record.

VersaForm also includes a complete mailing-label system and can handle formats of up to nine labels across. Even with its basic focus on numerical data, this added benefit makes it even more appealing and versatile.

The system recommends (and the software automatically checks) for a structured backup, but the feature is optional. You copy disk A to disk B, and B to C. Finally, you can only copy disk C onto disk A. This procedure eliminates the possibility of copying a bad disk onto your only backup.

We don't mean to imply that VersaForm is a piece of software that you learn to use in a few minutes. To get the greatest benefit from the program takes time and effort. To create report formats, in particular, requires considerable thought; and the package has its own quirks. Since it's written in Pascal (a language your 64K Apple understands), your usual Drive 1 is called Drive 4, your Drive 2 is called Drive 5, and if you have three drives, the third one is called Drive 9. The software itself should make this conversion for the user.

The new manual parallels the 1981 issue, but the company has added a special 29-page section that covers new functions, such as the ability to change form designs. For some unexplained reason, VersaForm refuses to tell you when to turn on your printer. All printing functions assume that your printer is on-line and running; if it's not, the system simply hangs and waits for you to remember to turn it on.

Although you can copy the disks with a system utility, you can only copy the Filing disk once. In all our contact with the VersaForm people, we found them knowledgeable and eager to help.

Finally, you must initialize your data disks with a special command. The Pascal language also requires you to name each disk. For some reason, although you select both functions from the same menu, once you complete the initializing process, you must press Reset to reboot the system before you can assign a name to a data disk.

Apart from having a few minor idiosyncrasies, VersaForm is a powerful and flexible piece of software. You can automate almost anything within the structure of alphanumeric data with this program. Thus, you may find that VersaForm can save you a lot of unnecessary paperwork and is worth the expenditure.

—*Gregory R. Glau*

HOME

Computers are moving into the home, and the programs reviewed in this category are designed for home use. With them, you can make music, play games and keep track of your personal finances.

REVIEW

Music Construction Set

If you are not a professional musician but would like to play with music on your computer, Music Contruction Set by Electronic Arts will allow you to compose and play your creations with little effort, and at a reasonable price. Used with a Mockingboard it produces excellent sound quality.

Music Construction Set is child's play to use. The ease with which you can see and hear what you have written makes music fun to experiment with and to learn.

The program follows the pattern of Rocky's Boots. You employ a hand-shaped cursor to pick up notes and place them on the staff. The note-values, rests, and symbols are constantly displayed on the screen making the program extremely easy to

use. You move the pointing hand with a joystick, the keyboard or a combination of the two. The joystick puts 16th through whole notes on the staff, while the keyboard positions 32nd notes. As suggested in the Reference Card, it is simpler and faster to enter notes with the keyboard.

In the Music Loading mode, you point the hand cursor to the place you want a note and press the number that corresponds to the desired note-length; the note appears in place on the staff. Then, by moving the pointer to the piano icon and pressing the Return key, you can hear what you have created. To change parts of your creation, you can easily erase and replace notes (point the hand to the note and press the Escape key).

By using the scissors and paste-pot icons, you can move notes or measures around on both treble and bass staffs. You can combine two separate pieces of music or experiment with rounds and harmonies. It is easier to use the cut and paste icons with a joystick rather than the keyboard unless your computer has repeat-key capability. Note: The program is written so that the hand must point to the bottom of the note desired. If it points to any other part of the note, the computer will register a different space or line and will not perform your chosen function.

Included on the screen is a counter that monitors the beats in each measure using any of the four allowed time signatures. It flashes to warn you of extra beats so that you can make corrections if you wish. Music Construction Set will play the music with or without the changes, so you are free to experiment.

The program can transpose music from one key to another, and you can use the Note Indicator to show the name of a specific note in a given key. The key is also displayed on the screen.

The Music Construction Set program is large, allowing each piece of music to contain a maximum of only 1400 notes. If your composition is written in both treble and bass clefs, this will limit the length.

Once written, your creations can be saved on a file disk, played by the computer or printed.

Music Construction Set stores music as binary files, and the music-generation program has been left open, so you can use the music you have composed with Music Construction Set in other programs — a valuable asset for programmers.

If you want printed copies of the music, you can consult the Reference Card for instructions. A simple print command sends music to the Apple Dot Matrix printer, the C. Itoh Pro Writer printer, or the NEC 8023 printer. Although instructions are given for setting the proper printer codes for other printers, instructions for setting

up some printers (such as the Apple Silentype) are not.

Since Music Construction Set is designed for use by beginning musicians, games and previously recorded music are provided. One of the programs challenges you to guess a simple medley when only the rhythm is played. Another plays scales. (You can transpose through the circle of fifths.) A third game allows you to add preset rhythms to different melodies and hear the results.

According to the back of the package, "The Apple version by itself can play up to 32 notes per measure, two notes at a time. But if you add a Mockingboard, produced by Sweet Micro Systems, you'll be able to construct chords of up to six notes each." This fact, plus the difference in tone transmitted by the stereo and Apple speakers, makes a difference in the final product.

The authors of Music Construction Set are aware of this fact, too. It becomes evident as your read the "Musical Table of Contents" listed on the Reference Card. Nine pieces of music are listed to be played with the Mockingboard. Only two were designed to be played through the Apple speaker.

These pieces can also be changed. Many players will appreciate this feature especially because the recording of "Turkey in the Straw," written in the key of C, ends in a series of chords containing C sharp — a jarring conclusion.

Although you can control the speed at which the music is presented with or without the Mockingboard, you can control volume and tone quality only through the Mockingboard, so the possibilities for complexity of composition contrast sharply.

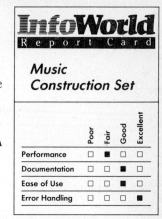

InfoWorld
R e p o r t   C a r d

*Music
Construction Set*

	Poor	Fair	Good	Excellent
Performance	☐	■	☐	☐
Documentation	☐	☐	■	☐
Ease of Use	☐	☐	■	☐
Error Handling	☐	☐	☐	■

Summary
Music Contruction Set is a group of educational games and composition aids that are easy to use, yet challenging enough so that beginning through intermediate musicians will enjoy using it. To work at full capacity on the Apple II Plus or Apple IIe computers, it needs the addition of a Mockingboard.

System Requirements
☐ *Apple II Plus or Apple IIe*
☐ *48K RAM*
☐ *One disk drive*
☐ *Supports some printers and is most useful with a Mockingboard*

Suggested list price: $40

*Electronic Arts
2755 Campus Drive
San Mateo, CA 94403
(415) 571-7171*

When music is played with the card in slot 4, the tone is comparable to that of a small synthesizer.

When music is produced by the Apple speaker, the second tone often carries with it annoying harmonics. Because of these harmonics, listening to the music is sometimes difficult.

The graphics are excellent, with only a few problems and limitations. Notes placed too close together form large blobs with stems; no bars are provided to link groups of eighth, sixteenth or smaller notes; and some notes carry with them unnecessary ledger lines. Triplets are unavailable, and the music will scroll as it is played only if the Mockingboard is in place.

The disk is accompanied by a manual and a reference card. Although the program is menu-driven, you should read both documents in order to take full advantage of Music Construction Set. The manual contains information about music theory, plus games and some instructions that do not appear on the screen. It is valuable and well-written documentation.

The Reference Card contains instructions and a list of the music already recorded on the disk. The instructions include keyboard shortcuts, printing directions and error messages.

If the program disk is damaged, you can obtain a new one from Electronic Arts for a fee of $7.50.

In spite of the problems mentioned above — most of which are minor — Music Contruction Set (especially when used with a Mockingboard II on the Apple) is a good product for its price. It can be a valuable tool for beginning programmers, and a good learning device for music students. It is fun for any computer user.

—*Janet E. Meizel*

REVIEW

The Home Accountant

The Home Accountant from Continental Software is efficient and reliable for people who require an accurate record of their personal finances. The program offers a variety of useful features for $74.95. It contains a well-written manual and one copy-protected program disk. The product is warranted for 90 days, during which time Continental Software will replace a defective program free of charge. To receive an extended, one-year warranty, you must return the warranty registration card with $20. The payment entitles you to telephone support, future-program improvements, enhancements and a free replacement disk.

If you decide against paying the $20, a replacement disk costs $17.50 if defects show up after 90 days. The manual states that Continental will not accept your telephone calls if you have not registered under the warranty program.

This ubiquitous program is available for the Apple II and IIe; IBM PC and PC XT; Osborne 1 and Executive; Atari 400, 800 and 1200; Commodore 64; TRS-80 Model III; TI Professional; Kaypro II; Zenith 110 and 120; and Epson QX-10, at prices ranging from $74.95 for the Apple version to $150 for the IBM version. We used the Apple version of the program for this review.

The program centers around the budget categories it requires you to create. You must set up categories for each asset, liability, credit card, income and expense item before you enter data. You can develop up to 100 budget categories. The initial budget setup takes some thought and is often a chore. Once the setup is organized, however, you needn't perform the task again unless you wish to change the categories.

The Apple version of the program keeps track of up to five checkbooks. It prints checks, balance sheets, summaries of income and expense, and net-worth statements. It also reconciles your bank accounts.

In addition, the program flags transactions to be recalled for tax purposes, and for search and display. It flags single or multiple transactions by date, check number, payee, amount, budget category, memo or any combination of these items.

You can enter up to five automatic transactions per checkbook per month. You can split or spread individual transactions over several budget categories.

You can also review bar, line and trend-analysis graphs. The bar graphs compare budget to actual expenses. The line graphs display a point-to-point plot of actual expenditures for up to three budget categories. The trend-analysis graph uses linear regression on transaction data to show the historical trend of any category. According to the publisher, the program works with the Tax Advantage, also published by Continental Software.

After entering over 600 actual transactions and creating 65 budget categories, we can say, without qualification, that the Home Accountant performs exactly as represented by the publisher.

The only negative aspect of the program's performance that surfaced in ten months of use was the amount of time required to load the various modules that the program used. The Apple program is written in Applesoft, and speed of execution suffers as a result.

The program is divided into seven modules: Budget, Transactions, Graphing, Printed Reports, Print Checks/Activity Report, Start New Year, Extend and Hardware/Start New System. Depending on the number of transactions involved, it can take more than four minutes to load modules such as Printed Reports or Transactions. You learn to compensate by fully using the features of one module before loading another.

The program is easy to use. Even with no prior computer experience, novices should have no difficulty after they familiarize themselves with the product. All menus are in a readable format and require one or, at the most, two keystrokes to activate a particular function. Each command is self-explanatory, and you need memorize no codes. Having completed the initial study required by the program, you rarely require further reference to the manual unless you wish to perform complicated tasks such as splitting a transaction between different budget categories, or saving a graph to disk.

Setup of the program is easy — just follow the simple instructions in the manual. The program requires either a 132-column printer or printer capable of compressing type to 132 columns on 8½×11 paper. The program handles errors efficiently. Using the program steadily, we had no problems. We recommend, however, that you follow the manufacturer's suggestion and make backup copies of the data disk.

The 140-page manual is professional, both in appearance and content. It is a well-written, easy-to-follow tutorial containing examples of how to use each function. Apart from an incorrect page reference, the

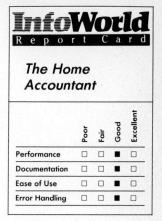

The Home Accountant

	Poor	Fair	Good	Excellent
Performance	☐	☐	■	☐
Documentation	☐	☐	■	☐
Ease of Use	☐	☐	■	☐
Error Handling	☐	☐	■	☐

Summary
Apart from the slow execution speed, the Home Accountant is a fine product. We recommend it.

System Requirements
☐ *Apple II, II Plus, IIe*
☐ *DOS 3.3*
☐ *48K RAM*
☐ *One or two disk drives*
☐ *132-column printer*
☐ *Video monitor*

Suggested list price: $74.95

Continental Software (a division of Arrays, Inc.)
11223 S. Hindry Avenue
Los Angeles, CA 90045
(213) 410-3977
(213) 417-8092

documentation reveals no mistakes. In addition to the tutorial, the manual contains a helpful, general-reference section, a troubleshooting guide, a glossary, an appendix and an index.

Continental Software maintains a customer support number in Los Angeles, and although it is frequently busy, once you establish contact, you receive information from a knowledgeable and helpful person.
—*William A. Feinberg*

REVIEW

Apple Games

No discussion of the Apple II would be complete without some mention of games. Although the versatility of the Apple hardware and the power of Apple-compatible software such as VisiCalc are widely believed to be the major reasons for the Apple's enormous success, the influence of games cannot be denied.

There are three reasons so many great games were written for the Apple. The first was the encouragement Apple Computer gave to software developers. Unlike many companies that tried to keep secret vital information about the operation of their computers, Apple published freely. When game developers know more about a machine, they are able to play up its strengths and avoid its weaknesses.

The second reason for the large number of good Apple games — the reason that caused some people to call the Apple a "game machine" — was the Apple's excellent graphics. Although many machines have since come up to the Apple's level, or surpassed it, the Apple was one of only a few early personal computers designed to treat graphics seriously. It contained such features as high resolution, color and shape tables.

Finally, the Apple was flexible enough to operate in both home and business environments. Buyers could excuse laying out $2000 for a system because they were "going to use it to save money at home and get ahead at work." In fact, many people ended up using their machines mainly for playing games. There were other game machines and other business computers, but few could fill both roles. Once buyers recognized that fact, the software development effort for the Apple snowballed. More owners meant a larger market for software so more was developed. More software meant even more reason to buy an Apple.

What's in a game?

A computer game isn't necessarily a *video-game* as that phrase is generally understood. If you picture a 14-year-old kid who is able to maneuver a shape of light past flashing obstacles and shoot up galaxies of aliens, yet is unable to stop his hands from twitching after the game, you've seen only one side of games. Plenty of those games, commonly termed *arcade-style games*, are available for the Apple II, and many are on the best-sellers' list. But they aren't the only games, nor the sole popular variety.

If you have played games in an arcade, you will notice a difference between those arcade games and home-computer games. Basically, a round of play lasts longer in a home-computer game than in an arcade game. The programmer is trying to entertain you, challenge you and encourage you to come back and buy another program.

The designers of arcade games have a quite different end in mind: quarters. The feeling you're supposed to get when you play an arcade game is, "Gee, if I try that just one more time and remember to miss the strange thing in the lower-left corner, I bet I can get to the next screen..."

Home-computer games give you more "lives" and more background, as well as more time to win or to learn. Of course, you can buy many arcade hours for the money you'll spend on a home-computer and software.

Games for home computers range from arcade-style, to sports, to "board games," to simulations, to role-playing fantasies to interactive adventure novels. Some require a joystick, some a keyboard. Fast reactions are vital in some games; others allow you to ponder your next move. The moral of the tale is: Look around. No matter how much you dislike one sort of game, there may very well be another that could surprise, challenge, educate or even enthrall you.

Arcade-style games

These are the most recognizable games. Most feature the hand-eye coordination that arcade-parlor owners tout. It's you against them, whoever they are. Some of these games are adaptations of arcade-parlor favorites. Others are copies, rip-offs. Still more were written originally for home computers.

Just because an adaptation is authorized doesn't mean it was well programmed. Game X may be your all-time favorite in the arcades and zilch on the home screen. So, if you can, try a game at the store or at a friend's before you buy it.

You shouldn't have much trouble finding the game you want for your Apple. Most popular arcade games have been translated for the Apple.

Frogger, from Sierra On-Line, Inc., is an example of an arcade adaptation. This easy-to-learn game makes you play the part of a frog that must cross a road and a river to reach home. Cars on the road can squash you or you can fall in the river and drown. On your journey, you pick up points by escorting another frog, eating insects and avoiding diving turtles. The music is limited, and the graphics aren't particularly sharp, but the simplicity of play — jumping the frog around dangers — makes Frogger an ideal arcade game for kids.

Choplifter, from Broderbund software, is an original for the Apple. You fly a helicopter into a desert to save hostages. This approach is a turnaround of the old shoot-'em-up theme, and with the game's superb attention to graphics detail, it is an all-time classic. Hostages wave to the copter, the blades whirl in response to the flight, and the pull of gravity forbids passive hovering. As you improve, the enemy gains new weapons and the game grows more difficult.

Old Ironsides, a two-player game, from Xerox Education Publications, uses high-resolution graphics to put you on a ship trying to sink an opponent. Fog, cannonballs and other touches add up to a gripping game.

Stellar 7, from Software Entertainment Company, is a three-dimensional tank game. The difficulties of presenting a 3-D image on a screen are evidenced in several new games. In this case, the approach is that of the arcade game Battlezone. Shapes are outlined. You can run into them or hide behind them. These graphics will undoubtedly look primitive in a few years, but for now they are an exciting game element.

Zaxxon, from Datasoft, was adapted from the arcade game of the same name. In 3-D (the game uses a different technique than that of Stellar 7) you fly a fighter into a fortress and attempt to shoot up everything in sight. The graphics are the game: the three dimensions are believable and are enhanced by such details as shadows. The fighter can fly up or down and side to side. Though this version isn't as good as the arcade original, it's exciting to see that third dimension.

Miner 2049er, from Micro Lab, is another example of an arcade-style game. The Miner (that's you) tries to conquer mining stations in a mine inhabited by mutants. This game was first made for a home computer and has a complexity of play often missing in arcade games. Each complete view on the TV or monitor is called a "screen." When the miner moves outside a screen's boundaries a new screen appears. Many different hazards crop up as you go through the various screens. As an added incentive, you race against a clock. This game is extremely popular, and you should play it only if you're sure you don't have anything else pressing to do. It may hook you.

Raster Blaster, from the Budge Company, and *David's Midnight Magic*, from Broderbund, are examples of a strange concoction we can only call "pinball simulations." In sound, feel and play they re-create the old pinball machines that video games replaced. The summit, to date, of this field of programming is the *Pinball Construction Kit*, from Electronic Arts. This program lets you build your own pinball game. A set of bumpers, tunnels, flippers and other such elements is displayed on the screen, and you place those elements wherever you wish.

Then you play the game. You can stretch the bumpers, trim them, paint them or change their elasticity; you can even change gravity.

Boards and sports

These games are re-creations of pastimes that were popular long before the advent of computers. *Golf, Football* and numerous other outside games are available in computer form.

Olympic Decathlon, from Microsoft, graphically presents the events of that competition. Several contests will give your fingers a workout, such as the 100-meter dash, while others depend on timing. This is another good game for several players. We hope your keyboard can take the beating.

Indoor games such as chess, checkers, backgammon and cards have been adapted to the Apple.

Chess 7.0, from Odesta, and *Sargon II*, from Hayden, are two of the best chess programs. You play against the machine. Although neither of these programs will beat a master, their multiple levels afford woodpushers a good workout. The more advanced levels take as much as five minutes or more per move.

Ken Uston's Professional Blackjack, from Intelligent Statements, is both a game to play against, and it is a teacher. Ken Uston is a card counter who has been successful enough at blackjack to be barred from many casinos. More recently he has authored some best-selling guides to video-game strategy. Professional Blackjack teaches card-counting by rule and practice.

Tactical Armor Command, from Avalon Hill, is a war game. That is, it simulates a combat situation in which you are one of the foes. These games, long popular in board versions, are well suited to computer play because of their complex rules. Tactical Armor Command is a re-creation of a World War II tank battle. Woods and fields, smoke and mines, infantry and artillery all give you plenty to worry about.

Education

The use of home computers in education is a field of intense interest to educators and entrepreneurs. Many of the educational programs are designed as games. The subjects range from spelling to shape-play. As these aren't truly intended as sheer entertainment, we won't discuss them in this section.

Adventure

Adventure games aren't represented at all in the video-game arcades, primarily because each game takes more than 30 seconds to play. These programs are almost all built around an area that must be explored — dungeon, maze or island. The object of the games can be to find treasure, or it may just be to find a safe escape.

Adventure, from Apple Computer, is an example of this genre. As with most adventure games, it is textual. Clues and descriptions of your surroundings are printed on the screen. You type in instructions to move or stay, fight or hide. Learning the instruction vocabulary is an important part of these games and will slow you down at first. Because they take so long to play, these games allow you to save your position on a disk.

Adventure, from Adventure International, is somewhat similar to the Apple game of the same name. It's not a rip-off from Apple; Adventure was around as a game on mainframe computers before Apple got to it. The plots remain the same but the rooms and dangers change.

Zork, from Infocom, is another adventure game that has the same theme of finding a treasure; however, the place and the dangers it contains, are different from those of either Adventure. More important, the program understands and accepts complicated instructions. Instead of terse directional commands — north, south, east, west — you can type in a more conversational tone. Zork was so popular that Zork II and Zork III were developed to continue the adventure.

Fantasy and role-playing

Have you played Dungeons and Dragons? These games are the computer versions of Dungeons and Dragons-type games. These are fantasy games involving spells, dragons, dwarves, warriors and the like. They are termed *role-playing* because you become a particular character. The strengths and weaknesses of your character, and of those of other players can be adjusted before play begins and are then modified in the course of the game.

Temple of Apshai, from Epyx, is built around a graphic dungeon with many rooms. Your role has intelligence, dexterity and other attributes you can use, enhance or exhaust. Different levels of difficulty and options create a game that is seldom the same twice.

Ultima, from California Pacific Computer, has much the same flavor as Temple of Apshai. The play progresses through phases, from swords to lasers, and was so popular that Ultima II and Ultima III followed.

Wizardry, from Sir-tech Software, more closely approximates the original Dungeons and Dragons board game. Six characters of five possible races and three possible outlooks (good, neutral, or evil) live in a world of monsters and spells. Building characters can be complicated, so programs such as *Wizmaker*, from ARS Publications, have no other purpose than to make *Wizardry* easier. You use menus to create, store and modify characters. Using Wizmaker is a little bit like cheating, but just call that an attribute, too. Wizardry, too, has its sequels.

Aztec, from Datamost, is an adventure in 64 rooms that seems directly inspired by Indiana Jones and *Raiders of the Lost Ark*. In superb graphics, the familiar figure finds his way into the ancient temple looking for treasure. There are dinosaurs and spiders, machetes and pistols, dynamite and finally treasure, all to be picked up or run away from — that is, if you don't find yourself in a room with no exit and the ceiling coming down to squash you before the water can rise to drown you. This is a hybrid game, both adventure and arcade. One note: it's easier to capture the treasure than to escape with it.

Simulations

Many computer simulations are designed for purposes such as predicting weather or traffic patterns. Some simulations, though, have both education and fun in mind. For example, *Flight Simulator*, from Sublogic, is a simulation of small-plane piloting.

Flight instruments and a windshield display a 3-D world in which you can practice simple flying or dogfighting. The imaginary plane flies as a real one would, and you can crash, though you can't get hurt.

—*Phillip Robinson*

EDUCATION

Computers are playing an increasing role in education, and school can be where your Apple is. The programs in this category are designed to enhance the education process. They range from math tutors to circuit-design programs.

REVIEW

Rocky's Boots

Rocky's Boots by Warren Robinett of The Learning Company transports you to Rocky's World, where you can learn how electricity flows through a variety of wires, logic gates and other devices. Once you become involved in Rocky's World, you use colors, shapes and sounds to build machines and wire circuits. Advanced users can try to wire circuits that make Rocky's boots kick specific targets of certain shapes and colors within a kicking or shooting gallery.

To use Rocky's Boots, you have to know how to place a disk in a drive, turn a computer on and read the directions on the screen. If you are using an Apple IIe, the Caps Lock key must be on. You need a color monitor to learn the program.

Rocky's Boots is a one-disk program for users aged 9 through adult containing simulations of electronic devices and 39 variations of a game using circuits that you build. The program uses the computer to simulate electronic devices on the screen. As you build circuits and machines, you play with them. The games simulate an electronic workshop.

An orange rectangle on the screen represents the user. You have the power to send electricity through any circuit that the rectangle touches. You move your marker with the I, J, K or M keys or a joystick. The joystick is good for fast movements, but the keyboard gives you more precise motions. Apple II Plus users can gain speed by using the Repeat key, but IIe users can simply hold down the keys for fast action.

Beginners learn about the program by going through an on-screen tutorial in Rocky's World. By pressing the space bar, you learn how to pick up and move

InfoWorld
Report Card

Rocky's Boots

	Poor	Fair	Good	Excellent
Performance	☐	☐	☐	■
Documentation	☐	☐	☐	■
Ease of Use	☐	☐	☐	■
Error Handling	☐	☐	☐	■

Summary
Simulations are great teaching tools and something that microcomputers do well. Rocky's Boots uses simulations and games to teach its users about electricity. You can also use the program to create your own games. The program's teaching function, combined with its game format, make it valuable for use in homes and schools.

System Requirements
☐ Apple II, II Plus, IIe
☐ DOS 3.3
☐ 48K RAM
☐ One disk drive
☐ Color monitor and optional joystick

Suggest list price: $49.95

*The Learning Company
545 Middlefield Road, Suite 170
Menlo Park, CA 94025
(415) 328-5410*

objects such as wires, noisemakers or sensors. Objects automatically connect when you place them near each other. A "splitter" that appears on the screen lets you disconnect simple or complex circuits.

Rocky's World contains the three basic logic gates of real electrical circuits, such as those found in computers. The AND gate requires electricity from two sources before a current can pass; the OR gate requires electricity from just one of its two inputs in order to have current flow out the opposite end. The NOT gate sends electricity out when none comes in and does not send any out when electricity flows in.

Once you have mastered the tutorials, you can play the Rocky's Boots game, providing you understand how the wires and the three logic gates work. The variations of the game provide you with three sensors containing symbols of specific shapes and colors. The shapes include diamonds, crosses, triangles and circles; and the colors are blue, green and purple.

As you play the game, eight targets with different point values pass by the three sensors. If the target has the same color or shape as the sensor, electricity flows out the other end. If your circuit works correctly and electricity enters Rocky's electrically activated boot, you can earn points by kicking the target. You must have your wires and gates arranged so that they activate the boot only when a target with a positive value comes along, because some of the targets have negative values.

When you achieve a score of 24, Rocky dances for you. You can see the targets and their point values before you wire your circuits. If you are

unsuccessful, you must modify your creation. Sound effects are optional.

You cannot rest on your laurels in Rocky's Boots. As you move on to more complex simulations, you'll need more complex electrical components. They include "flip-flops," "clocks" and "delays." A flip-flop is similar to a switch with two outputs and two inputs. An electrical current flows from one output at a time and flips to the other output when you turn on the second input. A clock has four outputs, and current flows clockwise from one output to the others. A delay slows down the current coming in from the side until the top input turns on.

In addition to these actual electronic parts, Rocky's World has some special machines. They include the "clacker," "thruster," "alligator detector," "bopper," "splitter" and "sensor." The names accurately describe their functions.

Once you have mastered the art of building machines, you can play Rocky's Challenge. You choose among easy, intermediate or very difficult games. Easy games require circuits that make Rocky's boot kick purple crosses or blue triangles. Intermediate games might have the boot kick diamonds or purple objects, but not purple diamonds. The program contains many different variations, and the most difficult have names such as Ann's Enigma, Rick's Riddle or Warren's Widget.

If you're extra creative, you can go to a separate room in Rocky's World where you can create your own games. Here you can choose the shapes and colors for the three sensors, plus the shapes, colors and point values for the eight targets. Unfortunately, you cannot save your games on the program disk or on a separate data disk.

Rocky's Boots is one of those special programs that demonstrates how exciting microcomputers in education can be. It emphasizes creativity while teaching complex concepts. Advanced users of the program can always design their own games and are limited only by their imagination.

We think that the program would be even better if students could save their own games, a step that would also help them gain a basic understanding of how computers function. Instead, the manual strongly urges users to make paper-and-pencil drawings of their games so they can reconstruct them later.

The program makes good use of color and sound. Schools need at least one color monitor to get started with Rocky's Boots. The option of using either a joystick or the keyboard to move and build circuits is welcome. Many school districts cannot afford a joystick for every system.

Rocky's Boots can become complicated, and trying to dismantle a "machine" that does not work is difficult. You must cut apart all the connections and carry the parts away. Rebooting the system is often the best way to save yourself time and avoid frustration.

Using the knife to disconnect connections is also tricky. If you get too close to any connection, you can break it, whether you want to cut it or not.

Many people can use this program to learn some basic concepts of electricity and logic. The beginning menu options for moving and building a machine are easy enough for children at the elementary level if they have had a little computer experience.

The more difficult features such as Rocky's Challenge seem more appropriate for students of junior- or senior-high-school age. High-school students who are familiar with programming can learn Rocky's Boots and proceed to the more complicated aspects in about 15 minutes.

The program catches errors well, and does not crash. It needs to get at the disk often, so you must keep the program disk in the disk drive to avoid input/output errors. Fortunately, the frequent disk accessing does not slow down the program's functioning. Some parts are written in machine language, apparently to achieve a fast and smooth performance.

Rocky's Boots comes with a 32-page, complete manual. It includes an overview of the program and tells you how to get started, move, build machines, use logic and flip-flops, play Rocky's Challenge, and create your own games. In addition, it contains Rocky's Boots solutions, a list of skills and concepts to be learned, suggested activities for experienced users, information on special keys on the Apple II Plus and IIe, and a glossary of terms. The manual refers to the keys on the IIe and the II Plus. (The computer gives you the correct commands.)

The manual does a good job of explaining how to move and build your machines. It contains a map of The World of Rocky's Challenge; the map supplements the instructions on the diskette in helping you find your way around.

Rocky's Boots has a 90-day warranty; the manufacturer replaces the program without charge within this period. If your disk is damaged after 90 days, you can replace it for $10.

Rocky's Boots is both an excellent product and a good value. It's an impressive learning tool that combines real-life electrical concepts with the interest of a computer-simulation game. With this combination of attributes, it can't help but be a success at school or at home.

—*Doug and Denise Green*

	Poor	Fair	Good	Excellent
Performance	☐	☐	☐	■
Documentation	☐	☐	■	☐
Ease of Use	☐	☐	■	☐
Error Handling	☐	☐	■	☐

Summary
Apple Logo is an excellent product and learning tool for all kinds of students. It is a complete programming language as well as a child's introduction to programming. The Sample Programs and Tool Kit add to its capabilities, but are made for experienced programmers.

System Requirements
☐ *Apple II, II Plus, IIe*
☐ *DOS 3.3*
☐ *64K RAM (Apple II 48K and 16K Language card)*
☐ *One disk drive*
☐ *Printer (recommended)*

Suggested list price: $100; Apple Logo Sample Program Disk and Tool Kit free or for duplication cost with purchase of Logo

*Logo Computer Systems, Inc.
220 5th Avenue, Suite 1604
New York, NY 10001
(212) 684-0710
Published through:
Apple Computer
20525 Mariani Avenue
Cupertino, CA 95014
(408) 996-1010*

REVIEW

Apple Logo

Many people consider Logo a valuable tool for teaching good programming habits, mathematical concepts, knowledge of computers and turtle graphics. Apple Logo is one of the many versions of Logo available for Apple II, II Plus or IIe computers.

MIT professor Seymour Papert developed the original Logo in the late 1960s and continued to refine it at MIT in the 1970s.

Apple Logo is a complete programming language that, like Applesoft BASIC, is interpreted rather than compiled. Although turtle graphics are the best-known aspect of the language, it has many other capabilities.

Logo lets you interact with a computer to accomplish set goals. The building blocks of the language consist of a definite number of inputs called *words* and *lists*. The combinations of words and lists form logical relationships called *procedures* or *programs*, with which you carry out your requests. You can define specific procedures that consist of primitive commands such as Forward and Right. Procedures can also include more complex primitive commands involving variables, user interaction and conditional statements.

You can make all kinds of shapes with turtle graphics. Beginners can easily draw figures by moving the turtle on the screen, while advanced Logo users can create complex and changing patterns. You can even use paddles or joysticks.

The Logo editor prepares your procedures and works like a simple word processor. A series of control keys handle cursor movement, simplifying the editing process. Unfortunately, you cannot see the graphics screen while you use the Editor.

Logo can use arithmetic operations, including trig functions, square roots and a random-number generator. In addition, conditions such as IF, IF FALSE, IF TRUE and REPEAT, plus the logical operations AND, NOT and OR are available. Recursive procedures, where a procedure calls upon itself, are also possible.

Owners of Apple Logo now receive, for no extra cost, the Sample Program Disk and Tool Kit disk. Two disks contain these enhancements and add extra capabilities to the language. The Tool Kit contains a word processor (of limited capability) and other utilities.

The Sample Program Disk and Tool Kit has many useful features written by Logo users. The sample programs contain turtle graphics, language programs and games. Most were written by students, and make good teaching aids. The turtle graphic programs are by far the most impressive.

Among other features, the Tool Kit includes programs for printing pictures, writing music, debugging programs and making primitive commands.

The sample programs and printing programs are the most useful and extend Apple Logo's versatility. Programs such as Teach and Zoom, however, fail to add to Logo's performance and are troublesome to learn, even though they were designed to make learning Logo easier. Textpro adds some extra word-processing capabilities to the Logo Editor. The limited capabilities of Textpro remind us of the early word-processing programs for uppercase-only Apple II systems from the late 1970s.

We often hear comparisons of the different types of Logos available. Some include only the turtle graphics while others are complete languages, like Apple Logo, with many frills. Apple Logo takes advantage of the excellent concepts behind the Logo language. The different versions of Logo each have their own strengths and weaknesses.

Logo stores more than one procedure in memory at a time. You can save a series of short procedures or programs under one filename on the disk. Applesoft BASIC users will find this a pleasant change from saving and loading each program by a separate name.

Logo filenames that you save on a DOS 3.3-formatted data disk are saved as text files with the Logo suffix for easy reference. While using Logo with your data disk, however, you do not need to type .LOGO to load a procedure.

Logo is a powerful language that requires time for both students and teachers to learn. Although students can learn much from Logo, teachers must realize that this requires a long-term commitment. Logo is more complex than most programs designed to assist in teaching subjects such as math or reading. We suggest that any teachers planning to teach Logo have in-depth training and be prepared to learn with their students. We do not recommend any version of Logo as the very first program taught to novices of any age or grade level, since there are easier programs available.

Nevertheless Apple Logo itself is easy to use. The manuals include step-by-step instructions. The Sample Program Disk is also easy to use, but the Tool Kit features, such as the Logo Assembler, are much more complicated. The Tool Kit enchancements are designed for more experienced programmers rather than for beginners.

Apple Logo has 42 error messages that help explain what you have done wrong. They would be even more useful if the reference manual briefly explained each one in the appendix. While using the product, we encountered no bugs and we could not make the program crash. You should save your procedures as you work as a precaution against losing data.

The programs contained in the Tool Kit are not as carefully written for error trapping as the Logo language is, but we did not encounter any serious problems.

Apple Logo comes with extensive and well-written manuals. For beginners, there is a 152-page manual called *Introduction to Programming through Turtle Graphics*. It slowly takes you through Logo, including the Editor, disk commands, variables, all shapes and colors and recursive procedures. It includes many good sample programs, but a few of the instructions are confusing. For example, one procedure tells you how to create different-sized triangles but refrains from explaining that you must set the heading or direction of the turtle first. Though not major, these errors frustrate new users.

The reference manual offers detailed explanations of the entire Logo language. It is well organized and informative. The explanations are technical, and you should use the introductory manual first. The error messages should be given additional explanation.

The Sample Program Disk and Tool Kit comes with a 64-page manual, which you can copy and edit, if you wish. The software contains much of the information for the sample programs.

InfoWorld
Report Card

Stickybear

	Poor	Fair	Good	Excellent
Performance	☐	☐	☐	■
Documentation	☐	☐	☐	■
Ease of Use	☐	☐	☐	■
Error Handling	☐	☐	☐	■

Summary
Overall, Stickybear Numbers and Stickybear ABC are beautifully designed programs that young children will enjoy. Their effectiveness can be enhanced even more by an interested parent or teacher working with an individual child.

System Requirements
☐ *Apple II, II Plus, IIe*
☐ *DOS 3.3*
☐ *48K RAM*
☐ *One disk drive*

Suggested list price: $39.95 each

Weekly Reader Family Software
A division of
Xerox Education Publications
245 Long Hill Road
Middletown, CT 06457
(800) 852-5000

The rest of the documentation for the Tool Kit is hit or miss. You must be willing to experiment and not expect the manual to give you all of the facts and examples you may need.

You receive two copy-protected Apple Logo disks, which come with a 90-day warranty and can be replaced if they're defective. Contact your Apple dealer if you encounter problems. Neither Apple Computer nor Logo Computer Systems provide individual-customer support.

—Doug and Denise Green

REVIEW

Stickybear

Imagine Stickybear vs. Big Bird in a ten-round, no-holds-barred fight for your kid's attention. Big Bird may be the champ in the educational division, but Stickybear is a serious contender.

Stickybear Numbers and Stickybear ABC are two separate programs designed for children from ages 3 to 6. Children using the program will probably need help putting the disks into the computer. Other than that, they just need to be able to press the space bar or any letter or number to see new pictures. All pictures are displayed in beautiful high-resolution graphics, a feature that makes a color monitor highly desirable.

Stickybear Numbers is a counting and number-recognition program contained on one disk. Full-screen, high-resolution pictures are displayed if users press the proper key. When a child presses a number from 0 to 9, a picture with that number of a given object is shown. The pictures are animated and come with sound effects. They feature a large variety of objects including cars, trains, rockets, birds, bears and ice-cream sundaes. If a child presses the space bar instead of a number, objects are subtracted one at a time until none appear on the screen. Then, if a child continues to press the space bar, a new object will be displayed one by one until none appear.

Stickybear ABC is a one-disk alphabet program. Each letter of the alphabet is represented by two different, animated pictures with sound. A child can press any letter, and that letter and a picture appear. Pressing the same letter again produces another picture and that letter. Users do not have to press letters in alphabetical order.

Both Stickybear programs provide an entertaining way to teach number, letter and object recognition to young children. They also serve as an introduction to the computer and offer practice with the keyboard. Using Stickybear ABC might result in a three-year-old learning the QWERTY version of the alphabet before learning the ABC version.

These programs ask for simple interaction from their users. Young users' experiences are much more successful when a parent or teacher offers guidance. Each program works best if only one or two children use it for about 10 to 15 minutes.

Stickybear Numbers appears to hold children's interest better than Stickybear ABC. Perhaps the combination of activities — pressing numbers and the space bar to make the number of objects change — accounts for this added involvement.

Sound effects include different songs for each letter or object being counted. The animation is peppy, but it understandably slows down as the number of moving objects on the screen increases. The quality of the graphics is impressive.

The Stickybear programs look much better in color than in black and white. On a black-and-white display, you lose excitement, as well as some details of the pictures.

We tried the programs on the Apple II Plus and the IIe. For younger children the II Plus works better because the keyboard is smaller, and the keys do not repeat. Children tend to leave their fingers on a key for several seconds while waiting for a result on the screen. On the IIe the pictures flash by if a key is held down too long. This drawback is especially obvious when children press the space bar on the Numbers program to make the objects appear or disappear.

Because these programs are filled with first-rate graphics, they require a great deal of disk activity. So the programs run somewhat slowly, but the slow speed doesn't detract from overall performance. Both programs are easy for parents to use and even easier for children. When Stickybear Numbers asks for numbers or the space bar, that's all it will accept. When Stickybear ABC asks for letters, it accepts no other input. A two-year-old was unable to make either program crash by pressing several keys at once, so we conclude that the programs are well designed.

Each Stickybear program comes with a 4-page guide of simple instructions, a poster of either the alphabet or numbers, eight Stickybear stickers and a short storybook.

The Numbers program comes with a book called *One Bear Two Bears* while the ABC program contains a book called

Look Book. These books contain beautiful artwork with labeled pictures. Nonreaders can enjoy the drawings, and beginning readers can learn to associate words and pictures. The books are an important part of the package, and we find that young children enjoy them as much as the programs.

Each copy-protected program comes with a 90-day warranty. Xerox Education Publications will replace or repair defective disks, and a toll-free number is available for ordering products from this company. These packages are so simple to use that no other support seems necessary.
—*Doug and Denise Green*

REVIEW

Memory Trainer

The Memory Trainer program is designed to increase your memory capacity by showing you how to develop well-proven memory aids. The program is based on the use of three aids to memory: visualization, association and linking.

Visualization involves making a mental picture; often the more ridiculous the picture, the better. Association is similar to visualization, but the pictures have a direct connection with the material you want to remember. Linking occurs when you join more than two items so that you can remember them in order.

Memory Trainer comprises three disks, containing five lessons in all. All of the lessons ask you to make associations, and they lead you through proven memory techniques for remembering names, long lists and

InfoWorld
R e p o r t C a r d

Memory Trainer

	Poor	Fair	Good	Excellent
Performance	☐	☐	☐	■
Documentation	☐	☐	☐	■
Ease of Use	☐	☐	☐	■
Error Handling	☐	☐	☐	■

Summary
Memory Trainer is a self-instruction program that teaches you techniques for improving your memory. If you are determined to succeed, then you will find this program to be an excellent tutor.

System Requirements
☐ *Apple II Plus, IIe*
☐ *DOS 3.3*
☐ *48K RAM*
☐ *One disk drive*

Suggested list price: $89.95

Alison Software Corporation
14937 Ventura Blvd
Sherman Oaks, CA 91403
(818) 905-8000

important dates and phone numbers. The package also includes a game called Memory Mix.

Lesson 1, Names and Faces, teaches you how to easily remember the names of people you meet. With the aid of high-resolution graphics, the program shows you how to associate an unusual facial feature with name reminders, called peg-words.

Lesson 2, Method of Loci, introduces you to the ancient art of memorizing long lists of information by making mental maps and placing the information at familiar "locations" (loci). Memory Trainer lets you extend your memory span for lists from 5 to 40 different items at a time, and you can even create, store and use your own personal set of up to 40 locations.

The peg-word system, the subject of lesson 3, teaches you how to translate numbers into sounds and then turn the sounds into visual information that is easy to remember. (For instance, the sound of the number 3 is M — picture 3 lying on its left side, and it looks like an M.)

In lesson 4, Important Dates, the program shows you how to extend the use of the peg-word system to remember important dates for birthdays, anniversaries, appointments or outstanding dates in history. You learn how to remember complete dates (month, day and year) and how to link any date with the person or event associated with it. Lesson 5, Phone Numbers, employs the techniques you have previously learned for the important everyday task of remembering phone numbers and the names linked with them.

Each lesson contains many examples and drills, randomly selected by the computer so that you never get the same sequence twice. The computer scores your performance as you progress.

Memory Trainer's display uses advanced techniques of movie-making, "wipes" and "dissolves."

Messages don't merely appear on the screen — they arrive through various animation techniques that heighten your enjoyment of the program. The color is not very effective, though. The program occasionally uses music — either to emphasize points or to augment congratulatory messages pertaining to your progress — but the quality is not good.

You couldn't ask for an easier program to use. You don't need to use the manual, as the entire program is self-instructing. Error messages are thorough and clear.

The manual is a 7×9-inch hardcover, spiral-bound, 130-page book. It is professionally printed on glossy paper, complete with illustrations. The index is thorough and includes biographies of people who collaborated on this memory-training project.

Within 90 days of date of purchase, Alison Software Corporation will replace any defective disks free of charge. After that, within one year, replacement of any defective disk will cost you $10 per disk.

Memory Trainer is an excellent example of computer-aided instruction. If you are serious about improving your memory skills and are willing to abide by the secrets of the ancients to accomplish your goal, then this program is for you.
—*Marty Petersen*

REVIEW

EduWare Games

EduWare publishes the three packages discussed in this review — Spelling Bee Games is published under the DragonWare trademark; and Hands on Basic Programming and Algebra Volume 1 are published under The Science of Learning trademark.

Spelling Bee Games, designed for children ages 5 to 10, consists of four interactive word games on one disk. To choose a game, a child presses a number from 1 to 4 on the Games menu. The object of the first game, Squadron, is to manipulate a high-resolution airplane so that it points to, and "zaps," the word that corresponds to the picture at the bottom of the screen. The child controls the airplane's movements with a game paddle. The program rewards successful matches with sound and adds points to the child's score. Two children can play this game together.

In the second game, Skyhook, the child must unscramble a word jumble. Up to four children can play this game simultaneously. Using a game paddle, a child moves a helicopter to a position above any letter in the sequence displayed on the screen and picks up that letter by using a hook on the underside of the aircraft. The child then moves the letter to the left-hand side of the screen and drops the letter in the appropriate location to correctly spell the name of the object that appears in the high-resolution graphic at the bottom of the screen. The players score a point each time they place a letter correctly. If they are incorrect, they lose their turn.

The third game, Puzzle, is similar to the television quiz show "Concentration." The program displays pictures on the screen for a few seconds. "Curtains" numbered 1 to 6 then cover the pictures. The name of one of the items appears on the screen, and the child must select the correct window number. If he or she is right, the child scores points. Wrong answers merit no points, but the correct picture remains uncovered for about six seconds so that the child can concentrate and remember the location.

The last game, Convoy, is designed for at least two children to play together. The program prints each child's name on a truck, and lines up the trucks at the left-hand side of the screen. A picture then appears, and the first player must correctly key in the first letter of the word that describes this picture. The player's truck inches forward a few steps if he or she selects the correct letter. The next player types in the second letter, and so forth. The player whose truck reaches the right-hand side of the screen first scores a point. All trucks in the convoy then return to the starting point, and a new graphic appears on the screen.

By using a Reconfigure option, parents or teachers can modify the difficulty of the games simply and easily. You can choose 22 units of words either individually or in blocks. These units include "shapes," "animals," "two- and three-letter words" and "difficult multisyllable words." Using the Reconfigure menu, adults can test the game paddles for reliability and range, and they can enter the names and numbers of players. You can save this information on the game's diskette.

The only snag we found was that the sounds the program generates during the games can be somewhat distracting in classroom use — we could not

InfoWorld
Report Card

Spelling Bee Games

	Poor	Fair	Good	Excellent
Performance	☐	☐	■	☐
Documentation	☐	☐	■	☐
Ease of Use	☐	☐	■	☐
Error Handling	☐	☐	■	☐

InfoWorld
Report Card

Hands On BASIC

	Poor	Fair	Good	Excellent
Performance	☐	☐	■	☐
Documentation	☐	☐	■	☐
Ease of Use	☐	☐	■	☐
Error Handling	☐	☐	■	☐

InfoWorld
Report Card

Algebra Volume I

	Poor	Fair	Good	Excellent
Performance	☐	☐	☐	■
Documentation	☐	☐	☐	■
Ease of Use	☐	☐	■	☐
Error Handling	☐	☐	☐	■

Summary

We can recommend all three of these software packages from EduWare. Potential users of the packages range from ages 5-10 for Spelling Bee Games, 13 and up for Hands on BASIC Programming and Algebra 1 for secondary-school students.

System Requirements

Spelling Bee Games, Version 1.1.1
☐ *Apple II, II Plus, IIe; Franklin Ace*
☐ *DOS 3.3*
☐ *48K RAM*
☐ *One disk drive*
☐ *Game paddles*
    Hands on BASIC Programming, Version 1.0
☐ *Apple II, IIe, II Plus; Franklin Ace*
☐ *DOS 3.3*
☐ *48K*
☐ *One disk drive*
    Algebra Volume 1, Version 1.6
☐ *Same as above*

Suggested list price: Spelling Bee Games, $39.95; Hands on BASIC Programming, $79; Algebra Volume 1, Version 1.6, $39.95

Customer Service
EduWare Services, Inc.
P.O. Box 22222
28035 Dorothy Drive
Agoura, CA 91303-0522
(818) 706-0661
Sales and Marketing
Peachtree Software by EduWare
3445 Peachtree Road
Atlanta, GA 30326
(404) 239-3000

discover how to turn the sound off.

Apart from this snag, all four Spelling Bee Games perform well and are easy to use. Leaving a game is easy — if you depress the Escape key, you return to the Games menu.

The software has provisions for input errors. For example, the program asks for a number from 1 to 4; if you enter some other character, the program does not respond.

The documentation consists of a clearly written, 20-page booklet. Children playing these games for the first time need some guidance. The last two pages of the manual, entitled "Handling Errors," help you troubleshoot problems that can produce error messages on the screen. If you can't discover the cause of errors, EduWare encourages you to call one of its representatives.

Spelling Bee Games comes with a 30-day limited warranty and unlimited service and updates for owners who fill out and return the registration card that accompanies the package.

Spelling Bee Games sharpen both spelling and reading skills as well as the powers of concentration and eye-hand coordination. The games are suitable for either home or classroom use, and, perhaps best of all, children seem to like them.

Hands on BASIC Programming is an interactive guide to the essentials of the BASIC language and computer operations. Any inexperienced computer user can benefit from this package since it is clearly written and easy to follow. We recommend this tutorial for ages 13 and up.

The package consists of a 185-page manual and a diskette containing the HOBASIC language — a language similar to Applesoft BASIC.

The HOBASIC manual is the guiding force in using this program. You have control of the computer's cursor at all times and, if you follow the manual, can quickly learn how to construct and debug programs. To further simplify this process, the HOBASIC language provides you with immediate syntax checking. The manual takes you from simple arithmetic operations to Print statements; loops; Read, Data and Restore commands; inputs; arrays; and branching.

Each section of the manual takes you step-by-step through the programming process. It includes many figures showing you what you should see on your screen display. Margin notes contain comparisons to Applesoft BASIC. Each section of the tutorial ends with a review and a table of newly encountered terms, commands and keystrokes. The manual also contains practice problems for you to try on your own and suggested solutions to these sample questions.

Although we found a couple of errors, the documentation is well written and serves as an excellent reference tutorial. Definitions are precise; explanations are clear and related to the world of everyday experience. In addition, the author injects a sense of humor into his writing, which takes the edge off what might otherwise be a pedantic approach to programming. Hands on BASIC Programming offers a logical approach to computer programming. This package is so well constructed that, if it had a few minor modifications, we would recommend it without reservation.

Algebra Volume 1 is the first in a series of six volumes of tutorials suitable for secondary or remedial-postsecondary mathematics students. This software provides an excellent medium for learning or reviewing first-year algebra. It covers the concepts of numbers vs. numerals, the number line, sets and rules for evaluating expressions.

This series of volumes is based on an instructional model that is clearly and precisely presented in the 17-page manual that accompanies the set. The program is fully consistent with the pedagogical model.

The program divides each major unit (for example, Sets) into concepts. You can learn each concept using four learning modes: definition, rules, examples and sample problems. Each mode reinforces the concept. Once you successfully complete the sample problems, you receive a congratulatory message. If you don't perform well on the sample problems, the program doesn't give you any negative feedback but highlights areas you should review with an asterisk.

A flowchart on the Main Algebra menu keeps track of your progress. It is composed of rectangles representing each unit — rectangles outlined in white highlight units not yet attempted; green highlights units successfully done; red, units attempted unsuccessfully; and blue, the unit recommended next. Although this flow diagram is an excellent means of charting your success, only students with color TVs or color monitors can take advantage of this feature.

During any practice session, students can change modes, return to the Unit menu or end with just a few, easily learned keystrokes. The program ignores unanticipated inputs (such as alphabetic characters substituted for numeric ones). The program records your progress on the diskette, so that you can return later and continue working where you left off.

A minor complaint is that the program uses a small rectangular character to designate multiplication, which can be confusing at first.

Nevertheless, Algebra Volume 1 presents concepts in a well-thought-out and instructionally sound manner, and we highly recommend this program.
—*Cynthia E. Field*

REVIEW

Ernie's Quiz

Ernie's Quiz is one of four Discovery Games developed by the Children's Television Workshop and is available from Apple. It incorporates the "Sesame Street" discovery-through-interactive-play approach to learning.

Aimed at children from ages four to seven, this colorful, animated program uses the familiar Muppet characters to provide experiences in counting, closure using parts and wholes, reasoning and creativity.

Ernie's Quiz is made up of four games: Guess Who, a game involving nine Muppets whose identity your child must guess as visual clues slowly appear on the screen; Jelly Beans, a counting game in which your child must count the jelly beans in a jar; Face-It, a body-parts game in which your child, using game paddles, can create a unique individual made up of a wide selection of head, face and body parts in a variety of colors; and Ernie's Quiz, a reasoning game consisting of three clues about different Muppet characters that tests your child's knowledge of the Muppets.

In addition to the four games in the program itself, the documentation includes follow-up activities to enable children to practice the skills they need in the games. For example, a suggested

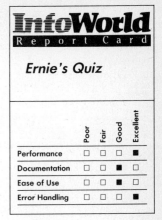

InfoWorld
Report Card

Ernie's Quiz

	Poor	Fair	Good	Excellent
Performance	☐	☐	☐	■
Documentation	☐	☐	■	☐
Ease of Use	☐	☐	■	☐
Error Handling	☐	☐	☐	■

Summary
Ernie's Quiz is a colorful, animated program designed for children from ages four to seven. Its four games use familiar Muppet characters to provide experiences in counting, closure using parts and wholes, reasoning and creativity. The documentation includes follow-up activities. Children should have hours of fun with this excellent program, which reinforces basic concepts they need for learning as they play.

System Requirements
☐ *Apple II Plus*
☐ *Integer BASIC*
☐ *48K RAM*
☐ *One disk drive*
☐ *Game paddles*
☐ *Color TV or monitor*

Suggested list price: $50

Apple Computer
20525 Mariani Avenue
Cupertino, CA 95014
(408) 996-1010

130

follow-up activity for Face-It is to make "fractured faces," using pictures of face and body parts cut from different magazines. Children can assemble them in any way they please and glue them onto another piece of paper to create a brand-new face.

The program randomly generates the number of jelly beans for counting, the clues in Ernie's Quiz, the visual clues in Guess Who and the face and body parts in Face-It, so that children cannot memorize a set sequence of reponses to each game.

The program gives auditory and/or visual feedback for both correct and incorrect responses throughout all the games — children can know immediately whether they have counted the jelly beans correctly or guessed the identity of the Muppet in Guess Who.

Ernie's Quiz requires adult assistance the first couple of times that your child uses it. Although the game is intended for young children, someone must usually read the on-screen directions and documentation to them at first. Once youngsters have memorized the directions, they only have to press the Escape key to signal a guess and type in the correct name (provided in the documentation) in Guess Who, press a number for the amount in Jelly Beans, use game paddles in Face-it and press a number for a guess in Ernie's Quiz.

They must press Return to enter their response — doing so is a basic tenet of good, interactive learning because players can set the pace of the game. To start a new game, they simply press Control/Reset and select a different game from the menu by pressing the correct number and Return.

Ernie's Quiz ignores incorrect responses, so your child's lack of typing ability has no effect. Pressing Control/ Reset to end a game is the only way to stop the program.

The documentation included with Ernie's Quiz is exceptionally well done. It contains step-by-step directions for loading and running the program, and it tells you what to do if nothing appears on the screen.

Children who can read at the second-grade level should have no trouble following the instructions. They are clear and contain many drawings that show you exactly what to do and which key to press. The on-screen documentation is in large, uppercase letters, and, again, is simple and easy to understand.

An unusual feature of Ernie's Quiz is that the original package includes a backup disk.

Ernie's Quiz is endlessly entertaining and, at the same time, encourages children to discover and practice the basic concepts they need for learning. Coupled with the follow-up activities that the well-conceived package includes, it is appropriate for the age level at which it is aimed.

—*Patti Littlefield*

COMMUNICATONS

Computer use need not be a solitary activity. The programs in this category allow your Apple to communicate with other computers.

REVIEW

Transend 2

Transend 2 is a data-communications program for the Apple II and IIe. It lets you send programs to and receive programs from another Apple equipped with Transend 2 (and a modem). Transend 2 also serves as an intelligent-terminal program with limited editing capabilities.

The program is menu driven, slow to load to the basic menu (it takes about 20 seconds) and equally slow to move to submenus. For example, it takes 15 additional seconds to load the terminal functions and then five more seconds to load information (telephone number, log-on instructions) about the number you plan to call. (Transend can store data for up to six systems.) In the Terminal mode, the system automatically defaults to parameters for

The Source. You may choose another default system, but you must always have one, whether you want to or not.

When you choose the number you plan to call, you also choose how many successive attempts you want to make to call that number. Once the connection is made, the computer responds with a tone; therefore, you need not watch the screen while you wait for the connection to be made.

Transend 2 stores the data you send or receive in a 14,000-character capture buffer. As the buffer becomes full, a clicking sound is emitted. If you do nothing, the first data you receive will be lost. If you want to save the data, you can stop the output, save the buffer data on disk, empty the buffer and resume transmission. This procedure takes about a minute and can be expensive if you are making a long-distance call or using an information utility such as The Source.

While data are in the capture buffer,

InfoWorld
Report Card

Transend 2

	Poor	Fair	Good	Excellent
Performance	☐	■	☐	☐
Documentation	■	☐	☐	☐
Ease of Use	☐	■	☐	☐
Error Handling	☐	☐	☐	■

Summary

Transend 2, a data-communications program for the Apple II and IIe, lets you send Applesoft files to and receive files from other comparably equipped Apples — and ASCII files to and from any computer. You can edit data in files that you receive, but the Editing mode is one of this product's weakest features. Another weak feature is Transend 2's manual. Despite these and other drawbacks, Transend 2 is an efficient file-transfer device.

System Requirements

☐ *Apple II Plus, IIe*
☐ *Applesoft*
☐ *48K RAM*
☐ *One disk drive (two recommended)*
☐ *Modem*
☐ *Printer, 80-column card recommended*

Suggested list price: $149 (included Source Membership)

*Transend Corporation
2190 Paragon Drive
San Jose, CA 95131
(408) 946-7400*

you may edit them. The Editing mode is one of Transend's weakest features. The screen shows you the material in the capture buffer. You can only delete material from the beginning or end; you cannot edit material in the middle or insert anything in the material you have captured. (Transend offers a substantial discount on the Magic Window word-processing program, but this discount does not compensate for the lack of internal editing.)

Transend comes in three versions: Transend 1 is an intelligent-terminal program, Transend 2 lets you send files to and receive files from another Apple, and Transend 3 allows you to send electronic mail on an unattended basis.

Transend 2's strongest feature is its ability to send and verify files. The other Apple must be equipped with a Transend 2, and you must be present during transmission. To send Applesoft, integer or binary files, the other Apple must also be equipped with Transend 2. Transend 2 can send ASCII files on a nonverified basis to any computer. The only thing it cannot send is information on a copy-protected disk.

You can estimate the time needed to send a file. For example, sending the text file of this review would take about 4.5 minutes at 300 baud and 1.5 minutes at 1200 baud. Transend sends large files slowly. A full disk of 43 files would take 69 minutes at 300 baud and 22 minutes at 1200 baud.

Prior to the file transmission, the two Apples can communicate to one another in the Terminal mode. While files are transferred, you are informed of the status of the transmission. An unobtrusive clicking sound tells you that transmission is under way, and the screen display shows you the status of the transmission.

Transend requires 48K and one disk drive, although a second disk drive will prevent disk swapping. It works with most major modems (300 or 1200 baud), 80-column cards and printers, but it does not display lowercase characters for Apple IIs with a lowercase chip. Hardware configuration is a simple process that you perform the first time you use the program.

Transend efficiently traps errors. If you press the wrong key, the program emits a warning beep. Transend double-checks each command, which permits new users to reconsider each entry. Once you are confident of your ability, you can eliminate much of this double-checking; safeguards are still present on critical commands, however. For example, the program always checks to be sure that you want to clear the capture buffer.

Transend's manual is deficient in several regards. Printed on glare-producing shiny paper, it is badly written and poorly organized, and it contains an almost unusable index. The manual's menu-order format often forces you to match the menu on the screen with the menu in the manual. On the other hand, telephone support (through a toll call to San Jose, California) is excellent. Transend also maintains an electronic bulletin board, where you can see the problems of other Transend users and the solutions they have developed.

The latest version of Transend has log-on and macro features, which may help some users. The log-on features let you send account numbers and passwords automatically for up to six different systems. The automatic log-on waits a specified time for a trigger character and then sends the required data. For instance, when you log on to Telenet, you need to send information when you see @. If Telenet is slow to respond, automatic log-on may not work. Internal macros are also available. By pressing Control-E and a letter while you're on-line, you may transmit several words. For example, to get the latest news about Apple, from the Dow Jones News Retrieval Service, you must type //DJNEWS and press (return) and then type .lAAPL 01 and press (return). With macros, you perform that operation in four keystrokes. For each of six numbers, you can have up to 26 macros, but you cannot print out a reference to determine what you have programmed for each macro.

Disk utilities let you lock, unlock or delete files. Print utilities allow you to print text files or to examine them on the screen.

The Transend package includes a backup disk and free membership in The Source. You can upgrade to a more complex level of Transend by trading in your version and paying the price difference.

Transend 2 would be a much better program if it had good editing capabilities, faster program loading, a larger capture buffer and a better manual. If you need a general-purpose intelligent-terminal program and want free Source membership, Transend 1 is worth the money. If you don't want free Source membership, consider other programs. To transfer files between Apples, Transend 2, despite its limitations, is a useful and efficient program.
—*Saul D. Feldman*

REVIEW

ASCII Express

ASCII Express "The Professional," is a telecommunications program for the Apple II family of computers and compatible machines. Although the publisher's advertising of the package contains some hype, after our review we feel that, indeed, this is a very well written, complete program that should meet most of your communications requirements.

As with any communications package, your first outing won't be a picnic. You have to complete certain fundamental steps before you can hope to begin transmitting or receiving data. You must set up the program so it matches your computer, your monitor and the modem you are using. You must tell it how you are going to pass information over the telephone lines, the characteristics of the program at the other end and the receiving computer's requirements. Additionally you have to consider whether the information going over the telephone is a program or text file.

ASCII Express can function with a large set of hardware devices such as modem cards, display boards, printer hookups, external modems and hard disks. It can communicate with computers that use special protocols or behave like terminals. It is compatible with Bell 103, Bell 212a and Vadic 3400 telephone-network protocols.

The program uses an extensive series of menus to allow you to choose the specific requirements for the hardware you have. Herein lies the problem for most novice "communicators." There are so many options, in so many permutations, that

InfoWorld
R e p o r t C a r d

ASCII Express

	Poor	Fair	Good	Excellent
Performance	☐	☐	☐	■
Documentation	☐	☐	■	☐
Ease of Use	☐	☐	■	☐
Error Handling	☐	☐	☐	■

Summary
ASCII Express, "The Professional", is a complete communications package for the Apple II family of computers. The documentation is overly technical, and setup of the program could be frustrating for novices, partially because the subject is complex in nature. The package itself is good, though.

System Requirements
☐ *Apple II, II Plus, IIe*
☐ *DOS 3.3*
☐ *48K RAM*
☐ *One disk drive*
☐ *Apple-compatible communications device that uses an RS-232 asynchronous serial interface*

Suggested list price: $129.95

United Software Industries
1880 Century Park East
Suite 311
Los Angeles, CA 90067
(213) 556-2211

program setup can be confusing. The manual contains a thorough discussion of all these options. The preset values are useful in many cases, so with some trial and error, you can successfully set up the program. Once you save the instructions, the modem program can use the information automatically the next time you run the program.

ASCII Express includes a tutorial in the manual that teaches you general operation of the program. The tutorial shows you how to set the profile of your own system. Once this is done, you are ready to use ASCII Express to communicate with another computer. The manual shows you how to dial a number, using your Apple's keyboard; log onto the remote computer; keep a record of the session; exit; and hang up the telephone. At any point in the program, you can get information on a given command.

We found the performance of ASCII Express to be exceptional in most areas. A trio of examples of the program's attention to detail are the Editor, Diversi-DOS and the utility diskette that come with the package.

The Editor can build or change standard text files. It is primarily line-oriented and provides you with commands to change uppercase and lowercase, insert characters and lines, reset margins, search and save or print the record of the session. Such a built-in editor is useful when you are transmitting files. You don't need a separate text processor to make the changes.

Diversi-DOS is a high-speed operating system facility that comes with ASCII Express and can be copied to other programs. This program automatically relocates DOS to upper memory if a RAM card is present. If you use this special Memory Management System, a much larger buffer size is available (28K versus 18K). With this

increased buffer, you have about 50% more room for input when uploading a file, for example.

You use the utility programs for changing files from one format (such as DOS) to another (such as CP/M) and for converting Applesoft BASIC or binary to ASCII text that can be transferred.

The main menu has several options, and you really don't use all of them often. It is comforting to know all those other options are there if you need them, though. You won't have to use different packages for text processing, editing, file conversion and telecommunications.

Even though the manual is descriptive, you will have to wade through a good deal of technical computer jargon in order to understand the program. This problem is exacerbated if the installation doesn't go smoothly and some preset values don't match your equipment. Once you have the preliminaries out the way, you can perform the basic operations of the program quickly, easily and logically. To assist you in case you become confused, the manual has a troubleshooting section. Its four parts cover connection problems, communications problems, transmission problems and command problems. This chapter is concise — perhaps a bit too much so. It would pay to expand this section to include some actual problems and their solutions. An on-line tutorial would be a great help; unfortunately, the program doesn't include one.

Once you are aware of and understand all the capabilities built into the program, though, you can complete any of your communications in exactly the way you want. Nearly everything you might want is right here. A good deal of error protection is built into ASCII Express. The menu construction helps to prevent you from issuing unrecognizable commands, and you can instruct ASCII Express to ask you to verify most commands you enter. You can also choose the Brief mode of operation if you want the program to execute your commands immediately. We recommend the Brief mode only for when you know, and really understand, what you are doing.

The program allows you to automatically save incoming data to disk. This procedure automatically creates several different files, as necessary, keeping up with the remote computer. Later you can merge all these files into a single file.

The documentation for ASCII Express is extensive. The manual consists of 339 pages containing 24 chapters divided into 9 sections, plus an index. The table of contents is long, as is the subject index. Troubleshooting is cross-referenced under both "Problems" and "Troubleshooting" in the subject index, and "Troubleshooting" is a full chapter listed in the table of contents. The manual is not written in the light, breezy style of an Apple manual. It usually is terse, meaty, technical and to the point.

When you purchase the product, you receive a copy with a unique serial number. You must notify United Software Industries that you are the holder of this particular copy. Once you are registered as the owner, you have access to a number to call directly with problems, technical or otherwise. You'll need your registration number to receive future revisions to ASCII Express.

We feel this is an excellent communications package for use with the Apple, especially for experienced users or users with extensive communications requirements. It is complete and works well with most hardware systems that work with Apples. Because of the complex nature of telecommunications today, however, the program's setup could be time-consuming and perhaps frustrating for novices.

—*Larry G. Leslie*

REVIEW

VisiTerm

VisiTerm is a program that lets you use your Apple as a very classy data-communications terminal. To do so you will need a 110, 300, or 1200-baud modem and an asynchronous serial-interface card (e.g., the Apple Communications Card, Apple Super Serial Card or the CCS serial card #7710A, Novation Apple-Cat II modem, Mountain Computer CPS Multifunction Card) or a D.C. Hayes Micromodem II.

VisiTerm shows outgoing and incoming data as a 60- to 70-character-per-line display on the high-resolution screen. You can define and select the character sets with both uppercase and lowercase letters and special symbols (foreign alphabets and mathematical and scientific symbols).

That's right, VisiTerm displays 70 characters per line with uppercase and lowercase letters — without requiring additional hardware.

InfoWorld
R e p o r t   C a r d

VisiTerm

	Poor	Fair	Good	Excellent
Performance	☐	☐	☐	■
Documentation	☐	☐	☐	■
Ease of Use	☐	☐	■	☐
Error Handling	☐	☐	■	☐

Summary
VisiTerm lets you use your Apple as a remote terminal to communicate with other computers. It uses both menu- and command-driven modes. VisiTerm is a useful if somewhat complex program.

System Requirements
☐ *Apple II, II Plus, IIe*
☐ *DOS 3.3*
☐ *48K RAM*
☐ *One or two Disk II drives with controller card*
☐ *Micromodem II or asynchronous serial card and 110-, 300- or 1200-baud modem*

Suggested list price: $100

VisiCorp
2895 Zanker Road
San Jose, CA 95134
(408) 946-9000

You control the formatting of the information on the CRT completely. Through the software, you can select half- or full-duplex, baud rate, parity, break-key duration and a host of other data-communication criteria. A Bell Column feature is available, as well as a soft click (with controllable volume) for every keypress.

You can "type ahead"; that is, you can continue to enter information to be transmitted even when the host computer is not yet ready to receive. When transmission is possible, VisiTerm pumps that backlog of characters out to the modem automatically — once again, without additional hardware.

You can use VisiTerm to define (and save to disk) "keyboard macros," or strings of characters that can be transmitted later at the push of a preselected key. This is a handy feature for log-on and log-off procedures, in particular, but it would also be useful whenever you needed to transmit a series of instructions repeatedly to the host computer. For instance, you might frequently need to access the same data base, file or report-generator program. VisiTerm makes up for the lack of a break key on the Apple keyboard by generating a break signal when the appropriate Escape-key sequence is pressed.

If you are using either the D.C. Hayes Micromodem II or the Novation Apple-Cat, you will be able to dial the telephone from your Apple keyboard while using VisiTerm.

One of the most useful features of VisiTerm is its ability to transmit, receive and generate printouts of disk text files. You can:

transmit long messages at high speed even if you're a slow typist (because you can type the message off-line and later transmit it at the maximum transmission rate);

exchange programs and data with other Apple owners via telephone;

produce a hard copy of information received off-line even if your printer prints much slower than 30 characters per second (cps) and has a limited input buffer;

receive information for later transmission to others.

VisiTerm does support the one-wire, "shift-key-to-game-port" modification of the Apple II and II Plus if you want to have the hardware changed to allow use of the shift key the way it works on the IIe.

When you boot VisiTerm, it goes directly into the Terminal mode with a blank screen, except for the cursor in the home position and the status line at the bottom. In this mode, VisiTerm is immediately ready for you to begin transmitting and receiving.

When you watch VisiTerm work, you get the feeling that the Apple has been transformed into a top-of-the-line intelligent terminal. About the only flaw is the slow scrolling speed.

Because VisiTerm uses software-based, high-resolution character generation, the scrolling routines are complex, so scrolling is slower than it is on the normal, hardware/firmware-based, "text-page one" system.

This slowness is exaggerated if you select the scrolling increment to be as small as possible — i.e., one line of the dot matrix per scroll. Even with this slight drawback, however, at 300 baud there is no noticeable degradation of performance when you're receiving.

VisiTerm is capable of working at speeds as high as 1200 baud. So if you have a serial-card/modem combination that can function at that speed, the actual throughput when printing to the CRT screen will slow a bit unless you change the size of the scrolling increment to five lines or greater.

From the Terminal mode, you can move to the Options mode by using a short Escape-key sequence. The Options mode gives you a menu of communications and screen-formatting options, including baud rate, data format, required break duration and vertical spacing between lines.

In the Options mode, you can also completely define the two character sets you want to use; you can save the entire configuration on disk; you can call a previously defined (or factory-supplied) character-set configuration; and you can dial the telephone (if you're using a Micromodem II or Apple-Cat).

In the Macro Definition mode, you can add new macros, change existing macros or delete macros in RAM. Each macro has a maximum size of 249 characters. The total memory space available in RAM is about 1400 characters, but you can save additional 1400-character blocks with each option configuration.

In the File Transfer mode, you can name, define, create, send and receive text files. When creating and receiving files, you are limited to about 18K of characters in RAM before you must stop putting characters into the disk buffer and write the buffer to disk. Thereafter, if you want to write again to a file of that name, you will be prompted to inform the computer whether to append or replace the preexisting disk file or to cancel the write process (and choose a new name for the next file).

About the only drawback with the File Transfer mode is that the text display is smaller and cruder than that of the Terminal mode. (It wouldn't

really have been an issue if the author hadn't already spoiled us with a fancy Terminal-mode screen.)

When you're about to print out a file, VisiTerm lets you send an initialization-and-termination string to your printer that defines the end-of-line pause duration and selects pagination or continuous printing, the page depth, extra line feeds, the form-feed string definition and the new page pattern. You can also select the starting page number and the numbering format, the left margin, the line length and the characters to ignore, and you can determine how to handle line overflow. You can save these printer configurations and retrieve them later.

VisiTerm is organized into both menu-driven modes and a command-driven Terminal mode.

The menus are easy to use, but the command-oriented Terminal mode forces you to refer back to the documentation continually to find the appropriate choices.

The command choices would be much easier to deal with if a list were always displayed at the top or bottom of the screen, much as Hewlett-Packard does with its function keys, or if the list were available on a separate screen that came into view when you asked for it by typing a ? or H for help.

Every operation except the high-resolution scrolling is fast and well organized. One problem with the Print program, however, is that it ends abruptly.

To send a text file to your printer, you must first get into the Options mode and "XEQ" the program named PRINT. Since the Print program and VisiTerm can't exist together in RAM, a nice touch would have been to be able to exit the Print program and return automatically to VisiTerm. Such is not the case, though. When you quit the Print program, the program clears the screen, erases itself from memory and jumps to the BASIC prompt.

If you are using VisiTerm with a Micromodem II, VisiTerm does not improve the Micromodem's normal method of dialing. You have to key in each digit slowly to allow Micromodem to keep up with you; you can't save the phone numbers within VisiTerm for later automatic dialing.

VisiTerm itself is well protected against errors. About the only potential problem could arise because the VisiTerm disk must be left without a write-protect tab when you need to save option configurations or incoming/ outgoing data files for later use.

This situation is particularly worrisome because VisiTerm is delivered without a backup copy and with relatively effective copy protection.

The manual provided with VisiTerm is professionally printed in black and white on 150 pages of 6×9-inch glossy stock and bound in a padded three-ring binder.

The manual has a clear and thorough table of contents, an index, a glossary and technical appendices. It takes you step by step through an explanation of how to use the package, and it gives you an overview of VisiTerm functions, a required-equipment list and a summary of how to boot the package and troubleshoot common mistakes.

The manual includes an easy but complete tutorial (with examples and sample CRT screens) of each of the operating modes and utility programs. A folded 7½×24-inch reference card is included; it's indispensable when you're "on the air." It even has illustrations of the CRT screen showing the different operating modes.

VisiCorp provides a well-staffed customer-support and technical-representative service at its main number in San Jose, California. Unfortunately, this number is not toll free.

If you fill out and return the warranty card, the firm will provide you with a free replacement disk if the original is found defective within the first 90 days from purchase. Thereafter, a replacement will cost you $20.

You can buy a backup at any time for $20.

At $100 VisiTerm is not inexpensive, but it is worth every penny. A software package this well conceived and effectively executed is a pleasure to have and use.

—*Donald S. Teiser*

REVIEW

Softerm 1 and 2

Softerm 1 and 2, software packages designed to help computers communicate, can give you top-notch performance.

Softerm 1 is for users who want remote access to timesharing host computers or information services, such as The Source or CompuServe, or who want to communicate with other computer owners. Softerm 2 has all the features of Softerm 1 plus the ability to make your computer "look" like one of many (19 at last count) CRT terminals to a host computer, including ADDS Regent, DEC, Hazeltine, IBM and Lear-Siegler.

The Softerm packages are flexible and, once you figure out how to run them, they do many things. People used to the constraints and limitations of some other programs will appreciate Softerm 1 and 2's well-thought-out features. You should decide at the outset whether you need the complexities of Softerm 1 or 2 or if you can meet your needs with a program that is simpler to use. The complexities are mostly a fault of the manual and not of the programs themselves. Softerm's on-screen menus are quite easy to understand and, for the most part, are self-explanatory. Softerm 1 and 2 will continue to satisfy your needs as they become more complex.

Softerm 1 and 2 each come with a "keyboard expander" board that plugs into any slot of your computer. A long, skinny cable connects the board to a small keypad. The keys on the keypad allow you to make direct use of some of the functions of Softerm. The disadvantage of the keyboard extender, however, is that it takes up an extra slot on your computer. The flimsy keypad needs to be affixed by adhesive pad to the computer, which means you can't move it or move the board from the computer any distance greater than the length of the wire.

Softerm 1's main feature is that it will handle DOS, CP/M or Pascal files. You don't need a coprocessor board in your Apple to be able to transmit or receive CP/M files, as the Softerm program can directly read the disks with its file-management program. As a result, you can also transfer, for instance, a DOS file in drive 1 to a CP/M file on a CP/M-formatted disk in drive 2 — drive B in CP/M terms. The file manager, which uses an enhanced disk-operating system, operates at speeds many times faster than Apple DOS.

Softerm 1, unlike other intelligent-terminal programs, operates at speeds up to 9600 baud in half- or full-duplex transmissions if your computer is directly connected to a host computer. (Normal telephone lines are incapable of carrying data that fast.)

Softerm 1 and 2 provide a menu for specifying the terminals you want to imitate. You can load, save or edit terminal configurations. You define your configuration by name rather than by technical specifications. If you don't find your particular hardware listed, you can query Softronic's on-line update service for its specifications. You can define as many configurations as you like and name them whatever you like. If you name a configuration "Softerm.INIT," it will automatically load when you start the program.

The Softerm packages have a nice solution to one problem modem users face — dealing with the different bit patterns different host computers use. The programs deal with this problem in their "phone book" utility, which allows you to name and maintain up to 50 telephone numbers in a directory.

When you enter the name, not only does the program automatically dial the number, but it automatically configures the bit-pattern protocol you previously specified. One of the minor annoyances of the phone book utility, however, is that you can add or delete names, but you can't edit them.

You can send incoming information directly to the printer with Softerm 1 or 2. You can also simultaneously store received data on the disk and print it. The Softerm programs provide a mode that stores all data received and a mode that stores each line on the screen after

InfoWorld
R e p o r t C a r d

Softerm
1 and 2

	Poor	Fair	Good	Excellent
Performance	☐	☐	■	☐
Documentation	☐	■	☐	☐
Ease of Use	☐	■	☐	☐
Error Handling	☐	☐	■	☐

Summary
Softerm 1 and 2, a pair of programs for communicating between computers, offer good performance to the technically experienced buyer who can follow the documentation. They are well-thought-out packages that solve many of the problems modem users face. If you don't understand modem communications, though, these package aren't going to help you very much.

System Requirements
☐ *Apple II, II Plus, IIe*
☐ *DOS 3.3*
☐ *48K RAM*
☐ *One disk drive*
☐ *Asynchronous port or any type of modem*
☐ *80-column board*
☐ *Clock board and printer (optional)*

Suggested list price: $135 for Softerm 1; $195 for Softerm 2

Softronics
3639 New Getwell Road, Suite 10
Memphis, TN 38118
(901) 683-6850

it is first displayed. You have to decide in advance what you want to save and how you want to save it. It would be better if you could make these decisions after you received the data and not before.

Softerm 1 and 2 use keyboard macros, which let you assign a predefined string of characters to a single key. Pressing that key then has the same effect as typing the whole string. You can save up to 18 individual keyboard macros, with up to 26 characters each. These macros may be "nested," that is, one macro can call on another.

The program has many other features. For example, all 128 ASCII codes can be generated from the keyboard. The XMODEM protocol for the CP/M users' group provided compatible file transfer. The Softrans file-transfer protocol provides CRC-16 error checking with automatic retransmission. Automatic binary encoding and decoding are provided; data compression makes maximum use of disk storage space. A FORTRAN 77 source program allows Softrans protocol compatibility with any host computer. There is a built-in patch utility for correcting user-reported problems.

The documentation is a contrast to the quality of the software. On the surface it appears to be very good. The manual includes appendices that detail the hardware the Softerm programs support, describes all of the error messages and explains the user-support policy, including the on-line update service. It concludes with a comprehensive glossary and index. It is thorough, but written by engineers for engineers. It's not that the information needed is absent; it's that nontechnical users will have a tough time understanding it.

Step-by-step instruction sequences would be useful, but most of the instructions throughout the manual are of the "if-then" variety: If you select *this* option, then *that* will happen. But if you don't know what option to select, you want to be given a model to follow by rote until you understand what's going on. Modem communications are far too complicated for software firms to expect new users to wade through manuals, technically comprehensive as they may be, without giving specific instructions.

We have just scratched the surface of the Softerm packages' many features. For a communications expert, Softerm 1 or 2 could be the ideal program. However, these programs are definitely not for people who don't already understand the technicalities of communicating with modems.
—*Marty Petersen*

REVIEW

P-Term

To communicate with powerful computers, all you need is your Apple II, a modem and P-Term, a versatile communications program.

P-Term communications software turns your Apple into an "intelligent terminal." With the right modem, you can automatically dial and log onto a variety of remote computers. Once logged on, you can transmit predefined strings of commands with only a few keystrokes.

When you're on line with the computer, simple commands let you turn your printer on and off. You can capture what you see in a buffer and save it on disk for later editing with a word processor. Simple commands let you send or receive files and programs with full error-checking.

P-Term supports all Apple-Pascal-compatible 80-column boards or external terminal drivers as well as the 40-column screen. With P-Term you can emulate a variety of terminals.

You can customize P-Term to change the characters used to stop and start the flow of data from one computer to another or to make your Apple send both a line feed and carriage return to your printer.

Its designer claims that P-Term supports all modems and asynchronous serial cards currently compatible with the Apple II computer, at baud rates up to 2400.

In addition to a variety of terminals and modems, P-Term supports all Apple-Pascal-compatible printer interfaces. Printer output is automatically buffered when you are on line to a remote computer, meaning that printers with speeds slightly slower than the transmission rate do not lose characters.

You can switch an 18K capture-buffer on and off while you're on line, thus allowing you to store incoming data in the memory of your Apple II at will. With an auto-save option, the buffer contents will be saved automatically on disk each time the buffer fills with data. You will not lose incoming data each time the buffer contents are saved.

P-Term provides a Conversation mode to enable you to communicate with other computer owners. What you type will be displayed both on your terminal and on a remote computer terminal.

It is often desirable to transfer data files or programs to another computer, but the risk of transmitting errors can defeat your purpose, especially when you are using telephone lines. Unlike most communications programs P-Term supports an error-checking/correcting protocol called Christensen Protocol. If you send a file or program when both computers have this protocol feature, errors in the transfer are recognized, and the program repeats the transmission until it is received correctly. This is an indispensable feature for any quality communications program.

P-Term also supports a variety of data-transmission options, including block send. These options become important if the computer you want to communicate with requires their use.

You can also operate P-Term remotely. You can call your unattended Apple with another computer and send or receive files, even if you are calling with a system that is not using P-Term. You can have P-Term send out a special sign-on message and require a password to access your Apple.

We used P-Term with a Micromodem II and an Epson MX-100 printer. In most cases, the program is self-configuring to a variety of peripherals; otherwise, P-Term guides you through a configuration procedure. You can also use P-Term with a single disk drive.

We were able to adapt our Apple to a variety of communications requirements while on line. P-Term provides utilities and instructions for modifying or customizing many other

InfoWorld
Report Card

P-Term

	Poor	Fair	Good	Excellent
Performance	☐	☐	☐	■
Documentation	☐	■	☐	☐
Ease of Use	☐	☐	☐	■
Error Handling	☐	☐	☐	■

Summary

P-Term is an easy-to-use program that lets your Apple communicate with a wide variety of computers, while causing a minimum of confusion and frustration. The documentation lacks a glossary — a drawback for novice users.

System Requirements
- ☐ *Apple II Plus*
- ☐ *Apple Pascal*
- ☐ *64K RAM*
- ☐ *Two disk drives*
- ☐ *Modem*
- ☐ *Printer and 80-column card optional*

Suggested list price: $129.95

United Software Industries
1880 Century Park East
Suite 311
Los Angeles, CA 90067
(213) 556-2211

systems. P-Term has many subtle features to enable you to streamline your data-communication abilities.

With P-Term, you don't have to wait for parts of the program to load during operation, and you don't have to journey through multilevel menus. All commands are simple keystroke sequences and take just a few seconds to execute. If you take into account P-Term's numerous features and commands, you will find the program easy to use.

The manual is conveniently divided into tabulated sections. It begins with a discussion of P-Term's features and instructions for getting started and for dealing with the Pascal operating system.

The manual has a brief, but adequate, description of each P-Term menu choice. It also provides an explanation of the use and design of the auto-dial and command-string features, including several examples.

The documentation contains a discussion of the various file-transfer protocols available in P-Term, along with a technical discussion of the Christensen Protocol. It includes information on customizing P-Term to communicate with a variety of remote computers. The manual also explains terminal emulation.

The manual does not contain an index or a glossary, but information is easy to locate. For a first-time user a glossary and a tutorial sample on-line session would be helpful.

Despite this flaw, P-Term is a well-designed package that meets its intended purpose with speed, accuracy and versatility.

—*Rik Jadrnicek*

GRAPHICS

If pictures are worth more than words to you, take a look at these graphics programs. They're not just for drawing pictures, either.

REVIEW

The Graphics Magician

The Graphics Magician and the Apple computer are a perfect hardware-software combination. With them, you can create the same multitude of special effects that more experienced programmers produce. A set of graphics editors and machine-language routines takes the pain out of adding impressive high-resolution graphics and controlled animation to both arcade and adventure-type games.

The Graphics Magician is a programmer's tool. To fully utilize its fast machine-language animation and picture-drawing routines, you must do some programming. The package contains two separate systems: the Animation system and the Picture/ Object Editor. The Animation system has three basic subsystems: the Shape Editor, the Path Editor and the Animation Editor. The Shape Editor is a screen showing seven identical frames with a command menu. Using the I, J, K and M keys, you create on the screen seven views of one shape, each view comprising one frame of an animated figure. The Path Editor lets you draw simple or complex paths for your shapes to follow. The Path Editor uses the same keys as the Shape Editor plus four extra keys for diagonal moves. You save the shape and its path on a disk and then bring them together in the third editor, the Animation Editor. There you assemble the shapes and paths for objects (the items that move) to perform the final animated display. You can animate up to 32 different objects simultaneously on the screen to create a carousel of movement.

With the Picture/Object Editor, you create full-screen pictures using a joystick, Apple graphics tablet, KoalaPad or any device that returns x

InfoWorld
Report Card

The Graphics Magician

	Poor	Fair	Good	Excellent
Performance	☐	☐	■	☐
Documentation	☐	☐	■	☐
Ease of Use	☐	☐	■	☐
Error Handling	☐	☐	■	☐

Summary
The Graphics Magician lets programmers of all skill levels produce state-of-the-art graphics and animation. People with little programming knowledge receive instructions to get them started; experienced programmers will appreciate the system's ease of operation. The Graphics Magician is a versatile tool that saves hours of programming.

System Requirements
- ☐ *Apple II*
- ☐ *Apple DOS*
- ☐ *48K RAM*
- ☐ *One disk drive*
- ☐ *Works with Apple Graphics Tablet, KoalaPad, joystick, or any analog device that returns x, y values directly through a game paddle*

Suggested list price: $59.95

Penguin Software
P. O. Box 311
Geneva, IL 60134
(312) 232-1984

and y values directly through the paddle's I/O. Within this editor you can draw a line, fill in an area, pick a brush from a selection of eight different sizes and even type letters onto your pictures. You pick from a palette with 108 different colors. The absence of a pen-draw capability, due to the coded file you use to save the picture, means that you lose a little detail. Your pictures are saved in a special compact format that lets you store, depending on complexity, more than 100 pictures on a diskette. A standard Apple bit-map screen occupies 34 disk sectors; Graphics Magician images occupy only 2 to 5 sectors. The Graphics Magician provides that space by storing the moves you make to create a picture rather than the entire screen image. Most adventure-type games need this compression feature. You see the picture actually redraw itself on the screen.

Even if you have only basic programming skills, you will soon be designing background screens with little creatures jumping all around. The Graphics Magician is a software-application tool designed to help programmers create and store graphic files they will call from their BASIC or machine-language programs. Novice programmers will discover a way to add computer graphics to their programs; experienced programmers will find a powerful and flexible tool that saves hours of programming time.

Since this software is designed for programmers, they should have no problem responding to errors. Beginning programmers encounter standard DOS messages when their entries are inappropriate. The absence of helpful messages is excusable because programmers are the main audience.

The 76-page manual is concise but designed for advanced programmers. A "quick" tutorial is short on defining computer-graphics terms. A good table of contents and a reference card are all a programmer really needs, anyway, and the documentation provides good charts, tables and program listings.

The Graphics Magician comes on a copyable disk — an outstanding feature for application software. You can make backup copies. The standard 60-day warranty covers defects; after 60 days, you pay a $5 fee. You don't pay a license fee to add routines to your programs, but you must get permission from Penguin Software.

The Graphics Magician is an inspiring piece of software. If you want to include high-resolution animated pictures in your software designs, consider The Graphics Magician.
—Karen A. Weiss

REVIEW

Apple Business Graphics

The use of microcomputers in the production of business graphics is rapidly growing in importance. Graphs are used in business both as tools for exploratory analysis of data and for presentation of data. Apple II Business Graphics is a command-driven graphics package that allows users to draw scatter, line, filled-area, vertical and horizontal bar and pie graphs from their data. You can enter data by hand, using the package's integral editing facility, or the system can read data directly from files maintained in a wide variety of data formats.

You can draw graphs produced by Apple Business Graphics on the Apple video display (in color when the CRT can produce it) or on the Apple Silentype printer, the Qume Sprint 5 daisy-wheel printer or the HP7225A/B and HIPLOT DMP-3 and DMP-4 pen plotters.

Business & Professional Software, Inc., the developer of Apple Business Graphics, sells a package called PIK that allows dealers to install drivers for any one of an additional 44 devices (including the Epson MX80 printer and the HP7470 plotter) as part of the Apple Business Graphics program.

BPS now supplies "PIKYs" to users; these are utilities for specific families of devices.
Volume 2 — Apple Plotter, HP family
Volume 3 — Roland plotters
Volume 4 — Mannesman Tally Plotters
Volume 4 — Panasonic

You can get the best-quality presentation of graphics with plotters, but few currently available Apple graphics packages support plotter output. Apple Business Graphics does — a significant plus.

Users create "take" files of Apple Business Graphics commands and can direct Apple Business Graphics to take its input from these files. This command facility is unusual in a microcomputer package.

You can use take files to automate significant parts of chart production with Apple Business Graphics. This ability is especially convenient when you undertake the time-consuming task of producing hard copies of charts. You can place the necessary commands in a take file and let your Apple run virtually unattended.

You can use take files, along with an Apple Business Graphics Wait command, to make live presentations. The program automatically draws on a TV screen and pauses when you need time to explain your charts and graphs.

The program provides a wide range of user commands to help you customize graphs. A comprehensive system of defaults spares casual users from the necessity of specifying their charts in full detail. Users can specify scales for graphs, center titles on either axis of the graph, or, using a "floating title" facility, they can put vertical or horizontal labels at any place they choose.

You can override the program's default color choices and can place vertical and/or horizontal grid lines on your charts. You have eight different marks to indicate points on scatter charts, which you can connect with solid lines or any of five different kinds of dashed lines.

With Apple Business Graphics, you can draw graphs of several different data sets on the same chart. Multiple-bar charts can have as many as four different bars side by side, and bars can be filled or unfilled. You can mix lines and bars on the same chart.

Although you cannot display more than one pie chart at any one time, you can specify the aspect ratio of pie charts and even create pies with missing slices.

The package supports exploratory uses of graphics by providing data-manipulation and curve-fitting commands. Simple English-language commands allow you to add and subtract elements of a data set, or multiply or divide elements of that set by a constant or by the elements of another data set.

Using the method of least squares, you can fit a line, logarithmic curve, parabola or sine curve to the data.

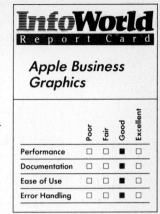

InfoWorld
Report Card

Apple Business Graphics

	Poor	Fair	Good	Excellent
Performance	☐	☐	■	☐
Documentation	☐	☐	■	☐
Ease of Use	☐	☐	■	☐
Error Handling	☐	☐	■	☐

Summary
Apple II Business Graphics helps you construct various graphs and charts using your data. The program is command-driven and operates with a variety of printers and plotters. Its output speed is limited only by the speed of the peripheral devices you use with it.

System Requirements
☐ *Apple II*
☐ *48K RAM and 16K RAM card*
☐ *Two disk drives*

Suggested list price: $175

Business & Professional Software, Inc.
P.O. Box 11, Kendall Square Branch
Cambridge, MA 02142
(617) 491-3377
(800) 342-5277

By using a Distribute command, you can create a new data set in which values are the percentage of a given data set's elements that fall into each interval of a given set of intervals. With this command, you can construct histograms of given sets of data easily.

Apple Business Graphics responds to user commands quickly and efficiently. It rapidly produces the graphs you tell it to draw on the CRT display.

The algorithm that decides the automatic-scale factors performs well. We tested Apple Business Graphics' automatic-scaling algorithm with a data set from a competing package. We wanted to see if the program would produce an inappropriate scale that would then require a deliberate override. We found that Apple Business Graphics automatically provided a viable scale.

When you display multiple data sets on the same graph, however, Apple Business Graphics requires you to build the graph in stages. Because you can't change the scale after you draw the first graph, and because the program cannot anticipate the scale required by the data sets that are first entered, you may have to set the scaling explicitly rather than rely on the automatic-scaling algorithm.

In drawing bar charts with negative and positive values, the program draws bars from the zero value in the appropriate direction — that is, it draws a vertical bar corresponding to a negative value from the zero point downwards and draws a bar corresponding to a positive value from the zero point upwards.

The program places the axis of such a chart at the low vertical point of the scale, instead of at the zero point of the scale. In our opinion, the chart does not look good.

Apple Business Graphics lacks some features that would increase its usefulness for some people. Although you can produce multiple-bar charts with bars side by side, you can't draw stacked-bar charts on plotters. On pie charts, you can't highlight a detached slice.

You have to enter labels for monthly data by hand; this graphics program does not generate them automatically. You can't frame a graph.

Other features of Apple Business Graphics make it a superior performer for other groups of users, however. For example, in filling in areas on graphs, you can elect to fill between the curve and the zero line or between the curve and the baseline of the curve.

The program delivers its hard-copy output with a speed that seems limited only by the speed of the devices and the interface you use.

Typically, command-driven packages are more difficult to use than menu-driven packages because of the initial effort required to learn the specific command names. Apple Business Graphics eases the burden for novices by providing a Help facility. If you type HELP, the screen displays a list of the package's major categories and advises you that you can obtain further help by typing HELP followed by the category name. The program has 14 such additional Help screens.

Once you learn its wide variety of commands, you will find Apple Business Graphics reasonably easy to use. The take-command file capability enhances the package's ease of use. You can save settings and titles for specific classes of graphs in these files and recall them automatically. Unfortunately, learning to use this command is difficult, and the documentation concerning this subject is obscure.

The integral editor is likewise difficult to use, but these difficulties are offset by the ease with which the package can obtain data from external sources. Users who don't like the editor can readily produce their data files using the screen-oriented editor of the Apple Pascal system and transfer that data to Apple Business Graphics.

Apple Business Graphics responds to incorrect commands with a beep from the Apple speaker and a message that reads: "? UNKNOWN COMMAND, TYPE "HELP" FOR HELP." Commands that would clear the current data are greeted by a message asking for confirmation, if you have not saved the data already.

On the whole, the package's designers have thoughtfully anticipated the usual run of user errors and have guarded against them well.

The documentation for Apple Business Graphics is uneven. Parts of it are excellent. For example, the manual begins with a tutorial that is well written and well paced. It can take a first-time user through most of the major features of the package in an hour or two.

On the other hand, the documentation often fails to give adequate explanations of some of the package's more difficult features (for example, the Set Virtual File command) and is marred by many errors that diminish its value.

One notable feature of the documentation is the thorough discussion of the package's internal file formats. The manual carefully documents ways in which you can have Apple Business Graphics interact with other programs. This kind of support is unusual in a copy-protected program, and it makes Apple Business Graphics a more versatile and more valuable product.

Business & Professional Software, Inc., the author of Apple Business Graphics, has a full-time staff member available for telephone support of the product. Unfortunately, none of the papers or documentation included in the Apple Business Graphics package indicates that this sort of help is available, and users who are less agressive may fail to discover it.

Apple II Business Graphics is a well-designed, powerful and advanced tool. It is more difficult to use than a menu-driven package, and less experienced users might not be comfortable with this program. For users who can take advantage of its substantial power, however, it is an excellent utility.
—*Joel Pitt*

REVIEW

VisiTrend/Plot

Anyone who uses microcomputers for personal or business reasons has probably heard of VisiCalc by VisiCorp. Following the success of VisiCalc, VisiCorp has developed follow-up programs that not only work with the original program but can also stand alone as fine programs, mimicking only the command and menu formats of the VisiCalc program. The VisiTrend/Plot program gives the VisiCalc family an important business dimension.

VisiTrend/Plot's analytical functions are designed for use in the calculation and determination of data

InfoWorld Report Card

VisiTrend/Plot

	Poor	Fair	Good	Excellent
Performance	□	□	□	■
Documentation	□	□	□	■
Ease of Use	□	□	■	□
Error Handling	□	□	■	□

Summary
VisiTrend/Plot is a trend-analysis and plotting program designed for "middle-management" users. Although it is of general use, the wider your background in finance and the more experienced you are with VisiCalc, the better are your chances of fully exploiting the program's abilities.

System Requirements
□ *Apple II or II Plus*
□ *DOS 3.3; controller must have 16-sector PROMs*
□ *Apple Language Card or Applesoft ROM for Apple II*
□ *48K RAM*
□ *Two 16-sector disk drives*

Suggested list price: $300

VisiCorp
2895 Zanker Road
San Jose, CA 95134
(408) 946-9000

relationships over time. The plotting function is independent of the trend-analysis function so that you can use it alone.

When you use them together, these programs produce graphs based on current information. You can also use them to plot ancillary time lines and to forecast trends based on the relationships of current independent variables to a known dependent variable.

For example, if you take current sales figures and graph them over a period of time and then plot expenditures for several different types of advertising over the same time period, you will notice that in some periods sales are higher than in others. You should also be able to see some relationship between one or more of the advertising methods to these higher sales peaks and you can then regress these independent variables to determine the highest average (mean) correlation to the dependent variable under consideration (in this example, it would be the sales).

This is known as performing a linear regression. When you use several independent variables, you can perform a multiple linear regression. After you perform the regression to find relationships, you can use this information to project sales based on this correlation to estimate future sales trends. You might also want to use this type of analysis to project future trends in the commodities or other markets.

The mathematics involved in this type of analysis is complex; it would take a great deal of time to perform without the aid of a calculator or computer.

Not only does VisiTrend/Plot perform regression and trend computations, but it also determines standard deviations, moving averages, smoothing, lag and lead, percent of change and many statistical relationships and constants. The package even calculates the Durbin-Watson statistic, an autocorrelation method involving residual values (deviations) of variables in a time series using the least-squares methods.

You can use VisiTrend/Plot to perform a series transformation based on your own equations. Your only limitations are those of Applesoft BASIC itself. You can also use certain logical operators, such as AND, OR and NOT.

The plotting portion of this program allows you to present data in chart format and includes line, bar, area, high-low and scatter charts. You can produce charts in color, with horizontal and vertical grid lines, without grid lines or with horizontal or vertical lines. You can label your graphs on the sides, top or bottom. You can place a movable title anywhere within the chart in normal or inverse video. You can also select a flashing title.

The chart or graph portion of the program also lets you plot a series of lines at the same time. You can compare bar graphs by overlaying graphs to produce graphs that are in half-left and half-right format. Bar graphs can be solid, outlined, dark or light.

Area charts are line charts with the area on the bottom side of the line filled in to make a solid area. Pie charts compare the values of different series at the same point in time on a percentage basis, and the plotting program can color the different portions of the chart differently for easy identification.

The program also contains a third feature: data entry and editing. This is not really an information-producing function, but you could not introduce your own data and variables without it.

VisiTrend/Plot performs many functions, and the analysis portion is complex. There are some limitations — based on memory size and the memory program's requirements for some of the computations — but they are insignificant when you compare them with the program's versatility.

The package handles up to 16 data series at one time, with a maximum of 645 data points. You cannot put all of them on one chart, however, because each chart is capable of holding only 150 data points.

The time required for loading some parts of the program into memory should not cause any problems unless you're impatient.

Time-series charts with many data points can take a long time to plot if you choose to use a bar chart. In a sample case, which required the program to plot data over several years with each year broken into twelve parts, the plot program took several minutes to produce a bar chart. Plotting the same information on a line chart took much less time, so you may want to exercise discretion in your choice of chart type.

We tested many of the available functions, and results were generally good. Most users will find the program more than adequate for their needs.

If you are equipped with a graphics printer that the program supports, you can save your charts in printed form. If you don't have a printer, you will have to replot your series each time you want to review it, but this should not be a problem if you save all the data series that are important to you.

The program allows for the transfer of data from your VisiCalc program if the data is stored in the data-interchange format supplied on your VisiCalc, version 1.37 or a later version. To effect this transfer you must have data that is presentable in a time-series format, and you must change any nonlinear data to linear before plotting.

The programs developed by VisiCorp have an unusual format that some new users have difficulty adjusting to. Some people have trouble with programs that have as many command functions and data entry/retrieval methods as this one. You need to remember numerous keys and characters to move freely throughout the programs and perform data entry. By its very nature, this program is not easy to use, but it would not be fair to say it's incredibly difficult either.

You must be fairly knowledgeable to fully utilize this program. You don't need an MBA in finance, but someone with that type of knowledge has a better chance of understanding the full implications of the data VisiTrend/Plot provides.

Many users would be more than satisfied with the chart-plotting capability of the program. The program is directed toward middle and upper management, so users with this kind of background will probably be able to use at least a portion, if not all, of the statistical capabilities of the program as well.

Most errors you're likely to make during data input cause the loss of the last item you input or, at worst, a transfer from the input mode to the highest available menu area.

Power failures can cause the loss of current entries and of any unsaved series in memory. Such a data loss is especially troublesome in areas of the program that require large amounts of data when you are using complicated formulas to perform computations.

This program does a reasonably good job of limiting data loss, but because there are so many input areas in this program, you should take care to make sure that you don't inadvertently lose any of your data.

As is the case with most VisiCorp products, the documentation consists of an extensive manual that is made up of a progressive series of tutorials. They are designed to acquaint users with as many aspects of the program as possible.

The manual also provides information the tutorials don't cover and is fully indexed. Its use of text and samples of what you can expect to see on the screen as you perform the different functions make it easy to follow. The book also contains an accordion-like pocket reference that gives you easy access to many frequently used functions and commands. The company has a large staff of people skilled in the use of its various programs, and they are helpful when you call them.

VisiTrend/Plot is a good program. It is unusual because it has both a general and a select user group. It is particularly useful for those who want to perform market forecasts, statistical analysis, trend analysis and stock/bond analysis. Most middle-management personnel should have no problems using the plot functions, although they may need a certain expertise to fully utilize the trend/analysis portion of the program.

—*Amanda Hixson*

DATA

The programs reviewed in this category keep track of data bases, a fancy term for lots of information. One of them even keeps track of time.

REVIEW

DB Master Version 4

If you've been wondering what to do now that you've outgrown the file-management package the dealer either sold or gave you when you purchased your Apple II or IIe, you would do well to look at the new version of DB Master by Stoneware.

Stoneware's DB Master is a carefully planned series of data-base construction, use and management programs. Version 4 is the second major update of DB Master for the Apple II since its introduction about four years ago. It works on an Apple II Plus, an Apple IIe or a Franklin Ace 1000 or 1200, all with a minimum of 64K. It is not as complete a rewrite as Stoneware's version of DB Master for the IBM PC. As a result, you can still expect some awkwardness when performing such tasks as creating report formats and rebuilding files.

You can use the files from your version 3 applications with version 4, but if you rebuild the file to take advantage of the new, longer alphanumeric fields, you won't be able to use version 3 again.

We believe, however, that there are marked improvements in version 4 over version 3 for the Apple II. Version 4 is easier to use, it runs faster and its documentation is better. Version 4 can be used with floppies that are produced by the hard-disk version.

One of the chief changes in the new version is the ability you have to create alphanumeric fields up to 100 characters in length. You can also edit, rather than retype, alphanumeric fields. You can make the edited record a second, new record instead of using it to replace the old record.

Improvements to report preparation will make it easier for you to create

InfoWorld
Report Card

**DB Master
Version 4**

	Poor	Fair	Good	Excellent
Performance	☐	☐	■	☐
Documentation	☐	☐	■	☐
Ease of Use	☐	☐	■	☐
Error Handling	☐	☐	☐	■

Summary
*DB Master version 4 is
Stoneware's latest data-base
program for the Apple II family.
Although it takes some effort at
the beginning, it is flexible and
can be used for a wide range of
simple to complex applications.
The improved documentation
and the simpler report formats
added make it simpler to use
than its predecessor, and the
improved file management
makes it faster.*

System Requirements
☐ *Apple II, II Plus, IIe*
☐ *64K RAM*
☐ *Two or more floppy disk
    drives*
☐ *Printer recommended*

Suggested list price: $350

*Stoneware, Inc.
50 Belvedere Street
San Rafael, CA 94901
(415) 454-6500*

standard reports. Improvements in the procedure for creating files make them easier to edit as you work, if you make errors.

A utility converter is available upon request to translate information created with PFS:File and VisiFile into DB Master Version 4 files. This is a promotional deal to influence those of you who have outgrown those file packages and may convert to DB Master if you don't have to retype your data. We used the converter together with version 4 to translate a 950-record, 17-field TV-movie file from VisiFile into a new DB Master file. Our 4 disks of data were converted into about 1½ data disks. The conversion utility is quick to use. This was our first use of the converter, and we translated the file, designed a simple one-line-per-record report and printed it in about two hours.

Performance improvements include faster screen displays, faster random searches and faster report printing. We tested the claims for speed improvements from version 3 to version 4 by typing the same set of records into each version. Although this, admittedly, was a rough test and would vary depending upon the file, we found a 20% improvement in our data-entry time.

The error handling of the program is excellent. In a program this size there are innumerable ways that you can go wrong, and some are more damaging than others. The safeguards at data-entry time prevent errors except for typos that a computer has difficulty distinguishing from the correct form of the entry. If you are using an Apple IIe, you can use both uppercase and lowercase. One problem with using the lowercase letters: you must remember that they are not interchangeable with uppercase when you are sorting records. The manual carefully explains

this hazard.

You face a lot of disk swapping if you use only two disk drives. If your time is important to you, we recommend using three drives.

The printed documentation is good. It comes in an attractive 5×8-inch notebook with index tabs for each major section. It has a table of contents, a glossary and a detailed index. The first sections tell you what's included, how to use it, what a data base is (with examples), what you need to use the software and how versions 3 and 4 differ.

An especially nice addition to the documentation is the section called File Design Guidelines. It is a minicourse in file design, and it describes the steps that you must consider before you are ready for the computer.

The tutorial section (177 pages) guides you through the creation and use of the employee records of the Nose to the Grindstone Travel Company. This section shows sketches of the screens, the records you use and those you produce.

The disks are copy-protected, and a backup copy of the program is included with the package. You must return the registration card to get technical support and to be notified of updates and additions. We received the file guidelines after registration, rather than with the original documentation.

Although version 4 of DB Master takes some learning to make optimal use of its features, we think this is a high-quality, general-use data base for the Apple II.
—June Brevdy

REVIEW

Quick File II

Quick File II, an easy-to-use file manager for the Apple IIe, is suitable for small files and reports. With Apple Writer, you can use file data to produce individualized form letters or to insert reports into text. Files that expand or grow in complexity, however, are outside the capability of this package.

Quick File II provides consistent screen messages and warnings and protection from many errors.

It is driven by four major menus; each menu screen shows the name of the file in use, which area of the program you are in, the area you will go to by pressing the Escape key and the current work options.

The program carefully guides you to define your file needs, start a new Quick File data disk, create the file, add and edit records, change the structure of the file if necessary and print reports. Each screen has a help list of available commands.

You do not specify a field size or type of data. The program makes basic assumptions, and you enter data in whatever format you like. Creating a file consists of naming the file and up to 15 fields, called "categories." The name of each category can be up to 20 characters in length, and the combined length of the category name and the associated data entry can be up to 77 characters long.

The documentation says you can have a maximum category length of 76 characters, but this is true only if you restrict the category name to one

character. The maximum record length is 1140 characters.

The documentation shows a maximum of 140 records per file for a 64K Apple IIe, assuming an average record length of 75 characters. If you have an extended 80-column card with an extra 64K, you can have 600 of those average-length records.

Quick File has two different working-screen-record displays — the multiple-record and the single-record layouts — and you can switch ("zoom" in or out) as you work. The single-record format shows all the fields for one record and is useful for creating or changing record formats, entering new records and editing data in a specific record.

The multiple-record format displays up to 15 records, one line for each record, and as many fields as will fit on the screen. Long fields appear in an abbreviated form. This format is for browsing through the file and making corrections.

You can arrange (sort) the record order in any way, and the records remain as sorted until you rearrange them again. There is no limit to the number of sort levels, since you arrange the records by each category individually, starting with the most specific category.

You can format reports in two styles: "table" or "label." The "table" format looks like the multiple-record screen layout revised to contain your selected fields.

The "label" format is a multiple-line-per-record format similar to that of mailing labels. You design it, based on the single-record layout, by deleting the fields you don't want and rearranging the remaining ones.

Reports can contain new fields computed from the contents of existing fields. The computation formula can be

InfoWorld
Report Card

Quick File II

	Poor	Fair	Good	Excellent
Performance	☐	☐	■	☐
Documentation	☐	☐	■	☐
Ease of Use	☐	☐	☐	■
Error Handling	☐	☐	■	☐

Summary
Quick File II is an easy-to-use file manager for the Apple IIe. The program and manual let novice computer users learn quickly how to construct files, edit them and print reports. You can save report formats in the file and can alter and resave them. You can also change the file structure to add or delete fields. The overall file size is relatively small, with a maximum of 140 records of an average length of 75 characters for a 64K machine or 600 records for a 128K machine.

System Requirements
☐ *Apple IIe*
☐ *64K RAM, 128K recommended*
☐ *Two disk drives*
☐ *80-column card*
☐ *Printer*

Suggested list price: $100

Apple Computer
20525 Mariani Avenue
Cupertino, CA 95014
(408) 996-1010

up to 20 characters long. The report can also include subtotals based on value changes in one category and grand totals for as many of the categories as you want.

You can select records for inclusion in either report by specifying conditions that specific record categories must meet, and you can sort the record order.

Quick File works quickly and it is convenient as long as the file is small, preferably with relatively short total-record lengths. The built-in defaults add convenience, but you can't change them. For example, the program automatically sets report column headings, and you cannot change them without changing the category name of the file.

When your fields get longer than just a few characters and you have many fields, it becomes more difficult to keep the whole record and report formats in mind. This, in turn, makes it more difficult to create effective report arrangements. You cannot use short codes and then substitute the complete information when you print the report.

The printer options allow use of a Silentype or Qume printer without special print instructions, but we recommend that you refer to your manual if your printer requires print codes different from the instructions. Check with your dealer if you have a printer that's not compatible with either the Silentype or Qume printers. Most printer manuals don't offer enough information for you to select special codes without some help.

Quick File provides file identity and escape options for each screen and watches out for major errors. As you exit from the program, you are warned to save the file if you have changed anything in it. The program also warns you before you delete anything and when you try to format a supposedly empty disk that actually contains data.

It is difficult to lose anything without a warning, and the Escape key lets you back out of most errors.

The documentation is an attractive, 7×9-inch, spiral-bound, 158-page book. It has a reference card you can tear out, a detailed table of contents, index and ten chapters that instruct you in the use of the program. Illustrations from the sample files help you follow along on the computer.

The appendix illustrates the preparation of individualized form letters and the use of reports with Apple Writer documents. The documentation is easy to follow, and an effort was made to use nontechnical terms. Some terms are so nontechnical that they confused us — e.g., "arrange" for sort, and "category" for field.

The manual has many screen pictures, which help you check how you are doing as you follow the examples. More information on the defaults would clarify the program's restrictions. As stated, the maximum length of category names is 20 characters and the maximum field size is 76 characters, but the combination has to fit into a space of 77 characters. Try to use both maximum sizes and you will run into trouble.

Quick File is not copy-protected, and you should copy both the program and the sample-file disks before using them. The package sells "as is" with a standard 90-day warranty in case you discover defects or an update comes out within the 90 days. Apple does not guarantee that you will receive notice of updates and advises that you check periodically with your authorized dealer.

We wanted to check some specifications that were not in the manual to determine maximum field- and file-size combinations. A large and famous computer dealer couldn't answer our questions, nor could the product-support people we reached at Apple. The point is that small, easy programs need to be very well documented and shouldn't omit information the manufacturer considers too complicated for users.

You can learn to use Quick File easily and quickly. It keeps short lists with short entries in neat files, and it's easy to look at them on the screen or to print the file for reference. If you want more than 15 fields, longer entries or files that will grow (as you discover more uses for the data you have put in the file), you'll have some problems.
—*June Brevdy*

REVIEW

Visidex

The Visidex program from VisiCorp is a combination filer, calendar, clock and personal secretary for Apple computers. You can get data by using keywords, which can be either alphabetic or numeric. You can also access data by numeric range.

You can also use the program to set up keyed templates, which you can call up at any time for particular formatted entries. You can use the program to develop mailing lists and labels, customer lists, ZIP code and phone lists, repair and work orders; you can also use it to get information that is similar and yet slightly different from template to template.

You can use the program as a calendar; it will even display a monthly calendar for any year in this century.

The program performs data access by establishing keywords for the different data screens prepared by users. A screen is 40 columns wide and 20 columns high. About three screens make up the average printed page. Keywords can be single or compound, and a screen may have many different keywords for searching by different data areas. A keyword may not be more than 38 characters long.

To illustrate the use of keywords, consider this example: Suppose you have a series of screens on postage stamps that are set up with only one country's stamps allowed on any one screen. You might use *stamp* as a keyword, or something such as *U.S. stamps* as a compound keyword. If you set both as keywords, you could use stamps to find all screens relating to stamps, or you could use the compound country-stamp combination to access all screens relating to only one country.

Users can also use wild cards to find more than one keyword or combination of keywords. To do this, you use hyphens and asterisks in keyword commands. This feature comes in handy when you are searching for certain combinations or cumbersome words. You use them in situations such as the following: you have 70 screens with chemical combinations on them and you have used *triglyceride* as a keyword on several. Using a hyphen, you can type in *tri-ide*, and the program will search for all keyword combinations that begin and end with these combinations. The ampersand is used to find keyword/ screenword combinations.

On screens set up as permanent templates you can get data by employing mathematical comparisons. You would do this by requesting

InfoWorld
Report Card

Visidex

	Poor	Fair	Good	Excellent
Performance	☐	☐	☐	■
Documentation	☐	☐	☐	■
Ease of Use	☐	☐	■	☐
Error Handling	☐	☐	☐	■

Summary
You can use this filing system from VisiCorp as a filer, calendar, clock and personal secretary. The product is well supported and alerts you to potential problems.

System Requirements
☐ *Apple II Plus or IIe*
☐ *DOS 3.3*
☐ *48K RAM*
☐ *One or two disk drives*
☐ *Clock card, printer, lowercase chip (all optional)*

Suggested list price: $199

VisiCorp
2895 Zanker Road
San Jose, CA 95134
(408) 946-9000

information such as customers with sales greater than $5000, but less than $50,000 or

CUSTOMER&SALES>= 5000&SALES<=50,000

The manufacturer makes no claim about this program other than to call it an electronic index card, but it does much more than just file and store information. It allows users to set up templates that won't be modified if other users need to input data; it keeps track of appointments and dates; and it performs all of the other mentioned functions.

VisiCorp informs us that within memory limitations, any exisiting Apple II Visidex data bases will run with the Apple IIe Visidex program. The company says you should not try to use just any data base created on an Apple IIe computer on an Apple II or Apple II Plus. The Apple IIe Visidex program is compatible with the Apple Super Serial Card and the Apple Parallel Interface Card. VisiCorp informs us the Apple IIe Visidex program uses any printer that Apple II or Apple II Plus Visidex programs used.

The data-input portion of Visidex may be confusing to first-time computer users. As in other programs by VisiCorp, Visidex has many commands and control characters. Extensive use of the program may be required before you completely master it. This is not to say that most people won't be able to use and benefit from the program, but some patience may be required.

This program also requires you to pay special attention to the printers, which may cause some users to become frustrated, especially if they have not had very much experience with their systems.

VisiCorp uses an unusual data-entry format, but the software company also provides maximum ancillary data in order to ensure minimum user confusion.

This program deals with only one screen at a time and requests user verification before continuing in most instances. The information on a current screen may be lost if there is some power failure or accidental reset, but it probably will not result in a serious disaster because the amount of information on one screen is not large enough to be a major burden to enter again.

As you progress through the program, it will often prompt for a response before it will allow you to continue. Most of these prompts are requests for a yes or no answer before the program deletes or posts a new or revised screen.

When you have deleted information, you can recover it in some instances because the program stores a certain amount of deleted information in a buffer. If you have not exceeded the limitations of the buffer, you can recover all of a currently stored screen.

One problem can occur when you enter or add data. It is possible to push data off the screen by exceeding the number of columns available in any direction. If this happens, you will find that you have donated your data to the bit bucket in the sky. You receive ample warning about this possibility, so it should not be a major problem.

The manuals provided with VisiCorp products are generally very good. They use an extensive tutorial approach that leads users through varying levels of difficulty. If you follow them step-by-step, you should have no problem discovering just what applications a given program has.

At the end of each tutorial is a summary of what you should have learned to do if you followed the tutorial correctly. This is a good feature because it gives you a fast method to refresh your memory if you haven't used the program for a long time. These summaries are convenient.

In addition to the summary at the end of each section is a standard pocket reference that comes with most of the products by this company. This reference provides a quick and easy method for finding command keys and remembering special control characters. Also included is a detailed reference section and an index.

VisiCorp has a large staff that is qualified to help with problems users might have with one of its programs. You do not need to be specially trained in order to benefit from Visidex. Many new users will enjoy some of the functions that are available, such as the reminders for special events or dates and the calendar display. Many clerical and secretarial personnel will be able to keep track of numerous items without the burden of an overstuffed file cabinet. Visidex is functional as well as fun.
—*Amanda Hixson*

PROGRAMMING

After you've had your Apple for a while, you might want to enter the realm of programming. The programs in this category give you a variety of programming possibilities.

REVIEW

Apple Pascal

Apple Pascal is a version of the Pascal programming-language dialect known as UCSD Pascal that was written at the University of California, San Diego, under the direction of Kenneth Bowles.

The Apple Pascal package includes four diskettes containing the operating system, P-code, an editor and a utility library. The program includes several units of code that take advantage of the Apple computer's graphics and sound-generating capabilities. You can easily incorporate or link units with your own program, giving you the best of the computer's and the language's functions.

The Apple Pascal program was designed to run on the Apple II and II Plus. It can also run on the IIe system if you reconfigure it to use the IIe's up and down arrows as cursor controls. You can transfer programs written on the IIe to the Apple II if you recompile them.

Pascal is a block-oriented language that encourages you to break one task down into many small logical tasks. You write a block of program code to solve each of the tasks and give each block a unique name. When you need to invoke a block, you can call it by name. The use of simple blocks of code to form a more involved program is called structured or modular programming.

As a development language, Pascal excels because you can transfer program blocks to other processors. Additionally, the language's use of program blocks or modules makes it easy for you to write and debug the various procedures and functions that form the total program. Once you have written blocks, you can store them in a library, ready for use in future programs.

Pascal is a sparse language — it has few reserved words, is easy to learn and to teach and is logically coherent.

Programs you create using Pascal's top-down logic are easier to understand than line-oriented programs that are cluttered with GOTO statements. (Pascal allows you to use GOTO commands at your own discretion, but does not encourage them.)

Nicklaus Wirth, the author of Pascal, originally designed it for a nonexistent CPU (central processing unit), hypothetically known as the P-code machine. Bowles began the development of P-code simulators for other computers, and such simulators have now been written for the 6502, Z80, 8080 and most other popular CPUs. Since the Pascal programming language exists above each of the system-specific simulators, after some modification, you can transfer uncompiled code between CPUs. UCSD Pascal's editor, like the programming language, is identical from one system to another, which makes UCSD Pascal a good instructional language when you want to use several different micros.

Pascal was originally written for large computers. Because micros have a more limited work space, Apple Pascal's operating system allows you to move (swap) blocks of code from disk to RAM so that you can execute large programs that may exceed your available RAM. Apple Pascal also adds a useful new variable type, String, to the UCSD Pascal — you would otherwise have to write an input routine to gather an array of characters and then build strings.

Apple Pascal allows you to enter input/output (I/O) functions from the keyboard and also gives you new, extended long integers. Apple Pascal attempts to automatically pack its

arrays as a default, thus eliminating Pascal's Pack and Unpacked commands. It does not directly support Pascal's Dispose function, but does use a new function called Mark and Release to reallocate memory. The operators SIN, COS, EXP, ATAN, LN, LOG, and SQRT are not built into the language, but they are available as library functions. You can reach library functions through software instructions.

Apple Pascal's editor provides you with good cursor movement and includes scroll, insert and delete, and copy/move commands — in fact, you can use these functions as a rudimentary word processor. You construct most programs at the editor level, which temporarily stores them in the SYSTEM.WRK.TEXT file. This file is usually updated on the disk whenever you leave the editor. You can lose the file, however, if you don't transfer it to another disk volume prior to editing another file. The transfer routine requires you to press several keys, but each keystroke should be similar to other commands and only represent variations of the normally used keystrokes.

The program's Filer allows you to move the input and output to and from RAM, disk and other volumes or I/O (input/out) devices attached to the processor by specifying path names. The Linking routine allows you to add previously written code to a program during compilation or execution, and the Execute and Run routines can either execute compiled code or compile, link and execute programs.

The diagnostic messages for compile errors are succinct but informative. Because one error can force future compile-time errors, the program's diagnostic system stops the compilation at the point of the error. You can then either continue your compilation or enter the editor at the line where the

InfoWorld
Report Card

Apple Pascal

	Poor	Fair	Good	Excellent
Performance	☐	☐	☐	■
Documentation	☐	☐	■	☐
Ease of Use	☐	☐	☐	■
Error Handling	☐	☐	☐	■

Summary
Apple Pascal is a version of UCSD Pascal that takes advantage of the Apple computer's graphics and sound-generating abilities. The package includes the operating system, a P-code simulator, an editor and a library of utilities on four disks. With the aid of the program's good documentation and diagnostic messages, even a beginning programmer should find it easy to use.

System Requirements
☐ *Apple II, II Plus, IIe*
☐ *64K RAM or more*
☐ *One or more disk drives*

Suggested listed price: $250

Apple Computer
20525 Mariani Avenue
Cupertino, CA 95014
(408) 996-1010

error occurred and make the corrections. The editor level of the system does a good job of trapping errors, such as commands typed out of bounds or sequence. When errors occur Apple Pascal issues a beep signal; in the worst cases (run-time errors are the most common), the system reboots. The messages are easier to interpret than those on most mainframes, making it easier for you to debug with Apple Pascal than with other versions.

The compile time for Apple Pascal is noticeably slower than that of mainframe Pascal — mainly because of the limits of the 8-bit address line and processor of the Apple's 6502 CPU. For short assignments, the compiler speed is not a problem, although for larger application programs it can be a major deficiency.

To use Apple Pascal, you insert a 16K RAM card into an Apple II or II Plus motherboard (the IIe already has the necessary RAM but does require you to modify the cursor controls in order to use the up- and down-arrow keys). The operating system and editor are easy to learn to use, and the package includes a tutorial to help you through the procedures.

Apple has a reputation for high-quality reference and tutorial manuals, although, in the past, its Pascal manuals have been an exception. This release, however, includes an excellent tutorial, written by Luehrman and Peckham, entitled "Apple Pascal: a Hands-on Approach." It is a well-written, instructional manual that is easy to follow and includes good chapter summaries and samples. This tutorial is excellent for instruction but weak as a reference. The other enclosed manuals are good references but poor tutorials. Together, however, the pieces of documentation supplement each

other to make an excellent package. The language and operating-system reference manuals are fine — easy to use and well indexed. The documentation in the package also includes updated corrections for the printed manual.

All four of the Pascal disks are unprotected. In fact, the tutorial advises you to make several backup copies of the disks before you use the package.

Apple Pascal is a good implementation of the UCSD version of the language. The diagnostic messages are adequate, even for beginning programmers. The compilation times for longer programs are noticeably slower than Pascal compilers on mainframes and minicomputers. The language is easy to use as both an instructional medium and a higher-level programming language. An added advantage of the Pascal language is its transportability — although Apple Pascal takes advantage of the special features of the 6502 processor, you can use programs written for other processors with only minor changes.
—*Tom Neudecker*

REVIEW

Aztec C

Manx Software Systems' Aztec C, a C-language development system for the Apple II, includes a new operating system command processor, or "shell," for the Apple; two C compilers; and a variety of operating-system tools and utilities.

With Aztec C, you can write the speediest high-level language code ever run on an Apple II, and develop programs for other microcomputers as well.

C is popular among program developers, partly because it is portable — C is easily transferred to other computers. C programs are usually written according to a single standard, described by Brian Kernighan and Dennis Ritchie in their book, *The C Programming Language.* C is a structured language, and knowledgeable programmers can produce efficient code.

In addition to two C compilers, the Aztec C package includes a text editor, two kinds of assemblers, a link editor, libraries containing standard input/output and utility functions, and a library of common floating-point functions. Finally, the package includes archival source-code files for many of the library functions and system tools, as well as utility programs for managing these archives and function libraries.

When you use the Aztec system for program development you work within its own operating environment. You issue commands through the shell, a command-line interpreter. The shell's operating environment is like that of the UNIX operating system. The shell goes a long way towards easing the complex task of program development.

The shell has file-management commands built into it. It considers the other programs supplied with the system and the programs you create as transient commands. When you enter a command name other than one that's built in, the shell looks for a file with that name on a disk. If it finds it, it then executes the code in the file.

The shell executes commands entered from the keyboard or from a command file. You can specify variables and other program criteria at run time. You can also redirect command input and output (I/O). For example, you can save assembly-language compiler output in a file instead of assembling it automatically. Ved, a small, quick editor supplied with the system, edits programs as long as 700 lines.

Both Aztec C compilers compile the full C language with the exception of the bit-field construct. Both compilers compile your C language source file to an assembly-language file; the native-code compiler produces assembly code for the Apple's 6502 processor, and the pseudo-code compiler produces assembly code for an interpreted pseudo-machine.

The true machine code, produced by the native-code compiler, generally executes faster than the interpreted code produced by the pseudo-code compiler. The pseudo-code is generally much more compact, however, and the pseudo-code compiler is faster than the native-code compiler.

After you've completed the compile/assembly process you still have to link your assembled code before you can run it. The Aztec linker can mix native-code and pseudo-code files. When you're linking a large program, pseudo-code libraries are useful because they employ less memory space than the native-code libraries. Aztec provides both native- and pseudo-code libraries.

You can run your Aztec C programs under the shell or standard DOS 3.3. When you run Aztec C under the shell, you can use its UNIX system-like features, such as I/O redirection and the ability to pass parameters to a program from the command level.

Ordinarily you link programs you develop for your own use so they can run under the shell. If you intend to distribute your program, however, you link to one of the special libraries that

InfoWorld
R e p o r t   C a r d

Aztec C

	Poor	Fair	Good	Excellent
Performance	☐	☐	☐	■
Documentation	☐	☐	■	☐
Ease of Use	☐	☐	■	☐
Error Handling	☐	■	☐	☐

Summary
The Aztec C language-development system gives program developers all they need to create new programs for the Apple or other microcomputers. It supports a UNIX-like operating system that eases difficult program-development tasks. The two compilers are fairly slow, but the code they generate executes much faster than any other high-level language available for the Apple. Using the Aztec C system means switching a lot of disks if you have a two-drive system.

System Requirements
☐ *Apple II, II Plus, IIe*
☐ *64K RAM (48K and language card)*
☐ *Two disk drives*

Suggested list price: $199

Manx Software Systems
P.O. Box 55
Shrewsbury, NJ 07701
(201) 780-4004

Manx provides for running programs under Apple DOS. Even pseudo code programs run under Apple DOS.

Both Aztec C compilers produce impressive code. Although the native code executes faster than the pseudo-code, both kinds execute faster than anything we've seen on the Apple, except for programs written directly in assembly or machine language.

Programs written in Apple's interpreted BASIC typically take about 2000 seconds to execute the Sieve of Eratosthenes benchmark program; a Pascal program running under the Apple Pascal operating system takes about 500 seconds; and programs using Forth take on the order of 200 seconds. The versions we compiled using Aztec C took 20 to 40 seconds. The pseudo-code versions were not appreciably slower than the machine-code versions.

This processing speed is not entirely without cost: you pay for it in compilation time. The pseudo-code compiler compiles programs two to four times faster than the native-code compiler, but a moderately large program can still take a long time to compile. For example, a 150-line program took four minutes of compilation and assembly time with the pseudo-code compiler, and more than nine minutes with the native-code compiler.

When you're using the C compiler for development, its lack of speed need not be a major problem. C is designed so that you can develop and test your programs in separately compiled modules, and then link them together. The Aztec linker is not blindingly fast, but it runs well.

The 125-page owner's manual has a tutorial introduction, which gives you step-by-step instructions for editing, compiling and running a sample program. Other sections detail the built-in shell commands; the compiler, editor

and other system programs; and the system libraries. The last section describes how to mix C programs and assembly-language code and other technical details. Unfortunately, there is no index.

The documentation is written for experienced programmers, and the manual makes no pretense of teaching you how to program in C. In fact, it directs beginners to Kernighan and Ritchie's text. It is reasonably well written, and often has a pleasantly informal tone.

Because the system is large, if you have a two-drive system, you have to do a lot of disk swapping in the course of editing, compiling, linking and testing a program, This problem is due to the physical limitations of your computer; nonetheless it makes the Aztec C system harder to use than it would be otherwise.

When the compiler encounters errors in your program, it displays on the screen the line number, the program text and an error number. The manual contains a table of error numbers and explanations. Occasionally the compiler was unable to recover from an error, and a torrent of meaningless error messages cascaded across the screen.

Manx Software Systems provides phone support for Aztec C owners. The support staff are eager to help, but often lack the detailed technical knowledge to do so immediately. On one occasion the author of the compiler provided advice. Manx sent a corrected version of the compiler in response to our problem report.

One omission in the package merits mention: no support library for the Apple's high-resolution graphics. Since graphics support is not a standard feature of C, this omission is not surprising. But given the importance of graphics programming for the Apple, and the importance of speed in graphics applications, library functions specifically written to support high-resolution graphics would be a valuable feature.

The Manx compiler is outstanding, especially if you plan to develop complex programs for the Apple. It provides by far the fastest code of any Apple high-level language we know of. For program developers, Manx also has compatible C compilers and cross-compilers for a variety of microcomputers.

—*Joel Pitt*

REVIEW

Einstein Compiler

For programmers who require the efficiency of machine language but who have only BASIC programming skills, there exists a product that facilitates the transition. The Einstein Compiler is especially designed to translate Applesoft BASIC into machine language, providing both programming convenience and speed of execution.

The Einstein Compiler will operate on an Apple IIe, II Plus, II or an Apple III. All you require is a single disk drive and DOS 3.3. Source programs up to 31K can be compiled. Larger programs can be reduced in size with a separate utility program (included on the compiler disk), or they can be broken down into separate program modules. When compiling program modules that are part of a global system, you can

designate program variables, including strings, as "local" to a compiled program or global to all compiled programs in memory.

During the compiling process, a complete listing of compilation and program statistics, including a complete symbol table, are displayed on the terminal and optionally recorded on the printer. Included on the compiler disk is a unique utility program called Remake Compiler Disk. If you inadvertently make a destructive error while operating the compiler, this utility program will restore the disk to working condition. Thus, when you delete a disk file, you don't really erase it but merely remove its directory listing. In an analogous fashion, the Remake program restores the directory information.

Borrowing a BASIC program written for a CPS multifunction card that displayed the time of day, we used that as a model to do a loop-and-print test. After we reprogrammed it, the modified program printed a starting time, went through 500 loops of calculations and printed the time, and then printed the ending time. We then used the Einstein Compiler to compile the program. It took only a few minutes to compile the program from start to finish. We ran each program and recorded the running times of each. The original BASIC program took 9 minutes and 10 seconds to complete, and the compiled version took 2 minutes and 47 seconds — that's one-third the time. There is a trade-off, though: The original BASIC program occupies 10 sectors of disk space. The compiled version takes up 24 sectors — 240% more space than the BASIC version.

Operation of the Einstein Compiler is simple. After loading the BASIC program you wish to compile into memory, the compiler will scan your program for about ten seconds to detect any syntax or other program errors.

InfoWorld
R e p o r t   C a r d

Einstein Compiler

	Poor	Fair	Good	Excellent
Performance	☐	☐	■	☐
Documentation	☐	☐	■	☐
Ease of Use	☐	☐	☐	■
Error Handling	☐	☐	☐	■

Summary
The Einstein Compiler is a convenient programming accessory that translates Applesoft BASIC into machine language. Although it utilizes a lot of disk space, it has the potential to speed up your programming.

System Requirements
☐ *Apple II, II Plus, IIe, (III, in II emulation mode)*
☐ *DOS 3.3*
☐ *48K RAM*
☐ *One or two disk drives*
☐ *Printer (optional)*

Suggested list price: $129

*Alison Software Corporation
14937 Ventura Blvd.
Sherman Oaks, CA 91403
(818) 905-8000*

Then it asks you if you want to use standard compiler parameters. If you answer Y, the compiler operates, completely automatically, and in a matter of minutes you have a compiled program ready to run.

Here are some of the compiler parameters, which you can alter if you so desire. You can set the printer slot number, declare a different program starting address or change the run-time library address. You can also choose whether or not to compress code (the compilation runs faster if you don't compress code, but takes up less memory space if you do). You can display addresses of the compiled variables (handy if you are printing hard copy), or you can pause on errors.

When the compiler is running, you get a running account of what line number of the program you are on, where the program counter is and a percentage of completion indication.

The different error messages that may result when you use the Einstein Compiler (the same type of common errors, such as syntax and memory-conflict errors, that are not tolerated by Applesoft during program execution) are detailed in the documentation in the same manner as the compiler parameters: each on its own page. The headings on each page are Error message, Definition, Example and Action Required.

The manual is clear and concise. We particularly liked the method of describing the compiler parameters. Each parameter is listed on a separate page. Each listing uses the same format. You can easily understand what the parameter is and what the values are. The documentation further offers a precise description of the parameter along with an explanation of reasons for changing it.

The quality of the documentation is professional — thick, glossy pages and clear type of many sizes and varieties. The manual includes such necessary features as table of contents, index, charts, diagrams and program listings.

The original disk is warranted for 90 days, during which time free replacement is offered. After 90 days and within one year from date of purchase, a damaged disk will be replaced for a $15 charge.

It is a pleasure to see quality in packaging and quality in performance. You have to decide whether you think the trade-off of larger memory requirements for faster operation is worth the speed of subsequent program execution, but if you do the Einstein Compiler is an excellent choice.
—*Marty Petersen*

REVIEW

Apple PILOT and SuperPILOT

Devising computer-assisted instruction (CAI) courses can be easy with either of these well-written programs from Apple Computer, Inc. PILOT (an acronym for Program Inquiry, Learning or Teaching) and SuperPILOT are systems for creating instructional programs.

These programs are designed for educators. They are relatively free of computer jargon and emphasize maintaining student interest and comprehension. PILOT programs include such attention-grabbers as sound effects, color graphics, animation and special character sets.

For educators, PILOT features a special lesson-text editor, file and program backups, answer counts, and instructions for effective lesson development.

The two programs are closely related. We will detail the differences between the basic system (Apple PILOT) and the advanced one (SuperPILOT) after covering features common to both.

The first PILOT, developed in 1968, was revised into an eight-command version called Common PILOT in the early 70s. Apple PILOT contains these eight basic instructions, plus other commands that take advantage of the Apple's sound-generation and color-graphics abilities.

PILOT supplies four editors for creating lessons:

—Lesson Text Editor
—Graphics Editor
—Character Set Editor
—Sound Effects Editor

An author uses the lesson-text editor to create the PILOT lesson by entering commands, which the students re-execute.

The graphics editor can create and store fairly detailed images in up to six colors, with a resolution of 280 rows by 190 columns. You can use the paddle to move the cursor around, as with the Etch-A-Sketch pictures you created as a child. You can fill in any enclosed area with a specified color.

The character-set editor allows you to assign a predefined image to a key on the keyboard. For example, by pressing the R key, you might display a white chess rook; pressing the q displays a black queen.

You can combine images to create large or complex pictures. For example, if you had defined

T to be the top of a rocket
M to be the middle section
B to be the bottom of the rocket

then the commands:

t: T
t: M
t: B

would display the full image of a rocket.

The character-set editor contains a file of standard characters and a file of large letters that you can use to replace only a few characters. You may want to change certain vowels to their umlaut form if you are entering German text, yet keep all the other letters the same. Interestingly, PILOT also includes Japanese katakana characters.

The character-set editor can shift any row of dots one-half space to the right, which makes for better diagonal line displays. They provide more visually appealing letters with diagonals, such as A and Z, and triangular shapes.

Apple PILOT supplies sound effects: for example, "sweep" (the sound starts at a given pitch and sweeps down or up to the next pitch) and "warble" (the sound varies between two given pitches).

Access to a full range of commands for text, response, control, computation, graphics, sound, special character sets and easy file handling makes this program valuable to CAI educators. Response times were acceptable, except when some graphics were drawn on the screen. You can solve this problem by storing the screen image rather than the drawing commands.

A beginner might have a problem getting to know the set of single-letter commands and how to combine them. These codes can be cryptic at first. On the other hand, single-letter entry keeps typing to a minimum, which is a boon to experienced PILOT programmers.

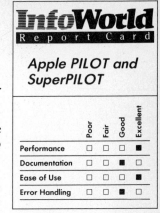

InfoWorld
R e p o r t C a r d

Apple PILOT and SuperPILOT

	Poor	Fair	Good	Excellent
Performance	☐	☐	☐	■
Documentation	☐	☐	■	☐
Ease of Use	☐	☐	☐	■
Error Handling	☐	☐	■	☐

Summary
These two related products are easy-to-use computer-aided-instruction (CAI) production systems. Designed for professional educators in any field, and based on the original PILOT (Program Inquiry, Learning or Teaching), they take advantage of the Apple II's sound effects and color graphics. SuperPILOT is an expanded version of Apple PILOT. Both cater to needs of authors who create a PILOT script and the needs of students learning from one. The documentation promotes a painless transition from novice to satisfied author. Overall, this is an excellent CAI authorship program.

System Requirements
☐ *Apple II, II Plus, IIe*
☐ *Language system or DOS 3.3*
☐ *64K (48K plus language card)*
☐ *one disk drive for lessons, two for authoring*
☐ *TV or monitor (high-resolution color recommended); paddles (optional)*

Suggested list price: $100 (PILOT); $200 (SuperPILOT and Co-Pilot); $50 (SuperPILOT Log); $35 (CoPILOT)

*Apple Computer
20525 Mariani Ave.
Cupertino, CA 95014
(408) 996-1010*

The program rates high marks for ease of use. For those of us with tin ears, the most challenging section is the sound-effects editor, where the entry of information about a note becomes arcane. On the other hand, the character-set editor is one of the easiest character generators we've encountered.

PILOT's sample program shows a typical student presentation, with text, questions, right/wrong answers, graphics, paddle input, color and sound. Beginners can review the code that produced the sample lesson. PILOT has no on-line tutorial, but the manual provides nice training sections that make using the system an easy process for beginners.

Error handling is excellent. The program recognizes only a limited set of commands, and errors divide into two types: those the "author" enters erroneously and those the user utilizes incorrectly. The original author has to plan, in advance, for students' incorrect responses.

PILOT provides a backup copy of the copy-protected author diskette. Users can back up any lesson diskette. The manual emphasizes the need for constant backups of lesson diskettes.

Documentation for Apple PILOT, like most Apple documentation, is extensive, well-written, illustrated and replete with warnings. The error messages are all in one section and are understandable. This document has a reference summary, a complete index and a useful quick-reference card.

Your dealer is your first support resource, but you may be better off getting assistance from another PILOT user or dealing with Apple directly.

SuperPILOT has extensions to the basic Apple PILOT. These include, among others, special record keeping for statistical analyses, more animation commands, high-resolution screen drivers and an external device control that allows the program to communicate with videodisks and videotapes.

Apple's enhancements to the academic PILOT exploit the capabilities of the Apple computer. The designers paid attention to what the producer of a CAI program needs: what it takes to design the module, debug it, test it, save it, and put it to practical use. The documentation is excellent, and a neophyte will soon be a satisfied user. SuperPILOT and Apple PILOT are excellent CAI-production systems.
—*Larry G. Leslie*

PERIPHERALS

Earlier, we said, "Software first, hardware second." Now it's time for reviews of peripherals — a variety of them. In this category, you'll find reviews of printers, boards, touch tablets, modems and other peripherals.

REVIEW

Daisywriter 2000

We have searched high and low for a good, reliable printer that would list programs, would print attractive manuscripts and would not break our bankbooks.

We were about to give up the image of the ideal printer when we saw it — the Daisywriter 2000. The Daisywriter 2000 uses a print mechanism similar to the one found in the Brother HR-1 — but that's where the resemblance ends. Without a doubt, this printer outperforms daisy-wheel printers twice its price.

The 2000 is packed with features. The Daisywriter was designed to be as universal a daisy-wheel printer as possible.

Daisywriter can imitate the protocols of almost every letter-quality printer now being marketed. It can change into a Diablo 630; Qume Sprint 9/11; NEC 3500, 5500 or 7700; or Centronics 737. You make these quick changes by merely flicking a few switches.

Not only does the Daisywriter understand computers that use different protocols but it also understands different "human" protocols. Twenty-five different languages range from American English to Finnish and Swedish. With a swap of the daisy-wheel, adjustment of a few switches and the use of appropriate software, you can print words in German, for example, umlauts and all.

If this weren't enough, the Daisywriter is also "hardware multilingual." It comes ready to connect to a Centronics 8-bit parallel, IEEE-488, RS-232C or 20-milliamp current-loop interface. All the circuitry is built into the Daisywriter. All you need is the correct cable, which is available from your dealer.

REVIEWS

InfoWorld
Report Card

Daisywriter 2000

	Poor	Fair	Good	Excellent
Setup	☐	☐	■	☐
Ease of Use	☐	☐	■	☐
Performance	☐	☐	☐	■
Documentation	☐	☐	■	☐
Serviceability	☐	☐	■	☐

Summary
The Daisywriter 2000 offers one of the best values in letter-quality printers of any on the market today. If you buy one, you will get a high powered, high speed, professional, buffered, daisy-wheel printer.

Features of unit tested
☐ *Z80-based, letter-quality printer*
☐ *Built-in, 48K print buffer*
☐ *Built-in self-diagnostic test*
☐ *Software controls for self-justification, proportional spacing, line spacing, characters per inch and other word-processing functions*

Suggested list price: $1495; $50 (cable); $150 (tractor-feed option); $595 (cut sheet feeder)

Computers International, Inc.
3540 Wilshire Blvd.
Los Angeles, CA 90010
(213) 386-3111

Then there's the built-in print buffer — 48K RAM. (The 2000 has 64K built in; the Z80 uses 16K.) A print buffer is memory that can store data quickly while the printer continues to print at its normal speed. The process, commonly known as *spooling*, allows your computer to transmit your document to the Daisywriter at maximum speed. Then you can use your computer for some other task while Daisywriter prints away.

You can reprint the contents in the buffer up to 255 times either by giving a command from the printer's front panel or by using a software command during spooling. In fact, the Daisywriter has more than 100 built-in software commands that change its operation.

Specifications such as form length, characters per inch and lines per inch are all front-panel/software-selectable. Form length can range from 1 to 255 lines per page. You have a choice of 10, 12 or 15 characters per inch and can select line spacing of 1, 1.5 or 2 lines per line feed — either 6 or 8 lines per inch.

You can also activate automatic margin justification and true-proportional spacing by software control and automatically center a line and reset the margins. The True Proportional Spacing feature uses an internal character-spacing table that is optimized to Linotype standards. You're not stuck with just the spacing table provided, however. Issue a software command, and you can generate your own spacing table.

The Daisywriter provides automatic baud-rate selection, of course. When you activate this feature, you need only transmit a carriage return to the printer and wait two seconds; then, the printer's baud rate is set to the data-transmission speed of your computer. You can manually switch-select the baud rate from the printer's front panel as well (50-19,200 baud).

The Daisywriter has subscript and superscript commands and even has commands for underlining, printing in either shadow or boldface.

Finally, using the software control, you can set the printer into a Graphics mode to permit absolute or vector plotting for drawing graphs or charts. The Graphics mode of the Daisywriter is compatible with Diablo Hyplot.

The printer mechanism Computers International uses in the Daisywriter is manufactured by Brother Industries. This mechanism, in production for two years, has some outstanding design features. A linear step motor drives the print carriage along a stainless-steel track, which eliminates the belts and pulleys that often cause malfunctions in other printers.

The mechanism uses a print-wheel cassette, available from Brother's typewriter dealers, that protects the print wheel from damage. By using a standard IBM ribbon cartridge, Daisywriter's designers have enhanced its reliability and simplified the search for replacements. By using four internal CPUs, they have reduced the number of moving parts and the number of electronic components. Usually, the fewer parts a printer has, the more reliable it is.

The printer is built for reliability. Although its case is made of plastic, it is of the same rugged quality you find in the NEC 3500 or Diablo 630. The use of a CPU-controlled linear step motor for driving the print carriage eliminates the chance of failure from stretching or breaking cables.

If you lift the Daisywriter 2000's lid, you discover an important undocumented feature that makes office or home use more pleasant — soundproofing. Pads of rubber are attached to the sides and top for sound absorption. In addition, flexible brushes close the slots through which the levers for bail and paper release are placed, thus allowing you to move the levers while keeping printer sounds from escaping. The acoustic cover, standard with the 2000, has a foam gasket around the bottom surface, further evidence of concern for reducing printer noise.

If you purchase a tractor feed, it is also supplied with an acoustic cover, another soundproofing feature. In our opinion, the operation of the Daisywriter is noticeably quieter than that of a NEC 3515. It is *far* quieter than a Smith-Corona TP-1.

The entire standard ASCII character set is decoded. Therefore, you can use it to list programs. Depending on your print wheel, however, some of the characters might differ. The Daisywriter 2000 comes with an American English Prestige print wheel. With this print wheel, the "caret" is printed as a superscript 2 and the backslash (hex 5C) is printed as a plus/minus sign. These minor differences should not cause you problems when you list programs.

We tested each of the software control features with the exception of the Hyplot-compatible graphics. Each worked as advertised. The biggest problem was getting a word processor to make use of all the features.

The advertisements say Daisywriter prints up to 40 characters per second (cps). A printer's actual speed is critically dependent on what you are printing. Generally, the more white space, the faster the printing speed. The Daisywriter's promotional brochure gives the fairest description of printing speed seen from a printer manufacturer. It includes a graph of various printing speeds you can expect for different applications. According to this graph, you can expect 20 cps for letters, 33 cps for statements, 40 cps for preprinted forms and 50 cps for columnar data.

With the Daisywriter's large print buffer, however, printing speed is far less important than with most printers because the buffer allows the computer to transmit its text at maximum speed. In any event, the print speed is comparable to that of an NEC 3500.

We ordered our Daisywriter from a mail-order distributor by phone. When we placed the order, the salesperson asked what type of interface we had. We gave the make and model and asked why she needed to know. She told us that each interface cable ($50 extra, we might add) was specific for the type of interface.

When the printer arrived, we set the function switch according to the manual, attached it to the serial port, fired up the word processor and tried to start printing. Nothing happened.

Now, we had seen this word processor hang before with another printer, and we had discovered the problem to be a missing "request to send" signal on pin 4 of the RS-232C connector. Could the Daisywriter's interface cable have the same problem?

Sure enough — the interface cable only supplied signals to eight of the 25 pins of the connector; and pin 4 was not one of the eight. A telephone inquiry to the distributor solved the mystery — but not the problem. Our interface was an earlier version than the one the dealer's cable guide listed. So for the cost of $50, we were granted the opportunity to rebuild a cable.

This is the weakest link in the

installation of the Daisywriter. It is absolutely critical that you give your dealer the model and revision number or serial number of the interface you'll be using. Computers International has supplied signals to all the pins specified in the EIQ RS-232C standard.

Now for the good stuff. Other than the confusion mentioned above, we found the Daisywriter easy to install and operate. The power switch is located on the left side near the front rather than on the back. All of the switch-selectable features are set by 24 switches located under a small door on the front panel. You don't have to "dig" around inside as you must with some other printers. The "on" position of each switch is marked clearly, so setup is easy and unambiguous.

The plastic print guard is marked with several red lines that show where characters will be printed. Line up these with the top of a sheet of paper, and the paper is properly positioned. If you are using cut sheets, you do not have to manually retract the paper bail for the first five lines, because the printer automatically retracts the bail until the sheet has advanced enough. Then the bail clamps down on the paper to prevent paper jams.

The enclosed print-wheel cassette is so easy to insert and remove that there is little likelihood you will break it by changing it.

A clearly marked type-position guide shows the location for 10-, 12- and 15-pitch typing. This guide really helps when you are resetting margins after you've changed pitch. The printer sounds different "bells" for paper out, print jam and cover open, and the printer even has three built-in self-diagnostic tests to help you identify printer problems.

A users' guide and information manual come with the Daisywriter 2000. Both are clearly written and provide complete information about the operation and features of the Daisywriter.

The information manual is more than 45 pages long. It clearly describes how to set the 24 switches to set up the functions you want. It explains each of the features along with the software commands to activate them. Both the ASCII and hexadecimal codes for each command are included, along with a special "Daisy-key" code, useful for some computer systems.

The manual also includes a clearly written table of contents and an extensive index. The appendices contain an American English ASCII table, a hex-to-decimal conversion table and a summary of the commands available.

The Daisywriter 2000 is designed to minimize failure; however, the printer is also designed to facilitate repair. The unit consists of five components: platen, carrier, controller, power supply and a single universal interface-emulator-buffer board. Loosen two screws and you can remove the cover for easy access to parts.

The manufacturer, Computers International, signed a national distribution agreement with ComputerLand, so servicing of the printer should be available at your local ComputerLand store.

The suggested retail price of the Daisywriter 2000 is $1495. It outperforms printers that list for much more. The interface cable is priced at $50 and the tractor-feed option is available for $125. You can get the printer from mail-order dealers for less than $1100.
—*Russ Adams*

REVIEW

Epson RX-80

The Epson RX-80 dot-matrix printer has the same physical characteristics as the Epson MX-80, which cost twice as much and had fewer features. It is lightweight (approximately 12 pounds) and compact (measuring about 15×12×4 inches). It uses a black-cloth cartridge ribbon that the manufacturer claims will last for 3 million characters or about 600 pages of total-density text. We have found this figure to be somewhat liberal if you consistently desire "new ribbon" blackness of print. If you examine the ribbon closely after using it for a while, you notice that the printer uses only one-half of the ribbon. If Epson incorporated a Mobius loop (half-twist) in the ribbon's continuous-loop design, as is the case with the ribbons that the Apple dot-matrix printer uses, the ribbon's life could be increased.

The RX-80 interface is compatible with that of the Epson MX series — it is a Centronics standard 8-bit parallel port. The bidirectional print speed is 100 characters per second (cps), an improvement compared with 80 cps for the MX-80. The RX-80 also has a Half Speed print-speed mode. Why would anyone want to run a printer at half speed? Half speed is desirable because the printer runs more quietly. In many instances, particularly when you are running an overnight batch job, speed is not important.

Whereas the original MX-80 came with only a 96-character ASCII set, the RX-80 sports a host of characters including 96 roman characters, 96 italic characters, 32 roman international characters (providing the special symbols and accent marks for a list of ten countries), 32 italic international

characters and 32 graphic characters.

You can also program the printer to produce Pica, Emphasized Pica (darker than normal but less dense than double-strike print) and Pica Expanded print. The print can range in widths from 40 to 80 columns. You can compress the print to 137 columns or compress-expand the print to give you a 68-column format. The printer can also produce an Elite print style, which is programmable with the same column-width options as the Pica.

Super/Sub Script is a character mode that prints small characters. It does not roll the paper up or down to produce these characters. You can program the printer's line spacing in increments of 1/216 inch in the Text and Graphics modes.

The manner in which the printer pulls through the form-feed paper is best described by comparing the RX-80 to the Apple dot-matrix printer. On the Apple printer, the form-feed mechanism comes first, followed by the platen. This arrangement means you can line up the printhead ready to print on line 1 of the first sheet of paper. With the Epson printer, the platen comes before the form-feed mechanism, and you can only set the printer to start printing on line 1 of the second sheet of paper. Thus, every time you finish a project and issue a Form Feed command, the Epson loses an extra sheet of paper.

The RX-80 has two DIP switches that you must set. The first enables or disables the international character sets; the paper-out sensor; 11-inch or 12-inch form length (in the U.S., 11-inch is standard, but in Europe, 12-inch is the norm); enables or disables the alarm beeper; and sets the graphics character set and print width.

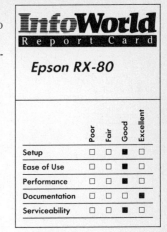

InfoWorld
Report Card

Epson RX-80

	Poor	Fair	Good	Excellent
Setup	☐	☐	■	☐
Ease of Use	☐	☐	■	☐
Performance	☐	☐	■	☐
Documentation	☐	☐	☐	■
Serviceability	☐	☐	■	☐

Summary
With its RX-80 dot-matrix printer, Epson offers an improved product with many more features and at a lower price than that of its original MX series of printers. This printer comes with excellent documentation and gives you good value for the money.

Features of unit tested
☐ *8K ROM*
☐ *256 bytes RAM*

Suggested list price: $399

Epson America, Inc.
3415 Kashiwa Street
Torrance, CA 90505
(213) 534-0360

The second DIP switch toggles the skip-over Perforation feature, automatic line feed, printer select (active or inactive) on power up and slashed or normal zero. As with the MX-80, these switches are buried inside the machine, and you must remove the top cover to get at them. At least the RX-80 offers one improvement in this cumbersome process, however. With the MX-80, you have to turn the printer upside down to get at four deeply recessed Phillips screws. With the RX-80, you only have two screws to worry about, and they are accessible from the top of the printer.

We were impressed by the outstanding improvement in the documentation that accompanies the RX-80 over the manual that came with the original MX-80. Epson has done its homework and has obviously heeded the comments of many Epson printer users over the years. The RX-80 manual succeeds in being all things to all people. It contains a detachable heavy-duty quick-reference guide with all the control codes, character sets and DIP switch settings you'd ever want to know.

If you already know about printers, this document may be all you need. If you are a novice, however, you're in for a treat. The manual contains lessons that not only teach you how to use the printer and how to write Microsoft BASIC programs to utilize or demonstrate its many features, but also teach you, in depth, about graphics. You can learn how to design graphics — from generating an array, calculating pin patterns and setting the graphics width to printing the figure you have designed. We're sure Epson could sell this manual separately in a bookstore, and it would make a bundle by itself — but it comes free with the RX-80 printer.

Epson's service and warranty policy is a one-year arrangement whereby you can return any defective merchandise to your dealer or to the service department. If you call (213) 534-0360, you can obtain explicit instructions. You are responsible for paying shipping both ways, however.

With the great number of low-cost, high-quality printers on the market now, consumers are the ones who benefit from the competition. Not all manufacturers, though, have Epson's tremendous marketing strength and can survive the ordeal of improving their product while at the same time reducing their prices. Epson printers always have been and will continue to be great value for the money. You can be sure that whatever software is developed that requires a printer as a peripheral, Epson printers are sure to be included on the list.

—*Marty Petersen*

REVIEW

Pro Writer

C. Itoh's Pro Writer is a 7×9 or 8×8 dot-matrix impact printer with either a parallel or serial interface. The printer uses both tractor- and friction-feed paper and has a platen width of 10 inches. When the printer detects no paper in the feed mechanism, it stops printing, and a warning LED on the front panel lights up. The printer uses cartridge-pack ribbons that are easy to change.

The Pro Writer has software toggles that enable you to control logic and incremental printing, line-feed amount (both forward and reverse), double strike, underlining, bidirectional printing, and tab and margin settings. You can adjust the printhead pressure for multiple carbon-copy forms.

You can choose six different character fonts through easily accessible switches. Among the character fonts you can use are Greek letters and block-graphic characters for making charts and other graphs.

The printer's software toggles also allow you to select between 10, 12 and 17 pitch and proportional printing. You can also produce double-wide characters in each pitch, but not double-height characters.

Pro Writer performs well — the characters it produces are crisp and easy to read in both the 10- and 12-pitch versions. The 17-pitch or condensed print appears solid, rather than like that formed by a dot matrix. Because each character has the same width, however, the wider letters (m and w, for example) are slightly blurred. The printer's proportional font is impressive.

By embedding escape-code sequences, you can print superscript numerals from the Greek character font. Special characters such as ½ and ¼ are also available. You can produce subscripts of numerals, but you must enter additional commands to adjust the printer's line feeds.

The Pro Writer's ability to produce block graphics is a nice addition, and it reproduces high-resolution graphics well. Although charts require considerable time to perfect, once you have established a basic format, you can save it for future use. Because you can change character fonts and width, you can create special forms and letterheads

and, again, save them for future use on a disk.

The Pro Writer's paper feed is easy to use and works smoothly. The printer provides automatic line advance and form advance; you can also make manual paper adjustments for narrow forms and paper advancement. The printer has a combination paper-tear bar and sound muffler that is held in place with a shim. The shim snaps into place so securely that the plastic can break if it's forced open — one of the two shims did shear off during our tests.

As with typewriters, rollers hold the paper firmly against the platen. If you use the tear bar to remove your output, the muffler sometimes restricts the remaining paper and causes a paper jam.

C. Itoh claims that the printer has a print speed of 120 characters per second (cps) at 10 pitch. We found that in "worst-case" situations, the printer slowed to 90 cps, but, when printing normal text, it obtained the 120 cps speed. When the Pro Writer prints graphics, it is much slower because the printhead has to move to each dot location on the line. When you use the printer's Bidirectional Print mode, alternating lines are printed slightly off center, resulting in ragged vertical lines. If you use the Unidirectional Printing option, however, this problem does not occur.

The documentation that C. Itoh originally supplied with Pro Writer was improperly entitled a "Users Manual." Although it contained all the necessary technical specifications, it was not indexed and the table of contents was dismal. Because of these weaknesses, Leading Edge Products now includes a

InfoWorld
R e p o r t   C a r d

Pro Writer

	Poor	Fair	Good	Excellent
Setup	☐	☐	☐	■
Ease of Use	☐	☐	☐	■
Performance	☐	☐	☐	■
Documentation	☐	■	☐	☐
Serviceability	☐	☐	■	☐

Summary
C. Itoh's Pro Writer dot-matrix impact printer performs well and produces crisp, easy to read characters. It has either a parallel or serial interface and can produce six different character fonts of differing widths, as well as block graphics. Compared with other printers on the market, it offers good value for its low price.

Features of unit tested
- ☐ *7×9 dot matrix*
- ☐ *Parallel interface*
- ☐ *Tractor and friction feed*
- ☐ *Platen width: 9½ inches*

Suggested list price: $495; $745 with serial-interface option

Leading Edge Products, Inc.
225 Turnpike Street
Canton, MA 02021
(800) 343-6833

new manual with the printer, which is a vast improvement over C. Itoh's documentation.

The new manual is divided into three functional sections — the first is a well-written tutorial for beginning users; the second, written in the same style, explains the use of the special software commands that give advanced users complete control of the print; and the last section is a series of appendices. Unfortunately, this new manual is not indexed.

The Pro Writer delivers good crisp printing at a reasonable speed. Its special features are easy to use via software commands. The low price of the Pro Writer, compared to the prices of its sisters marketed by NEC and Apple, makes it a good buy.

—*Tom Neudecker*

REVIEW

Number Nine Graphics System

When the Apple II was first released, one of the most astonishing things about it was its graphics. The Apple high-resolution screen, with its six colors — eight if you counted both blacks and whites — inspired the imaginations of both designers and consumers, contributing in no small way to the machine's early success.

Its high-resolution screen wasn't, however, truly high resolution; jaggies and stairsteps abounded. In addition, the colors interfered with one another in ways that were sometimes difficult to predict.

Time marched on, as did technology; but Apple graphics remained, sadly, much the same — until the development of the Number Nine Graphics System (NNGS), from Number Nine Computer Corporation.

The NNGS board plugs into one of your Apple's peripheral slots and connects to an RGB (red-green-blue) monitor. Depending on which of several hardware options you select, it allows you to have either 16 simultaneous colors with a resolution of 512×512; four colors with a resolution of 724×724; or two colors with a resolution of 1024×1024. (Compare those numbers to standard American television, with its 525 scan lines, and to feature film, which has a resolution of about 1000 lines.)

Furthermore, you aren't restricted to only 16 colors — 16 colors simultaneously, yes, thanks to limitations in the way an Apple accesses memory — but if you add an RGB Analog Module to the NNGS card, you can choose your 16 colors from a palette of 4096. If that still isn't enough, you can link multiple cards to create a palette of up to 16 million colors.

The system we tested consisted of an option 1 NNGS board with 128K of on-board RAM and an attached RGB Analog Module, giving two separate video outputs with which to experiment. We ran the RGB TTL (transistor-transistor logic) signals from the board to a Taxan Vision 420 monitor, using an IBM PC-style cable. (The right cable is critical. This output creates 16 colors with signals that individually control red, blue, green and intensity; some monitor cables don't allow for the intensity signal, thus cutting your available colors in half.)

The RGB Analog Module has three individual analog video outputs and requires a monitor with separate control inputs for the red, green and blue color guns. We used an Amdek Color IV. With everything connected — and four new cables added to the Apple — we were then ready to insert the Interpreter disk that comes with the NNGS, boot the system and go.

Booting the NNGS Interpreter disk gives you a white cross-hair target and a strip of the system's standard 16 colors — black, white, red, light red, green, light green, brown, yellow, blue, light blue, magenta, light magenta, cyan, light cyan, light gray and dark gray.

The brain of the NNGS is its NEC 7220 VLSI (very-large-scale-integration) Graphics Display Controller chip. This controller is a mixed blessing. For some things, such as drawing circles, it is a whiz. For others, such as filling those circles with solid colors or operating fast enough for arcade-style action, it is not.

Moving images come when you type BRUN DEMO.SLOT7 and watch as the NEC chip is put through its paces. Although the chip is slow, it is fast enough to create some animation effects and to create enough movement to bring shapes and structures to life.

During the demo, flashing, pulsing concentric circles and colored rectangles grow and move in overlays (until they look as if they'd been painted by Vaserely) and gradually expanding spheres appear. The display is all in glorious 16-color splendor and completely free of the jaggies and color anomalies usually associated with graphics on an Apple.

Discovering how to use the board to create your own displays is not a simple matter for novices. Number Nine's primary goal is to market the NNGS board to various application-software

companies, who can then design their packages around it. The board's documentation is no help, because it assumes that you have prior knowledge of Apple assembly language. If you are not a computer expert, you'll need to make repeated trips back to your Apple manuals.

A CALL -151 command puts you into the Apple's monitor, and from there you can easily control the color palette of the RGB Analog Module. You type in a string of numbers at the appropriate memory location for each of the color guns and "blend" colors out of them. You can adjust the intensity of a gun to 16 levels, from 0 to F in hexadecimal. Setting all three color guns to F, or greatest intensity, puts white in that slot in the RGB Analog Module's lookup table, and setting them all to 0 leaves you with black.

The possibilities for different shadings are amazing — fluorescent pinks, corals, dark forest greens and mauves. If you get tired of typing in numbers, you can write your own subroutines to step through possible color choices.

You can also pursue the graphics commands available in the primitives of the NEC chip itself. For example, you can build colored bar charts to test your color creations. More complicated programming is possible, if you have the expertise. Alternately — and here's the wonderful part — you can buy software to use with the system.

Although the NNGS system successfully maximizes the NEC 7220's strengths and minimizes its flaws, the software available from Number Nine is not oriented toward computer users, as opposed to computer experts. This isn't

InfoWorld
R e p o r t   C a r d

Number Nine Graphics System

	Poor	Fair	Good	Excellent
Setup	☐	☐	☐	■
Ease of Use	☐	☐	■	☐
Performance	☐	☐	☐	■
Documentation	☐	■	☐	☐
Serviceability	☐	☐	■	☐

Summary
The Number Nine Graphics System board allows you to produce high-resolution graphics displays in a large range of colors, the number of colors depending on the system option you buy. The system is easy to use once you discover how to use it — its documentation is designed for computer experts and assumes prior knowledge of assembly language. For novices, software to accompany the board is available from other companies.

Features of unit tested
☐ *NEC 7220 VLSI Graphics Display Controller*
☐ *128K RAM*
☐ *RGB Analog Module*

Suggested list price: option 1, $895; option 2, $1095, $1195 or $1295 depending on configuration; RGB Analog Module, $295

*Number Nine Computer Corporation
691 Concord Avenue
Cambridge, MA 02138
(617) 492-0999*

a strong complaint — the company achieves what it set out to do, which is to fill a hardware gap.

Other companies, though, are busy providing the software. Visual Data Enterprises of Los Angeles, California, has the most extensive set, including painting, typefont design and television camera-scanning programs, not to mention a set of machine-language subroutines, called VPRIMITIVES, that allow you to access the NNGS board's power directly from Applesoft BASIC. Scot Steketee of Philadelphia has developed a Pascal driver with turtle graphics for the NNGS. 21st Century Typesetting in Northern California is working on a preview system, using the NNGS board at its highest resolution, that will allow designers to see what a page of typesetting *looks* like before they set the real type. TW Systems, maker of CAD-APPLE, is preparing a version of its product that takes advantage of the NNGS's resolution and color capacity.

In short, the Number Nine Graphics System board is creating a new kind of Apple graphics, and the quality of the product is superior. Users not interested in digging into Apple assembly language may have to wait for software packages for their specific needs. But for others, the NNGS is a wonderful tool and toy.

—*Freff*

REVIEW

Premium Softcard IIe

Because of its early acceptance by the embryonic personal-computer industry, CP/M has become the de facto standard operating system in the 8-bit world. Although the Apple II has a huge software base, it cannot handle CP/M application programs because CP/M requires a Z80 microprocessor, and the Apple uses a 6502. Several manufacturers, however, manufacture Z80 coprocessor boards that plug into the Apple II. Microsoft's Z80 hardware/software system for the Apple IIe is the Premium Softcard IIe.

The Premium Softcard IIe combines a Z80 coprocessor, an 80-column card, and 64K of extra memory, all on one board. Although you can add the card to your system at any time, the best time to consider purchasing one is before you buy your Apple. As part of its bundle plan for starter systems, Apple includes an 80-column card worth $125 or, optionally, an 80-column card with an extra 64K of RAM worth $295. Each of these cards partly duplicates the functions of the Premium Softcard IIe and resides in the same slot (0). If you can talk your dealer into packaging your IIe system with a Premium Softcard II instead of an 80-column card, you may be able to apply the $125 value of the 80-column card toward the $495 price of the Softcard.

The Z80 coprocessor section of the Premium Softcard IIe circuit board contains circuitry for communicating with the Apple IIe I/O bus, allowing you to run CP/M programs as well as Apple DOS programs.

The 64K bytes of RAM on the board can be used by either the Z80 or 6502 microprocessors. The memory section permits large application programs (up to 59K bytes) to run under CP/M. You might be confused by these memory-size statistics, thinking that with the Softcard plugged in you have 128K bytes in your Apple. In fact, the Z80 microprocessor runs at a higher clock speed than the 6502 and therefore requires higher-speed RAM to function properly. While the 6502 can use the Softcard's RAM and therefore access up to 128K, the Z80 can use only its own 64K of RAM. The 80-column Videx video display section automatically configures itself for 80 columns when CP/M is engaged. When Apple DOS or Apple Pascal programs are running, the circuit board can display either 80 or 40 columns under software control.

In addition to the hardware, the Premium Softcard IIe package contains software and documentation. The software includes the CP/M operating system referred to as CP/M-80, the Microsoft BASIC interpreter and a small collection of utility programs. You can copy Apple DOS files to your CP/M disk with the APDOS program, create startup disks with the AUTORUN program, configure CP/M for specific I/O devices with the CONFIGIO program, and format and copy disks with the COPY program. The package also includes a utility program that allows you to copy files in a single-drive system without causing BDOS errors each time you exchange disks.

The documentation consists of four manuals; three are included in the package. The fourth is mailed when you send in the registration card. The Installation and Operation Manual describes how to install the hardware and how to load and use the CP/M operating system. The manual itself is of high quality: hardcover, small three-ring binder, thick pages, table of contents and complete index. The only lacking feature is a chapter number at the top of each page, so you never know where you are when you leaf through the manual.

The Microsoft BASIC Interpreter reference manual provides an alphabetical reference for all of the language's commands, statements and functions. There is a slight difference between this manual and the one that accompanies the regular Microsoft BASIC for the Apple II (the nonpremium version). On the nonpremium version (a card without 80-column capability or extra memory), BASIC is called MBASIC. Another version, called GBASIC takes advantage of the graphic capabilities of the Apple. The premium version of the card, has no MBASIC, and the whole interpreter, including graphic capability, is called GBASIC.

The third manual in the package is the *Osborne CP/M User Guide* by Thom Hogan, an excellent book that guides you step by step through the different functions of CP/M.

The fourth manual, Premium Softcard IIe System Programmer's Manual, is the one sent to you when you return your registration card. It's meant for users who want to connect nonstandard I/O devices or to use software requiring patches to CP/M. It's unfortunate this book is not included in the package, since you won't be able to use the Softcard IIe with nonstandard devices until it arrives.

Other than the annoyance of waiting for the Programmer's Manual to arrive, setup of the system is easy. The card plugs into slot 0, and if you don't know where that is, a photograph in the manual shows you. In fact, the manual devotes five pages to plugging in the Softcard board.

A table describes what accessory boards you can plug in and what slots they should occupy. Besides the Apple

InfoWorld
R e p o r t   C a r d

Premium SoftCard IIe

	Poor	Fair	Good	Excellent
Setup	☐	☐	■	☐
Ease of Use	☐	☐	☐	■
Performance	☐	☐	☐	■
Documentation	☐	☐	■	☐
Serviceability	☐	☐	■	☐

Summary
Premium Softcard IIe expands the Apple IIe system to include a Z80 coprocessor, an 80-column card and 64K additional RAM. It allows use of Microsoft BASIC and is justifiably popular.

Features of unit tested
☐ *Z80 coprocessor*
☐ *80-column card*
☐ *64K additional RAM*

Suggested list price: $495

Microsoft Corporation
10700 Northup Way
Bellevue, WA 98004
(206) 828-8080

disk II controller, the Softcard will support the Apple Communications interface, high speed serial interface, Silentype printer interface, parallel printer card, firmware card and super-serial interface. It also supports the California Computer Systems (CCS) 7710A serial interface. After describing proper hardware installation, the manual shows you how to back up your system disk and boot CP/M and BASIC.

After these programs are running, you can run the CONFIGIO program, written in BASIC, with which you can modify the system further. With CONFIGIO you can reconfigure the screen functions (specify control sequences needed by external terminals), redefine keyboard characters, and load user I/O driver software. For instance, if your printer is standard, you can use this utility to load the printer driver software that operates the printer.

Perhaps the biggest advantage to having a Softcard Z80 coprocessor board, as opposed to owning one made by another company, is that only the Microsoft card will operate Microsoft BASIC. Nevertheless, Microsoft BASIC has become a de facto industry standard, and many people believe it is the best BASIC interpreter available.

In conclusion, the Microsoft Premium Softcard is a good system among several good systems on the market. You need to decide what's most important to you in a Z80 microprocessor. If you want the convenience of a Z80 microprocessor sharing a slot with 80-column capability, if you want to use Microsoft BASIC and if you want to buy the most popular card on the market, then the Microsoft Premium Softcard IIe is for you.

—*Marty Petersen*

REVIEW

CP/M Card

Digital Research's CP/M operating system is the oldest of the commonly used operating sytsems for 8-bit microcomptuers. A vast library of software is designed to run under its various versions. Its ability to use this software, which includes such well-known and widely used programs as WordStar, dBASE II and SuperCalc, makes it desirable to have a computer that can run CP/M.

This requirement presents a problem for Apple owners, because the 8-bit versions of CP/M and the software written for it can only run on computers with CPUs that are compatible with Intel's 8080 CPU chip. (These include the Intel 8080A and 8085 as well as the Zilog Z80.) The Apple II use the MOS Technology 6502 CPU, which is not a member of the 8080 family, but the Apple II's expansion slots allow it to use peripheral cards with other CPUs. Several manufacturers (Microsoft, Advanced Logic Systems, Personal Computer Products and Applied Engineering) have introduced expansion cards for the Apple II with CPUs that can run CP/M software.

The CP/M Card, marketed jointly by Digital Research and Advanced Logic Systems, is one of two expansion cards manufactured by Advanced Logic Systems (the other is the older, less expensive Z-Card). The CP/M Card is the only currently available Apple II expansion card that runs CP/M Plus, the latest version (3.01B) of the CP/M operating system.

The CP/M Card uses the Z80B processor, an improved version of the Zilog Z80 that can run at an internal clock speed of 6 MHz. If you're not technically inclined, it may help to know that Microsoft's SoftCard and ALS's own Z-Card, which both use the earlier, less expensive Z80A chip, run at 2 MHz — one-third as fast. The Z80B processor runs so fast that it cannot communicate at full speed with the Apple's main memory, so the CP/M Card includes 64K of its own fast RAM. The board also includes a real-time clock.

The CP/M Card is sold as a complete system that includes the CP/M Plus operating-system software, hardware, utilities, a CBASIC compiler and Digital Research's GSX-80 graphics-support software.

One of the most important reasons to purchase the CP/M card instead of its less-expensive competitors is the opportunity to use CP/M Plus. A number of features distinguish CP/M Plus from the 2.2 and earlier versions of CP/M.

CP/M Plus is a major update of the earlier versions of CP/M. The version supplied with the CP/M card supports banked memory, which allows your applications programs to use more memory, and permits programs to run more quickly by using disk buffering. The command-line editing facilities are improved considerably from earlier versions, and you can enter more than one command per line.

The Submit batch-processing capability of CP/M has been greatly enhanced. Applications running under Submit may obtain data from the batch-command file, and conditional execution of Submit commands is possible.

All of the built-in commands of CP/M 2.2 are available in CP/M Plus, and enhanced versions of several of

these commands are available as transient commands.

For example, the built-in DIR command has a transient extension that lets you request a directory listing with certain optional characteristics. Typing DIR by itself invokes the standard built-in DIR command, and CP/M Plus lists the directory of your default disk.

When you append the option SIZE to your DIR command, CP/M Plus attempts to load additional code from a disk file DIR.COM and, if it can, will include file sizes in its directory listing. If CP/M Plus cannot find the file DIR.COM, it informs you that the required disk file is unavailable.

Other major new features include an on-line Help facility that lets you ask for information about any CP/M command and optional time- and date-stamping of files. To use the latter feature, your system must, like the CP/M Card, have a built-in real-time clock.

CP/M Plus' disk-handling facilities are a distinct improvement over earlier versions. You no longer have to log in disks; CP/M Plus automatically logs in new disks when they're mounted. The annoying errors that so often occurred when users failed to log in disks when they used earlier versions of CP/M are now a thing of the past.

You can even use a special transient command, SETDEF, to specify the order in which CP/M Plus searches your disks for transient commands. You can configure your system so that CP/M Plus searches for transient commands on disks other than the default disk, even if you don't specify the disk on which the command can be located. CP/M is also more lenient in how it lets you enter built-in commands. It allows you, for example, to abbreviate the ERASE command as ERA.

On a hardware level, the most attractive feature of the CP/M Card, at

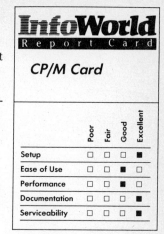

InfoWorld
Report Card

CP/M Card

	Poor	Fair	Good	Excellent
Setup	□	□	□	■
Ease of Use	□	□	■	□
Performance	□	□	■	□
Documentation	□	□	□	■
Serviceability	□	□	□	■

Summary
The CP/M card from Advanced Logic Systems is slightly more expensive than its competitors, but it is the only Apple II expansion card that lets you use CP/M Plus. The CP/M card is sold as a complete system that includes CP/M Plus software, hardware, utilities, a CBASIC compiler and graphics software. CP/M Plus is a valuable system that improves the performance of SuperCalc and WordStar.

Features of unit tested
- □ *2803 CPU*
- □ *64K RAM*
- □ *CP/M Plus*

Suggested list price: $399

*Advanced Logic Systems
1195 E. Arques Avenue
Sunnyvale, CA 94086
(408) 730-0307*

least in theory, is the enhanced processing speed permitted by its use of the fast 6 MHz clock speed with its Z80B processor. Although this CPU can operate three times as fast as the 2 MHz processors on the SoftCard and Z-Card, it must slow down to 2 MHz whenever it communicates with the Apple's on-board memory. All input and output from the processor (whether it's to your disk, screen or printer) must go through the Apple's on-board memory, so few programs actually run three times as fast on the CP/M Card as they do on competing cards.

If you're thinking of buying the CP/M Card to increase the speed at which your Apple-CP/M system processes a specific application, try it with that application software first. The ratio of processing time with the CP/M Card to processing time on other cards depends heavily on the amount of input and output activity required by a given application.

There's another reason to check the performance of the software you'll use on the CP/M Card before you buy it: not all CP/M software that is available in an Apple-disk format will run on the CP/M Card.

For this review, we ran many CP/M programs on the CP/M Card. Many worked, among them WordStar (Version 3.01), dBASE II, Condor and DataStar. Even MBASIC runs on the CP/M Card, but you can't use the System command to return to CP/M.

The speed of the CP/M Card significantly improves WordStar's performance. When run at 2 MHz, WordStar often drops characters when it wraps words on the screen. This doesn't happen when WordStar runs on the CP/M Card. Similarly, WordStar's printer spooling works effectively when it runs on the CP/M Card.

Several programs did not run on the CP/M Card. They included the other more popular and widely used packages; the most notable was the communications program Z-Term, the Professional. ALS has assured us, though, that a new version that will run on the CP/M Card will be released shortly.

The software included with the CP/M Plus system contains some excellent programming tools. Digital Research's fine relocating macro assembler, RMAC, replaces the assembler ASM, which was included with earlier versions of CP/M. The original CP/M debugger, DDT, is replaced by the improved SID (symbolic interactive debugger). The package also includes a compiler for CBASIC, which offers some valuable features for business programming. As a compiled language, however, it is more difficult to use for program development than interpreted basics like MBASIC, and the code it generates does not execute more quickly.

The extra 64K of RAM on the CP/M Card is used exclusively by the CP/M Card's processor and is unavailable when you use the Apple in its standard 6502 mode. It's disappointing to find that Digital Research and Advanced Logic Systems do not include software that allows programs running in 6502 mode to take advantage of this extra RAM, perhaps as a pseudo disk.

Installing the CP/M Plus system is easy. You need only put the CP/M Card in slot 4 or 7 of your Apple, and it's ready to run. (You can use several others slots, too.) If you have an 80-column card, the operating system automatically takes advantage of it. Several utilities let you easily copy and create system disks and install WordStar on the system.

Not all of the new operating system features on CP/M Plus are easy to use. To use the date- and time-stamping, for example, you must run a utility to reorganize the disk directory and turn date- and time-stamping on. This is a nuisance.

The limited capacity of the Apple's floppy disks creates another problem. To take advantage of most of the new operating-system features that CP/M Plus offers, you must have disks containing the program code for those features on line. The amount of disk space these programs require severely limits the disk space available for other applications.

The CP/M Card is reliable, but on some occasions programs hung up when an uncooled Apple overheated. The CP/M Card is 8 inches long, about 3 inches longer than the Z-Card. We expected that its greater length might interfere more with an Apple's ability to dissipate its internal heat, while its greater complexity would cause it to generate more heat. As a reasonable precaution when you use the CP/M Card, turn on a fan to cool your Apple.

Advanced Logic Systems offers a one-year warranty on its hardware. Its product support is quick and responsive.

The documentation for the CP/M Plus package is impressive. It's contained in an attractive binder that comes in a library slipcase. The four manuals inside the binder are well written and nicely printed.

On the whole, the CP/M Plus system is a good and valuable product. If you want to gain experience on the latest version of CP/M and if you own an Apple, it's an excellent buy; its $399 price is only $45 more than the price of the CP/M Plus software alone. It also includes a variety of excellent development tools for CP/M programmers.

If your objective is to obtain better performance from the CP/M programs you run on your Apple, CP/M Plus may not be your best choice. Many, but not all, CP/M programs perform significantly better when they run on the CP/M Card than they do on the slower, older Apple CP/M Cards. Check how much the more expensive card improves the performance of your applications before you buy it. For your particular applications, a slower, less expensive card may be adequate.
—*Joel Pitt*

REVIEW

Appli-Card

If you own an Apple II, II Plus or IIe, a Franklin Ace 1000 or other Apple-compatible machine, and if you are considering using CP/M, then you should consider Appli-Card from Personal Computer Products, Inc. (PCPI).

Appli-Card is hardware and software that converts your Apple into a Z80 computer that lets you run the thousands of CP/M application programs now available.

The hardware consists of a board that can plug into any slot of the Apple. Because of restrictions on some slots for dedicated purposes, however, such as slot 0 for ROM/RAM, slot 1 for a printer, slot 3 for an 80-column card and slot 6 for a disk drive, the

InfoWorld
Report Card

Appli-Card

	Poor	Fair	Good	Excellent
Setup	☐	☐	■	☐
Ease of Use	☐	☐	☐	■
Performance	☐	☐	☐	■
Documentation	☐	☐	■	☐
Serviceability	☐	☐	■	☐

Summary
If you want to run CP/M application programs on your Apple or Apple-compatible computer, you should consider Appli-Card. It comprises hardware and software that converts an Apple into a Z80 computer. The hardware consists of a board that plugs into any slot; the software consists of two disks, CP/M 2.2 and a utility disk. It is easy to install.

Features of unit tested
☐ *Z80A or Z80B*
☐ *CP/M 2.2*
☐ *PCPI Utilities version 2.0*
☐ *64K RAM*
☐ *2K PROM expandable to 8K*
☐ *Expansion interface connector available for extra memory or serial or parallel interface*
☐ *70-column uppercase and lowercase without extra hardware*
☐ *Menu-driven setup*

Suggested list price: $375 (6 MHz); $595 (6 MHz with 128K RAM extender)

*Personal Computer Products, Inc.
11590 West Bernardo Court
San Diego, CA 92127
(619) 485-8411*

manufacturer suggests that you use slots 4, 5 or 7.

Depending on the price you pay for the system, the board contains a Z80B (6 MHz) microprocessor that gives you either 64K of on-board RAM or 128K additional with the RAM extender option — a significant advantage since Appli-Card does not have to share Apple's memory.

The Appli-Card uses the Apple as an input/output processor only, borrowing the use of its keyboard, video display, disk drives and various ports. It leaves the Apple's 6502 and memory alone. That way, both the Apple and Appli-Card can run independently. When not in use (but still plugged in), the Appli-Card has no effect on the normal operation of the Apple.

Also on board is 2K of PROM (programmable read-only memory), expandable to 8K, and an expansion interface that can accommodate extra memory or a serial or parallel port. The expansion-interface port supports either a 64K or 128K RAM extender option. This extra memory, plus Appli-Disk software, turns the Appli-Card into a RAM, or pseudo, disk for both Apple DOS and CP/M. The expansion port can also provide networking and communications capabilities.

Included in the hardware is a shift-modification device, a short cable with a DIP plug connector on one end and a clamp-type connector on the other. The shift-modification device allows you to use the Shift key instead of the Escape key to shift from uppercase to lowercase during word-processing operations. The use of the modification, however, disables the caret key (above the 6), which you use in math operations as the exponent key.

The software consists of two disks, CP/M version 2.2 and a utility disk. Besides the CP/M utility programs, there are four PCPI utility programs for disk initialization and disk maintenance and for system-configuration functions for the Appli-Card.

The PCPI utilities include COPYFRMT, a program that allows you to initialize a CP/M disk, copy an entire disk or copy just the CP/M system tracks from one disk to another. ADOSXFER transfers the files between Apple DOS and CP/M format disks.

The product has several interesting software features — notably SoftVideo. The Apple computer is not an 80-column machine although expensive peripherals do exist to make it so. SoftVideo gives you some options to allow you to simulate the benefits of an 80-column display without having to buy expensive hardware.

CONFIGSV is one of the included utility programs that customizes the Appli-Card's SoftVideo features and configures CP/M input and output to match your Apple hardware.

Install is the utility program that modifies Appli-Card CP/M to include new or altered drivers, such as the SoftVideo Driver that the CONFIGSV program creates.

One of the special functions available with SoftVideo is horizontal scrolling of the Apple's 40-column screen. This function gives you a "window" of text that can be up to 255 columns wide. The scrolling can be automatic (following the cursor) or under manual control.

There is also a HIRES (high resolution) mode that fixes the screen at 70 columns by 24 lines. You don't usually need all of the 80 columns in an 80-column display, since margins account for 10 to 15 characters. You can run a program such as WordStar, which requires only 65 columns, without an 80-column card. Appli-Card does, however, support the popular 80-column cards now on the market.

A key-click added to the Appli-Card system gives you audible feedback while you are typing. By pressing Control-C and operating the arrow keys, you can raise or lower the key-click volume from silent (0) to loud (10). The default setting is 2.

Other SoftVideo controls include Toggle shift-lock, Toggle uppercase as inverse video, Toggle shift modification and Toggle lowercase modification. These controls allow you to control Appli-Card primarily in systems where you may have existing hardware that duplicates some of Appli-Card's functions.

Z80 cards that must rely on Apple's memory have less room for users' programs than does Appli-Card, which has its own on-board memory. Translated to actual numbers, the other systems have 49K RAM available for users' applications, compared to Appli-Card's 56K.

Appli-Card's major competitor is Microsoft's Softcard, so it is not surprising that Microsoft designed its de facto standard BASIC to run only on its CP/M card. If you want to run Microsoft BASIC on Appli-Card, buy the 8-inch disk version and send it along with a blank 5¼-inch disk to PCPI, which will download the disk for you for a $10 charge. Also check with your local Apple dealer, which may provide the service.

One of the concerns you may have about any plug-in peripheral to your computer is the power consumption. The Apple power supply delivers, at most, 5 amps, and heat can be a problem if all of the slots are stuffed and the cover is on. The Apple has no built-in fan, but several manufacturers make outboard units. The current drain for Appli-Card is ½ amp.

InfoWorld's general abuse testing includes running the hardware (leaving it on in an operational state whether in use or not) for ten consecutive hours for three straight days. The board performed flawlessly during this test.

The Appli-Card user's manual starts out with a good preface to help you feel at ease. Next comes the table of contents, which lists the major and minor chapter and paragraph headings. The chapters are in correct logical order: Installation, System Checkout and Operation, the PCPI CP/M Operating System, Appli-Card SoftVideo and Appli-Card Utility Programs. The appendices contain a troubleshooting guide and application notes. The manual has no index, however. Included with the documentation is the ever-popular *CP/M Primer* by Murtha and Waite.

PCPI warrants its product to be free from defects in workmanship for 90 days from the date of purchase. After 90 days and up to two years, the company will make any necessary repairs for $50. After two years, the buyer pays for all parts and labor. If service is required, you should mail Appli-Card, freight prepaid, to the manufacturer.

The installation and setup are adequately detailed in the users' manual. Three pages of instructions make sure you plug in the board correctly, so that even novices will have no trouble. After you have plugged in the board, you insert the CP/M master disk into drive A. When you turn on the Apple, the CP/M automatically loads.

The program then instructs you (with words and pictures on each screen, as you progress) to format blank disks and make backup copies. This is a two-step process; you format the blank disk first, and then you make the backup copy.

The last part of the setup procedure is to decide what aspects of the SoftVideo system you want to adapt to your system. With the utility disk in drive A, you can type CONFIGSV and select from the menu whether you want a 40- to 225-column screen, a 70-column screen or an 80-column screen.

Choosing one of the options then leads you through a series of menus, where you decide on such things as shift lock, click volume, auto-scroll and screen-width.

When you have chosen all of the options you want, you type INSTALL and configure all of the above criteria to your Apple system.

If you want to bring the CP/M operating system to your Apple or Apple-compatible computer, then you should consider Appli-Card. There is considerable competition in the market with Softcard, the Z-Card and a card from ALS, but Appli-Card can hold its own against any of them.

—*Marty Petersen*

REVIEW

212 Apple-Cat II

Novation produces a complete modem package, the Novation 232 Apple-Cat II, that fits in the accessory slots of an Apple II and provides high-speed data communications, along with many other features.

The 232 Apple-Cat II uses the Bell 232 signaling scheme specified for 1200-baud service on information utilities such as The Source and CompuServe, and data carriers such as Telenet. It is a complete communications package that includes a two-board modem set, support software routines in ROM and a terminal software program and utilities on a floppy disk.

The two 232 Apple-Cat II modem boards are each designed to fit into an Apple II accessory slot. You can buy the basic Apple-Cat II board separately and use it alone to provide 300-baud service with the Bell 103 signaling scheme and 1200-baud service using Bell 202 signaling.

Bell 202 signaling is a high-speed transmission method that allows transmission only one way at a time. Some corporate communications systems, amateur-radio operators and Apple-Cat owners use the 202 signaling scheme, but the information utilities and transmission services don't use this method of transmission.

The second 212 Apple-Cat board provides 1200-baud two-way service using the Bell 212 standard. This board plugs into the Apple II next to the basic Apple-Cat board. You can purchase it separately and add it to an existing Apple-Cat board, or you can purchase the entire 212 Apple-Cat II package.

The two boards connect through an 11-pin ribbon cable. If all the slots in your Apple II are full, you can mount the 212 upgrade card on top of the Apple power supply. The Novation package includes a plastic mounting board that you tape to the top of the power supply and a power cord that you insert in series with the Apple II's main power cable to provide power for the board.

If you use two accessory slots to hold the modem cards, installation of the 212 Apple-Cat II takes less than five minutes. If you mount the 212 board on the power supply, installation takes a few minutes longer. You do have to check the position of two DIP switches, but you don't have to make any other adjustments.

Other standard features of the Apple-Cat II include an RS-232C port for you to connect other peripheral devices and a telephone handset adapter. You can use the telephone handset for normal voice communications. The computer and the interface software control the handset's connection.

The Novation Apple-Cat II boards are well made. The bus connections are gold-plated; and the majority of the integrated circuits have sockets. There are no jumpers on the back of the board, and all solder connections are shiny and neat.

Novation uses several custom-designed integrated circuits, and the total parts count of the modem set is considerably less than that of earlier devices. The boards run without any hot spots or other electrical problems.

The Apple-Cat II has several special hardware options. These include an interface module, a BSR controller, a cassette-recorder interface, a Baudot communications ability and a tone-decoding receiver.

The interface module mounts on the back of the Apple II and provides a neat cluster of connectors for the RS-232C port, phone line, handset, recorder and other devices.

The BSR controller allows the Apple II to control lights and appliances remotely, through special receivers connected to the electrical power line.

You can use the cassette-recorder jack to record voice messages received before or after data transmissions.

The Baudot option lets you connect the Apple-Cat to the Baudot communications networks, which persons with hearing disabilities use. The modem can operate at the 45.4-baud speed that these systems use.

The operational features of the 212 Apple-Cat II are as diverse as the hardware configurations. The modem can automatically dial and redial the phone line and answer a ringing line. It can use either tone or pulse dialing. It contains special circuitry to detect both a dial tone and a busy signal; it does not simply use a set waiting period and then assume the presence of a dial tone.

The tone-decoding option for the Apple-Cat II allows the modem to determine the value of tones transmitted to it from a push-button phone. It reports the received value to the computer and normally displays it on the screen. An application programmer can use these values to cause the computer to perform various functions by remote control. This option has numerous possibilities for security and remote-control applications.

We ran the 212 Apple-Cat II through its paces with several different information utilities and communications systems. Our system did not contain all of the options so we could not evaluate such things as Baudot operation, tone decoding or BSR remote control.

The modem combination worked well with all of the communications systems we tested. The 212 Apple-Cat II has several self-test features that you can use for software and system tests.

Novation bundles its Com-Ware terminal package with the hardware (although several available software packages can use the Apple-Cat II). This software is a menu-driven terminal-emulation package. It provides a conversational "chat" capability from the keyboard and can also capture

InfoWorld Report Card

212 Apple-Cat II

	Poor	Fair	Good	Excellent
Setup	☐	☐	■	☐
Ease of Use	☐	☐	■	☐
Performance	☐	☐	■	☐
Documentation	☐	☐	■	☐
Serviceability	☐	☐	■	☐

Summary
The 212 Apple-Cat II is a complete modem package that you can install in the accessory slots of the Apple II. It is a completely integrated hardware and software system that comprises a two-board modem set, software routines in ROM and Novation's Com-Ware terminal-emulation software and utilities on a floppy disk. It is easy to install; has good documentation and the performance and flexibility you need for either business or home use.

Features of unit tested
☐ *Two-board modem set*
☐ *Bell 212, 202 and 103 signaling schemes*
☐ *300 and 1200 baud*
☐ *RS-232C port*
☐ *Telephone handset adapter, interface module, BSR controller, cassette-recorder interface, Baudot communications option, tone decoding receiver*
☐ *Support software routines in ROM*
☐ *Terminal software program and utilities*

Suggested list price: $695

Novation, Inc.
20409 Prairie Street
Chatsworth, CA 91311
(818) 996-5060

received data on a disk file and transmit disk files through the modem port. It can transfer the files between two Com-Ware-equipped systems using a special error detection and retransmission scheme that ensures accurate file transmissions.

The Com-Ware terminal program has all of the needed terminal abilities, but few frills. The software provides a simple interface between the modem and disk system. You can easily transmit and capture files with the software menu commands. The software disk is formatted in DOS 3.3.

The file-transmission routine gives you the option of inserting a variable delay between transmitted lines of characters. This option can make it a little easier for you to send files to certain mainframe computers and information utilities. It does not provide any method for inserting the delay between characters, which can also help in some file-transfer situations.

In the dialing process, the program only allows you to dial manually from the keyboard. It does not provide you with an electronic telephone directory or the ability to store and retrieve other commonly used data strings.

The Com-Ware disk comes with utilities that convert between Applesoft or Integer BASIC programs and binary files and can transfer the binary file between Com-Ware-equipped machines.

If you want more frills and fancy features, programs such as those in the Professional series from Southwestern Data Systems and Softerm from Softronics all support the 212 Apple-Cat II.

Installation of the Novation Com-Ware software is a simple operation driven by questions the programs asks. The program asks what option you have installed and what type of printer you are using with the system. The well-defined menu simplifies the operation of the Com-Ware program. The program makes good use of status display lines on the bottom of the screen that tell you whether the system is connected and what communications parameters are in use.

The manual is a 35-page pamphlet-size publication, printed on good stock in two colors. It has a good table of contents and a glossary, but no index. A separate manual for the 212 upgrade board and a detailed, 35-page programmer's guide, which describes the RAM memory locations and how Apple-Cat II accesses them, augment the principal manual. The programming manual includes several routines and demonstration programs.

Printed update sheets containing information on program changes further supplement the manuals. Novation obviously intends to document every aspect of the 212 Apple-Cat II.

Despite the presence of a schematic in the manual, users, and even dealers, can probably do little servicing of the 212 Apple-Cat themselves. Novation fully guarantees this system for one year from the date of purchase and provides all follow-up service.

The 212 Apple-Cat II has the performance you need for business use and enough flexibility to warm the heart of any hacker. It is a completely integrated hardware and software system. If you can use some of the special functions, it can serve you as a multifunction device, for the price of a modem alone.

—*Frank J. Derfler, Jr.*

REVIEW

Accelerator II

Is your Apple II (or II Plus) too slow? If your answer is yes, you may be interested in the Accelerator II, a peripheral board for the Apple II made by Titan Technologies. This 7½-inch board contains a fast 65C02 microprocessor that can execute all the operations that the Apple's standard 6502 processor normally executes. Thus, any programs that run on the Apple's own central processing unit (CPU) can also run on the Accelerator's CPU. Because the Accelerator's processor operates at a clock speed of 3.6 MHz compared to the 1.2-MHz speed of the standard Apple CPU, any processing that the Acccelerator performs on the Apple occurs three times as fast as it normally would.

The Accelerator board comes with 64K of its own RAM, and its 65C02 processor can only operate at full speed when it's communicating with this memory. When data has to be transferred between the memory on the Accelerator board and the Apple's motherboard, the Accelerator has to slow down. All input and output to the Apple must take place through its motherboard, and so the Accelerator does not generally operate at full speed all the time. For most applications, however, it can carry out enough of its processing at full speed to result in considerably faster program execution.

In the course of using the Accelerator, we tested it with a wide variety of Apple II software. We found, not surprisingly, that it was particularly useful in speeding up the execution of programs that involved considerable amounts of computation — the most noticeable improvement in Apple performance occurs when you use the Accelerator to run statistical programs.

We also used the Accelerator with the Aztec C compiler and several Applesoft compilers and found that it increased their processing speed considerably, too.

The Accelerator provides an important shot in the arm for the Apple Pascal system. The basic code for the Apple Pascal system is written for an ideal machine called a p-machine, and a special interpretive program, called a p-machine emulator, carries the load of executing Apple Pascal programs. Running this underlying interpreter program requires processing time, and thus Apple Pascal programs execute more slowly than programs that compile directly to 6502 machine language. The Accelerator's enhanced speed helps to cancel out this effect.

For certain types of programs the speedup that the Accelerator offers is undesirable — many arcade-type games run so fast that they're virtually unplayable. Other games, though, are improved with the Accelerator's added speed — for example, Wizardry.

On the whole, the Accelerator makes the Apple II a much more exciting and productive computer. As you might expect, the board's effect is least noticeable when you use it with programs that require considerable amounts of input and output, especially when that input and output processing is to disk.

Data-base programs, in particular, gain the least from the use of the Accelerator. Word-processing and spreadsheet programs generally run noticeably faster, but, because rewriting output to the Apple screen is a major function of both of these types of programs, neither improves as noticeably as do statistical programs.

InfoWorld
R e p o r t   C a r d

Accelerator II

	Poor	Fair	Good	Excellent
Setup	☐	☐	☐	■
Ease of Use	☐	☐	☐	■
Performance	☐	☐	☐	■
Documentation	☐	☐	■	☐
Serviceability	☐	☐	☐	■

Summary
The Accelerator II is a peripheral board for the Apple II and II Plus that can execute virtually all Apple software at up to three times the Apple's normal speed. The board is useful if you want to run programs requiring considerable amounts of computation, but not so useful for programs that require large amounts of input and output. At its present price, it is a major investment, but it's worth the money if you have a large Apple software library.

Features of unit tested
☐ 65C02 CPU
☐ 3.6 MHz clock
☐ 64K RAM

Suggested list price: $599

Titan Technologies
310 West Ann Street
Ann Arbor, MI 48104
(313) 662-8542

For hardware devices, reliability is a major performance consideration, and we found the Accelerator worked consistently and well over long time periods.

Installing and using the Accelerator is relatively straightforward. You can use it in any Apple II slot, although using it in slot 0 involves some problems. You must place any Apple II peripheral boards whose performance is time-dependent, such as disk controllers and modems, in slots 4-7. Thus if you have a modem board, for example, you may have to relocate it when you install the Accelerator. Finally, you have to set some switches to tell the Accelerator about the other peripheral boards that your Apple contains — this process is clearly explained in the manual that accompanies the board.

Not all Apple software can use the Accelerator directly. Any programs that run in the Apple's 48K of RAM can load directly onto the Accelerator board, but code that is designed to run in the upper 16K of the Apple's memory address range requires special software to load it into the Accelerator board's memory.

Titan Technologies supplies software that can transfer the Apple's Applesoft and Integer BASIC interpreters to the Accelerator's memory, and it also supplies a program that allows the Apple Pascal system's P-code interpreter to load into the Accelerator's memory, too. Thus virtually any Apple software — with the possible exception of modem software, which often requires your modem to be located in a specific slot — should run the Accelerator board.

The 23-page operations manual supplied with the Accelerator gives clear and concise instructions on how to install and use the Accelerator. It offers two explanations: one for users who are impatient to install the board and use it with their software, and another for users who'd like to understand some of the theory behind the board's operation.

The manual also includes several lists of software that the manufacturer has tested and used with the Accelerator and specifies the preboot software that you should use with those packages that require it.

Titan warranties the Accelerator to be free of defects in material and workmanship for a one-year period from date of purchase. It will repair or replace defective boards at no cost within that period.

Several other kinds of hardware products exist — including alternate processor and arithmetic coprocessor boards — that can speed up Apple performance, but, unlike the Accelerator, none of them can run virtually all Apple software. At its present price, the Accelerator is a major investment, but if you've got a large library of Apple software, it could well be worth the money.
—*Joel Pitt*

REVIEW

KoalaPad

First there were arrow keys that allowed you to move the cursor around the screen. Joysticks and game paddles then appeared to make it even easier to push that cursor around. Then came the "mouse," a little creature, that, by rolling around on a flat surface, also let you position the cursor. Now, there's the KoalaPad, a device that lets you move the cursor by moving your finger on a pad.

Two items are reviewed here: a touch tablet called KoalaPad (the hardware) and KoalaPainter, an application program (software) for the KoalaPad.

The KoalaPad is a position-sensing device that converts finger or stylus pressure and movement into electronic signals for controlling computers. It is particularly useful for drawing pictures and pointing to images on your TV screen. To get started, you simply plug the KoalaPad into your computer's game port.

The touch tablet comes in versions — each with a different plug — for the Apple II family, the IBM Personal Computer, the Commodore 64 and VIC 20, and the Atari 400 and 800.

We reviewed the KoalaPad and KoalaPainter for the Apple II.

The KoalaPad is six inches wide, eight inches deep and one inch high. The active drawing surface area is 4¼ inches square. The resolution is limited by the host computer's analog-to-digital hardware. The Apple computer offers a grid of 256×256 points.

Two buttons sit on the top of the tablet. The left button activates the switch 0 function, and the right button activates the paddle 1 function. Moving your finger or a stylus from left to right across the pad's surface simulates turning the paddle 1 control, and moving your finger or a stylus from top to bottom across the pad's surface simulates turning the paddle 0 control.

The KoalaPainter software is an example of state-of-the-art application programming. Designed to show off the features of the KoalaPad, it is a drawing program that — except when saving and loading picture files from disk, at which time you must key in a name — uses only the KoalaPad for total control of the program. A color TV or monitor definitely enhances the enjoyment of this program.

The menu gives you three choices — a Command option, a Brush Set option and a Color Set option. In the Command Set mode, you can choose from many styles or methods of drawing, including freehand, points, lines, circles, boxes and frames. You can fill in areas, erase sections and even magnify the screen to look at your artwork in close detail.

Using the Brush Set option, you can choose any type of brush you want, from fat to skinny. The Color option lets you pick from among 18 different colors.

A program that works in conjunction with the KoalaPainter is Coloring Series II — Crystal Flowers and Snowflakes. This program is a series of picture files (14 on each side of a double-sided disk) you can load into the computer and color. The language Logo was used to create these files; if you have Logo, you can create your own shapes using turtle graphics, for coloring via KoalaPainter.

Another application program for young children is KoalaGrams. Also included in the package is a program called Spider Eater. This program has an overlay that fastens to the surface of the KoalaPad. The overlay contains a picture of a piano keyboard. The idea of the program is to teach you how to recognize or correlate musical sounds or tones with their keyboard and musical staff representations. Spiders move from the bottom of the screen to their web at the top; however, they must cross a musical staff in the middle of the screen. They rest momentarily (for a duration you select) on a note position on the staff. If you press the correct piano key on your KoalaPad, the Spider Eater eats the spiders, thus preventing them from getting to their web.

If you want to write your own programs to work with KoalaPad, you

InfoWorld
Report Card

KoalaPad

	Poor	Fair	Good	Excellent
Setup	☐	☐	☐	■
Ease of Use	☐	☐	☐	■
Performance	☐	☐	☐	■
Documentation	☐	☐	■	☐
Serviceability	☐	☐	■	☐

InfoWorld
Report Card

KoalaPainter

	Poor	Fair	Good	Excellent
Performance	☐	☐	☐	■
Documentation	☐	☐	■	☐
Ease of Use	☐	☐	☐	■
Error Handling	☐	☐	☐	■

Summary

The KoalaPad is a touch tablet that helps you draw or create images on your screen. Using your finger or a stylus on the tablet's surface, you "sketch" images. The KoalaPainter software makes it possible for you to use the device with your Apple, as well as with an IBM PC or a Commodore 64.

Features of unit tested
☐ *256×256-point grid*
☐ *4½-inch-square drawing area*
☐ *KoalaPainter software*

Suggested list price: $124.95

*Koala Technologies Corporation
3100 Patrick Henry Drive
Santa Clara, CA 95050
(408) 986-8866*

can — with the help of the Instant Programmer's Guide. This program is a series of BASIC-language applications on a disk. The Instant Programmer's Guide shows you how to modify the applications to suit your own purposes.

The KoalaPad does its job of letting you use finger or stylus, on a flat surface, as a paddle-operation simulation. You'll find, however, that the tablet's touch sensitivity to the bottom, or pad, of your finger is not very pronounced. You'll have to press hard to get a response. The tablet's surface is not very slippery and offers resistance to movement if you press hard. Another drawback is that it will accept input from only one pressure point at a time. If two points are touched, the Koalapad will use the averaged point in between them. The drawing surface itself is too small for many graphics applications.

The best way to use the tablet is to curl your finger and use the tip of your fingernail on the tablet's surface. In this fashion, you only need a light touch, and your finger glides effortlessly across the surface.

The performance of the KoalaPainter software is outstanding. You can create pictures just for fun, or you can create pie charts, graphs or drawings for business purposes and save them on disk.

You probably won't ever have to read the manual that comes with the product; that's how easy KoalaPad is to use. You boot the software, and the screen displays a menu of choices. The menu appears as an assortment of boxes instead of the usual list of words. Inside each box is a picture illustrating the function you can perform. The boxes are similar to the symbols on the palette of the LisaDraw screen on Apple's Lisa.

As soon as you put your finger on the touch pad, a blinking cursor appears on the menu screen at a place relative to your finger's place on the pad. To make a menu choice, you simply move your finger to the appropriate box (such as Draw Freehand or Draw Circles) and push the button on the top of the KoalaPad.

The computer makes a little beep to acknowledge the selection, and a little white triangle appears and remains in the upper right-hand corner of the box you selected, as a visual reminder of your current choices.

When you leave the menu to go to the drawing screen, you first put your finger on the tablet so you can see where you are. Then, when you move your finger to where you want to be, you press one of the buttons on the tablet and hold it down while you draw your line (or whatever function you have selected).

You never use the keyboard, except when you want to save a picture or load a previously saved one.

The only errors that can occur are DOS errors that come up if you are loading or saving a file and don't have the currect disk in the drive. If you do insert the wrong disk, the program will not crash.

The manuals for both the KoalaPad and KoalaPainter are brief but entirely professional and adequate for the job. There are plenty of photographs that show you exactly what you are supposed to see and step-by-step instructions that describe in detail what you are supposed to do. The manuals lack indexes, however, and the back of the software manual contains a meager attempt at a glossary, but that is all. The hardware works so effortlessly and the software so easily, though, that you hardly need manuals.

If you have a malfunction in the package, Koala Technologies will honor a 90-day warranty. You pay a one-way freight charge, and the firm makes the repairs free of charge. After the warranty expires, you pay a flat $25 fee for service and shipping.

The KoalaPad and KoalaPainter set new standards in computer technology. You would be missing a lot if you did not try them out. We highly recommend them, both for sheer fun and excellent value they offer.

—*Marty Petersen*

REVIEW

PowerPad

Like people, computers need input. For many people, the computer's keyboard, its most common input device, serves only as a barrier that prevents nontypists from making productive use of a microcomputer. This situation is especially true for young children. In an attempt to remove this barrier, Chalk Board offers you the PowerPad, a large, sturdy input device that opens the microcomputer world to people who can point more easily than they can type.

Chalk Board also offers several software packages that rely on the PowerPad. These packages can turn your PowerPad into a graphics tablet, a piano keyboard, a jigsaw puzzle or different game boards. For this review, we used Micro Illustrator, the PowerPad Programming Kit and Leo's Links. The Programming Kit is for experienced programmers who are interested in creating their own software for the PowerPad.

The PowerPad's touch-sensitive surface covers a 12½-inch square. This surface is enclosed in a rugged plastic case with dimensions of 19×17×1½ inches. The case has a convenient carrying handle.

By touching the active surface, you can supply an x,y supply location that any custom-designed program can use. Both x,y axes on the PowerPad can contain 120 different positions, meaning that you can supply 120×120, or 14,400, different values to your computer using this device.

You can think of the PowerPad as a grid of on/off switches covered by a smooth surface. Since the active surface is indented by about ½ inch, you can place an overlay on this surface. Programmers can design such overlays so that anyone using a PowerPad program will know what each region on the pad's surface represents.

To use the Apple PowerPad, you must purchase the Apple Software Starter Kit. This starter kit supplies the connecting cable for your computer, a disk called the Micro Illustrator, and the required pad overlay.

The PowerPad's connector cable plugs into the game input/output port inside the computer, and the other end of the cable plugs into the pad. This cable is the same type that you will find on your telephone. It is easy to connect, but be careful not to pull too hard on the PowerPad or you will disconnect it.

With the Micro Illustrator, the PowerPad becomes an inexpensive graphics tablet with many of the features and capabilities that you would expect from a tablet costing much more.

By using your finger, or the stylus provided, you can create, store or modify high-resolution graphic pictures. You start the Micro Illustrator disk's menu from which you select your color, brush size and drawing mode. You have 18 different solid colors and shades to choose from, and eight different brush sizes. Using these colors and brushes,

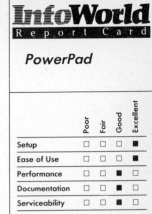

InfoWorld
R e p o r t   C a r d

PowerPad

	Poor	Fair	Good	Excellent
Setup	☐	☐	☐	■
Ease of Use	☐	☐	☐	■
Performance	☐	☐	■	☐
Documentation	☐	☐	■	☐
Serviceability	☐	☐	■	☐

Summary
With PowerPad, Chalk Board has created an inexpensive graphics tablet with a drawing surface area and capabilities similiar to more expensive versions. The PowerPad's sturdy appearance in conjunction with its low list price seems too good to be true. Remember, though, that you must purchase on Apple Starter Kit to use the pad.

Features of unit tested
☐ *12½-inch-square surface*
☐ *120 positions on each axis*
☐ *Micro Illustrator program*

Suggested list price: Power Pad, $99.95; Micro Illustrator, $49.95; Leo's Links, $39.95; PowerPad Programming kit, $24.95

*Chalk Board, Inc.
3772 Pleasantdale Road
Atlanta, GA 30340
(404) 496-0101*

you can draw freehand or select one of the 14 modes.

The other modes allow you to make circles, rectangles, points or lines. You can fill in enclosed areas with a color, make four-part mirror images of any pattern you draw or magnify a section up to seven times its original size. Magnification lets you work on fine detail. Finally, a drawing option, called Scale, allows the entire pad to represent only one quarter of the screen area.

The PowerPad's resolution is 120×120 dots. This number means that it has fewer possible input values than the Apple high-resolution screen has the ability to produce. As a result, the finest lines that the Micro Illustrator draws are more than one dot wide and seem a bit thick. If you want more detail, you must use the pad's Magnify option.

As with other tablets we have used, freehand drawings look like the work of a five-year-old child. The Apple II's so-called High Resolution mode is not all that high, but the PowerPad does not allow you to push the High Resolution mode easily to its limit.

The packaging of the pad and the software is colorful, attractive and large. We are not sure why Chalk Board has placed one disk, one 5½×8½-inch manual and a 12×12-inch overlay in a large 14-inch-square box.

The PowerPad is a durable piece of hardware. Although Chalk Board suggests that parents teach their children to treat all hardware with respect, this product looks as though it can withstand a great deal of abuse. The plastic surface can be scratched, though, if you use sharp objects, instead of using the stylus or your finger. The same extremes of temperature and humidity that could damage your computer can also affect the pad.

The PowerPad Programming Kit

contains a 46-page guide to programming the PowerPad, a blank overlay, two felt-tip pens and no diskette. You can add the lines of code listed in this book to any program you design that uses the PowerPad. Chalk Board also provides two sample programs to get you started. You must type any of the listed programs onto your own data disk.

Out of the list of application programs that are advertised with the PowerPad, we evaluated Leo's Links. This program allows you to design and play on your own computer golf courses and emphasizes the mathematical concepts of angles and degrees.

The manuals included with each of these products are well written and easy to understand. They feature about 40 pages of high-quality print, useful illustrations and good organization.

Other software packages for the PowerPad stress the creative aspect of the learning process and cover such topics as visual arts, music, math, science, language arts and social studies. At this writing, about 14 products are available, but Chalk Board plans to offer a total of 20 packages by the end of 1984. Some of the more intriguing titles include Leonardo's Logo, Micro Maestro, GeoPuzzles, Boolean Blueprints, Bach to Jazz, Gideon's Idioms and The Emperor's Clothes.

Like many other quality pieces of hardware, the PowerPad's performance depends on the quality and design of the software you use with it. We suggest you ask your dealer to let you look at several packages in action before you buy.

Your PowerPad, connector cable, disk and overlay are covered under a 90-day warranty if you return your registration card. Within 30 days, Chalk

Board will replace any part of the product at no charge. For the next 60 days, the company requires you to pay a $5 handling charge. When you use Micro Illustrator, Chalk Board advises you to make a backup disk.

After 90 days, Chalk Board will replace the PowerPad with a new one at a cost of $50 and will replace damaged overlays for $6. Although the pad looks as if it can be taken apart for servicing, ChalkBoard's policy indicates that the manufacturer intends to replace defective units rather than repair them.

The PowerPad saves inexperienced users from having to hunt for keys and lets them point to clearly labeled areas on a flat surface. Judging from the Micro Illustrator and Leo's Links, we think PowerPad's software is easier to use than similar products that rely on keyboard input. The pad can also reduce the wear and tear your keyboard may get from children, and it can relieve the frustration that the Apple IIe's Auto-Repeat feature can cause.

Chalk Board is offering a quality piece of hardware at an irresistible price in the hope that you will keep coming back for more software. If the software is good, this marketing approach may work. In any case, the PowerPad is a good product and an input device that is much easier to use than a keyboard.
—*Doug and Denise Green*

REVIEW

Smartmodem

The Smartmodem is a handsome modem packaged in a 1½×5½×10-inch "stackable" case. It is compatible with any system having an RS-232C serial port. The unit uses a standard Bell 103 transfer system at any baud rate from 0 to 300 baud. (A Smartmodem that has transfer rates of up to 1200 baud is also available.) Full- or half-duplex operation is possible, as well as Originate or Answer modes. The unit performs auto-answer and auto-dial functions, should you need them. The unit is FCC-registered, meaning it can be directly connected with any modular-jack telephone system.

A closer look at the Smartmodem reveals a few features that you might not notice or expect in a low-cost modem. Inside, for instance, is a Z8 microprocessor with 2K of ROM. Underneath, is a built-in speaker.

On the back panel, you find a volume control for the speaker. Behind the smoked-plastic front panel, seven light-emitting diodes monitor modem-ready, terminal-ready, send-data, receive-data, off-hook, carrier-detection and auto-answer functions.

So far, nothing out of the ordinary — the Smartmodem has most of the standard features modem users desire. But that Z8 processor really makes the Smartmodem, well, a smart modem. And the 17 option switches you select through software make it flexible.

You command the modem by sending simple ASCII command sequences. For instance, to dial a number and establish connection to a remote computer, you type "AT D###-###-####" at your computer's console, substituting actual numbers for the # signs. The *AT* stands for attention, and the Smartmodem usually ignores things you type that don't start with or contain the AT command.

To check out the Smartmodem, we logged on to a remote computer that worked at variable baud rates. Using software that allowed switching baud

InfoWorld Report Card

Smartmodem

	Poor	Fair	Good	Excellent
Setup	☐	☐	☐	■
Ease of Use	☐	☐	☐	■
Performance	☐	☐	☐	■
Documentation	☐	☐	■	☐
Serviceability	☐	☐	☐	■

Summary
The Hayes Smartmodem contains a Z8 processor with 2K of ROM and has 17 option switches controlled through software. You need only an RS-232 cable and a direct telephone connection to put the Smartmodem into immediate operation.

Features of unit tested
☐ *Serial, binary, asynchronous transmission; 7 or 8 data bits; 1 or 2 stop bits; full- or half-duplex; odd, even or nonparity modem*
☐ *Transfer rates of 0-300 bps*
☐ *Touch-tone or pulse dialing*
☐ *Seven LEDs for monitoring signal status*
☐ *Built-in speaker*
☐ *Z8 microprocessor and 2K ROM*
☐ *Bell 103-compatible*

Suggested list price: $289

Hayes Microcomputer Products, Inc.
5923 Peachtree Industrial Blvd.
Norcross, GA 30092
(404) 449-8791

rates in mid-conversation, we tried several baud rates. You haven't seen "slow" until you're logged on to a remote computer at 1 baud! The Smartmodem performed baud-rate switches perfectly.

You can modify all of the timing parameters, such as how long you should wait for a dial tone before dialing. All worked as described in the manual. One unique feature relates to the switching between traditional pulse dialing and touch-tone dialing. If your office is on a PBX-type system, you can differentiate between the two. You might have to "dial" the PBX (usually the number 9), pause for a new dial tone and then proceed with the final dialing using the touch-tone method. The Smartmodem performed as advertised, without producing any problems.

That built-in speaker is a nice touch. The Smartmodem automatically plays the hookup dialogue through the speaker at the volume you set. You hear the number being dialed, and you hear if the remote unit is busy or if it's not. Furthermore, you can turn it off.

The ASCII text-command strings make the Smartmodem simple to use. It took only five minutes to write a BASIC program that automatically did all the preliminary work, redialed the phone if a connection was not made and saved the conversation in memory.

The manual for the Hayes Micromodem series was one of the better pieces of hardware documentation when it first came out. With one qualification, the manual accompanying the Smartmodem is better than or equal to those of Hayes' earlier products.

Every command is nicely described in the pocket-sized booklet, every specification is carefully detailed, the manual is typeset, accurate and easy to read; and it even features some fine appendices. What the manual lacks, however, is some examples of how the Smartmodem fits into typical data-communications scenarios. The appendices include two such examples: "local networking with two Smartmodems" and "monitoring a low-speed data line."

In all other respects, however, the Smartmodem documentation is first-rate.

You connect the Smartmodem to your computer with a standard RS-232 cable. A three-wire cable will do nicely although you lose the ability to turn the Smartmodem on and off using the data-terminal-ready line (DTR) and carrier detect by your computer. Neither of these last features is necessary, but some software might make good use of them.

With all modems, the manufacturer must repair the unit in order for the Federal Communications Commission registration to remain valid. Our past experience with Hayes' services has been good. The company has returned units promptly and without paperwork foul-ups. The Smartmodem unit has a two-year limited warranty that covers the usual "defects in materials and/or workmanship" clause.

We were impressed by the Hayes Smartmodem. We used it on four computers, and it performed well. It is extremely convenient and eminently portable and requires only a three-wire RS-232 cable and a direct telephone connection to work.

Hayes also has a companion product, an RS-232 clock. Combining these, you end up with a "stack" that performs both auto-answer and auto-dial functions based upon the actual time.

—*Thom Hogan*

REVIEW

Hayes Joystick

Joysticks are useful for more than just playing computer games. You can use them for cursor control on certain software packages or for creating shapes and pictures in high-resolution graphics while saving wear and tear on your keyboard. Many educational packages have a joystick option, which greatly facilitates cursor movement for students who are not experienced keyboard users. The Hayes Mach III joystick is suited to all of these applications. It is a durable product that can help give you precise cursor control for a variety of software applications.

For this review, we tested the Mach III on an Apple IIe. This unit also works on the other Apple II systems. A different Mach III that plugs into the outside panel on the Apple IIe also functions with the IBM PC. Hayes makes a less expensive Mach II, but it has only two push-button switches, whereas the Mach III has three.

The Mach III joystick controls your computer's cursor by translating the stick position into x and y coordinates on the screen. The controls have two linear potentiometers. One reads the x-axis; Applesoft BASIC accesses the potentiometer using the PDL (0) command. The other potentiometer reads the y-axis using PDL (1).

For greater control, the Mach III contains three push-button switches. One brown and one orange button are on the top of the joystick box, and the other orange button, the "quick-fire" button, is at the tip of the control stick.

In addition to the three push buttons, the joystick offers fine-trim adjustments. To help you cope with different types of software, these independent trim levers, located near the control stick, let you finely tune the cursor position on the x or y axis. Without this ability you may find that your cursor can never get to one edge of the screen, or your cursor may not begin to move from the left side of the screen until you move the control stick far right. Each trim lever points in the direction of its axis.

Located on the bottom side of the joystick are four different adjustments for self-centering and positive true positioning. You control these self-centering adjustments with reference pins that look like small plastic screws. By rotating the reference pins, you can get many combinations of centering and positive true positioning.

Among these combinations is the ability to have the stick move to the center position when you release it. You can also have it stay where it is when you let go or limit the movement to only the x- or y-axis.

The Mach III is a superior joystick, but it is in the same price range as many others on the market. Initially designed for professional computer programmers and computer-aided designers rather than hobbyists, it is now available to anyone at a reasonable price.

The joystick case is made of hard plastic. We accidentally dropped it several times from our computer table, but it remained intact.

In general, the Mach III is well made. The control stick has a relatively substantial diameter of 7/8-inch at the top. The three buttons are built like keyboard keys, rather than cheap push buttons. The bottom portion of the control stick is steel and has a 7/16-inch steel pivoting ball at its base.

The extra button for paddle 0 on the top of the stick gives you extra control for many applications.

InfoWorld
R e p o r t   C a r d

Hayes Joystick

	Poor	Fair	Good	Excellent
Setup	☐	☐	☐	■
Ease of Use	☐	☐	☐	■
Performance	☐	☐	☐	■
Documentation	☐	☐	☐	■
Serviceability	☐	☐	■	☐

Summary
The Mach III joystick from Hayes Products is a durable accessory for the Apple II lines of computers. It offers high quality at a competitive price.

Features of unit tested
☐ *Versions also available for IBM PC, the PCjr and TRS-80 Color Computer*

Suggested list price: $54.95

*Hayes Products
1558 Osage Street
San Marcos, CA 92069
(619) 744-8546*

A tiny three-page manual contains all of the information you'll need to use the Mach III. This small but complete booklet tells you about the joystick's design, how to install it, how to operate the fine-trim and self-centering adjustments, and about the warranty.

Original users of Hayes products get a 90-day warranty. During this time, Hayes will repair or replace your joystick free of charge if it has not been damaged by improper use or altered in any way. You can send damaged products back to the company for repair with a check for shipping and handling. We are not aware of any local dealer who will repair this product.

After six months of exposing the joysticks to constant use in several schools, we have not been able to break any of the 15 units we purchased.

This joystick is as easy to install as any other game paddle. If you are a novice, you should consult the Apple IIe owner's manual for a detailed diagram of the game socket's location.

Hayes promotes the Mach III as a "Space Age Control Joystick." This joystick may not transport you far away into the cosmos, but it will give you first-class performance here on earth for a long time.

—*Doug and Denise Green*

REVIEW

Soundchaser

More music systems are built for the Apple computer than for any other computer. The Soundchaser Computer Music System from Passport Designs is one of them. It consists of the Mountain Computer Music System, a musical keyboard and software that enables you to produce four-track sound-on-sound recordings. It works with any Apple II, II Plus or IIe, as long as your computer has an auto-start ROM with Applesoft and at least 48K of memory.

The Soundchaser system's basic hardware is Mountain Computer Music System, which consists of two synthesizer boards that plug easily into slots 4 and 5 of your Apple. The package also includes Mountain Computer's own software. The two boards together contain 16 digital oscillators that have programmable waveforms, amplitude and frequency.

You can tune the synthesizer to match the pitch of an external instrument, such as an organ, in 0.5 Hz increments. The system's digitizing rate is 32 kHz, which produces a maximum audio output frequency of 16 kHz. This capacity is perhaps barely adequate, as some audio experts believe a sound system should be able to produce frequencies up to 20 kHz.

The first of the Mountain Computer system's boards provides audio outputs (eight oscillators per channel) that you can use as the stereo input to your audio-amplifier system, instrument amplifier or powered headphones. As the supplied cable is only 6 inches long, you might need to buy a longer cable to connect the computer and your amplifier. The second board has an attached light pen that you can only use with Mountain Computer's software. The light pen does not, however, respond to the Apple monitor's green screen but works only with a black-and-white monitor or color monitor of sufficient intensity.

The Soundchaser Music System's musical keyboard, which Passport Designs calls a Klavier to distinguish it from your computer's keyboard, is a 49-note, four-octave, C to C, AGO (American Guild of Organists) standard keyboard. It is housed in a finely crafted cabinet made of African walnut. By using appropriate software, you can expand the Klavier's range to a full nine octaves. You can connect the Klavier, using a short ribbon cable, to an interface card that plugs into slot 7 of your Apple. Passport Designs has recently added a five-octave keyboard to its catalog, as well.

The software that comes with the Soundchaser system's basic package allows you to make up to four tracks of sound-on-sound recordings and holds over 4400 notes.

When you boot the software disk, ten preset sounds load into memory, and you can instantly access any of these sounds by pressing the computer's 0-9 number keys. These ten sounds constitute a "master" file. The disk contains five master files for you to choose from, giving you a total of 50 preset sounds. You can create your own waveforms and save them as waveforms, or you can add ADSR (attack time, decay rate, sustain level and release time) information and save them as preset sounds. You can then add to or change any preset sound in any master file to create your own master file. Thus, depending on the number of disks you want to use, you can create as many waveforms, preset sounds or master files as you wish.

The number of oscillators that the synthesizer boards contain governs the number of individual sounds that the system can produce at any instant. Since the boards contain 16 oscillators, the system can only produce 16 sounds simultaneously. If you want to produce stereo sound, however, the system uses two oscillators to produce each preset sound channel, and you can then play only eight notes simultaneously.

Soundchaser's software provides you with a computer monitor display containing some parameters that affect the sound you produce when you play the Klavier. One of these, keyboard-0, means that the default preset is 0. If you press any other number keys on the Apple keyboard, you obtain a different preset sound. You have access to the other parameters if you type the one- or two-key prefix that identifies it, and then press the arrow keys to raise or lower the parameter. The range variation is 256 units.

As an example, the display contains two release-time parameters — R1 for the left channel and R2 for the right channel. Release time is the length of time that a sound takes to die, measured from the moment you release the key, and is the parameter you usually associate with reverberation or echo. By manipulating the left- and right-arrow keys, you can increase or decrease the release rate and thus control the amount of echo that the sound produces. You can control the left and right release independently and thus create an infinite variety of echo effects.

The display's O parameter controls the octave associated with the depressed Klavier key you are pressing. By manipulating the arrow keys, you can shift the key to any of nine octaves. You can "warble" the notes (vary or modulate the pitch) within a range of 256 speed variations — from fast (when the note sounds like a vibrato) to slow (when the note sounds like a police siren).

By typing the code letter(s) of the parameter you desire and operating the left- and right-arrow keys, you can control both the rate and the amount of pitch variation. In the same manner, you can also control the attack time (the length of time between the moment you strike a Klavier key and the point of

InfoWorld
Report Card

Soundchaser

	Poor	Fair	Good	Excellent
Setup	☐	☐	☐	■
Ease of Use	☐	☐	■	☐
Performance	☐	☐	■	☐
Documentation	☐	■	☐	☐
Serviceability	☐	☐	■	☐

Summary
The Soundchaser Computer Music System consists of two synthesizer boards, made by Mountain Computer, a Klavier keyboard and various software packages. It is capable of real-time operation, and you can use it to produce and edit four-track recordings. It performs well, is inexpensive and is easier to use than similar systems currently on the market.

Features of unit tested
☐ *Apple II, II Plus, IIe*
☐ *Applesoft in ROM*
☐ *DOS 3.3*
☐ *48K (64K optional) RAM*
☐ *One or two disk drives*
☐ *2-channel stereo system with auxiliary input, instrument amplifier or powered headphones*
☐ *Any dot-matrix printer using Grappler or Prometheus interface cards*
☐ *Game paddles or joystick*
☐ *Drum machine (Roland, Korg, Drumulator)*
☐ *Linn or Oberheim for Sync Drum option)*

Suggested list price: $1190 for hardware and 4-track software

Passport Designs, Inc.
625 Miramontes Street,
Suite 103
Half Moon Bay, CA 94019
(415) 726-0280

maximum sound), the decay time (the time the sound takes to go from maximum amplitude to the sustain amplitude), and the sustain level itself. You can save any preset sounds on disk by giving them names and preset designations.

To create sound-on-sound recordings, you press the Escape key, and the monitor display changes to a four-track-status monitor that shows you the status (record, play or off) of each channel and the preset currently assigned to each channel. You press the space bar to start, stop or rewind the sequencer. You can record sounds, using one channel at a time, and save the four channels as a Traks file. Your Traks file then contains not only the music information on each of the four tracks, but also the preset information. You can produce a five-channel event if you add a fifth channel "live" while you are playing back the recording.

Passport Designs also produces many other software options. One of the best of these is the 4-Track Editor, a tool for those who want to do more with a music system than just play it like an organ. You can use computer-music systems in one of two ways — you can either play notes on a keyboard in real time, which is fast, or you can laboriously type in the pitch and duration of every note. The 4-Track Editor takes the best features of both methods and can so achieve both speed and accuracy.

For example, you can create a Traks file and then use the editor to correct any errors. You select the track you want to edit, and the editor then lists each note you have played by pitch and duration, including rests. To fix an erroneous note, you can delete the note and type in the correct pitch and/or duration.

Another of the editor's useful features is the smoothing feature which

adds or subtracts time from a string of notes to make your composition consistent. This feature is not a cure-all for your poor keyboarding, but it is effective for minor or moderate timing inconsistencies.

As well as using the editor to insert or delete, you can use it to add commands that create loops when you want to repeat musical phrases.

Another useful program is Traksplayer, which allows you to collect up to 12 of your favorite recordings and put them on an album, complete with a "jacket" that lists the selection of songs. The great advantage of a Traksplayer album is that you don't have to boot the 4-track master disk — you just insert the Traksplayer album, make a selection and listen to the music. You can select the number of repeats you want for each individual selection and the number of total album repeats you want (up to 100).

Passport Designs could improve this software, however. You must specify all the repeat numbers and the number of songs in an album before you play it back, and once you have created an album, you can't add more songs to it or modify it in any way. The program continually asks you how many disk drives your system contains. Also, when you play an album number, you can't play along on the fifth track as you can on a conventional Traks file, nor can you give an album selection a name different from the original name of the Traks file.

One of Passport Designs' most exciting programs is Notewriter. Designed for the musician who likes to spend more time creating music than writing it on paper. The screen displays a blank musical staff with key signatures and timing marks that you can select. A metronome clicks at a rate you specify before you start playing the Klavier. As you play each note, its image appears on the staff. After you have composed your masterpiece and seen it on the screen, you can produce a hard copy of your efforts on a printer. With its companion program, Notetools Utilities, you can convert your newly created file to a Traks file that the four-track performance software can then play.

If four-track performance and recording ability isn't thrilling enough, you might be interested in another addition to the Soundchaser system: Turbo-Traks, a 16-channel performance- and recording-software base. Your Apple must have a 64K memory if you want to use this program. Turbo-Traks resembles four-track software, but more channels are available — your master file of preset sounds can now contain 16 sounds instead of 10. You can select them by pressing the 0 through 9 number keys and the A through G keys.

You can choose any note on the keyboard as a dividing line to split the keyboard, which enables you to use one preset below and a different reset above this dividing line. You can also turn on an automatic loop that, on playback, ties the first and last notes that you played. During playback, you can also raise or lower the pitch of the entire work without affecting the tempo, or you can change the tempo without affecting the pitch. Disappointingly, this program does not allow you to program a Control track that could memorize all of these pitch and tempo changes.

Turbo-Traks' Sync-to-Drum Option allows you to use a Drumlator, Rolan, Korg, Linn or Oberheim drum machine with the Turbo-Traks software. With a cable you connect the computer's game paddle I/O socket to the clock, and you connect the start/stop connectors on your drum machine with a cable. During the recording process, you can use the drum machine to set the beat of the recording. The drum machine automatically plays along in synchronization with your recording and even shuts itself off at the end of the piece.

Passport Designs also produces educational music programs. Notes-and-keys is a set of eight interactive instructional programs designed for beginning keyboard students. Another, Music Tutor Series, Version 2.0, drills you in the use of chords, intervals, matching and tuning. Melodic Games is a game similar to "Simon Says" — the computer plays a note, then two, then three and so on, and you have to match the notes.

The object of the game is to see how large an interval you can play back correctly. These programs all have excellent graphics.

The documentation for these programs now includes screen diagrams and cartoons to liven things up and contains a humorous appendix. The documentation is fair — none of the manuals has an index, and they are poorly organized.

Error handling is also fair. For example, when you use the Notewriter program and inadvertently choose a command for which there is no file on the disk, the program returns you to BASIC.

The Mountain Computer Music System alone has no provisions for real-time operation — you must use computer coding — and this is why both alphaSyntauri and Passport Designs have chosen to improve this system. The Soundchaser Music System is easier to use than the alphaSyntauri. It performs well and is inexpensive.

—*Marty Petersen*

REVIEW

Summary
The Amdek 300 video monitor is a fine product. It works with many home and small-business computers.

Features of unit tested
☐ *Stand-alone monochrome video monitor*
☐ *Cable hookup for Apple II; also available for IBM PC, Atari 800; simple modifications make use of TRS-80 Model I and other systems with composite-video available.*

Suggested list price: $179 for green screen; $199 for amber screen

*Amdek Corporation
2201 Lively Blvd.
Elk Grove Village, IL 60007
(312) 364-1180*

Amdek 300 Video Monitor

The Amdek 300 Video Monitor is a high-quality display unit compatible with most computer systems in the home and small-business market. It is a general-purpose, stand-alone, monochrome video monitor that accepts standard composite video signals — so it is usable with the majority of home and small-business computers.

The screen measures 12 inches diagonally and uses the green P-31 type phosphor or an amber P-134 type phosphor. A very fine nylon mesh covers the screen surface to minimize reflection from ambient light sources in the room.

The video electronics were designed for high resolution, and the display features a vertical bandwidth of 18 MHz.

Brightness and contrast controls are mounted on the front panel of the monitor, and the pull on/off switch is incorporated into the brightness knob. There are also controls for horizontal hold, vertical size, vertical linearity and vertical hold on the back of the monitor.

Standard 120V AC, 60 Hz line voltage powers the monitor, though a minor wiring change within the unit makes the unit compatible with 220V AC, 50 Hz power. (This modification, though simple, does require the services of a qualified technician.) Power consumption is 28 watts. The unit weighs approximately 17 pounds, and a carrying handle is integrated into the molded-plastic case.

Without a doubt, this is one of the best monochrome monitors we've seen. First of all, the screen display is crisp and clear. Even when you use a high-resolution, programmable character generator as a video source, the Amdek consistently has excellent dot resolution and definition. Another common problem, video "pulling," is conspicuously absent in the Amdek 300.

It is also clear that the power supply circuits in the monitor are well designed. Some monitors are affected by slight changes in primary power from the outlet, typically evidenced by the display shrinking size as the line voltage drops. The Amdek 300 never showed this problem.

Nylon mesh over the tube surface is also extremely effective in reducing screen glare. This mesh, in combination with the green phosphor, makes for an extremely readable display. The display minimizes eyestrain and allows you to use the monitor comfortably for extended periods.

The front-panel controls have large, comfortable knobs on them. Several of the rear-panel adjustments, however, require you to use a screwdriver to turn them. This requirement can be frustrating if the monitor is situated with its back panel near a wall. In order to make the adjustments, you must pull out the monitor, adjust it and then place it back into position to view the results.

It is clear that a great deal of thought went into the styling of the Amdek 300. Not only is it attractively styled, but the mechanical packaging takes the human factor into account.

The unit we tested was seated on top of a Lobo LX-80 interface for the TRS-80. This interface is roughly the same height as the Apple II, for which the monitor was originally designed. At this height, you can view the screen easily with a minimum amount of head movement. This detail may seem trivial, but as anyone who has used a monitor for extended periods can attest, it is a great factor in reducing eyestrain and headaches. In particular, office personnel who must use a display all day long will love the Amdek 300.

The monitor comes with a four-page, fold-out sheet of instructions, warranty-registration card and complete schematic diagram. No instructions are provided for connection to specific computers, but this operation should be self-evident to most users.

The Amdek 300 is covered by a two-year warranty on parts and labor and a three-year warranty on the CRT itself. The internal construction of the monitor is good, with plenty of room left for access to the internal adjustments. Virtually all the electronics are contained on one printed circuit board that is mounted to the bottom of the case.

In every respect, the Amdek 300 is a top-quality monitor. It compares favorably to monitors that cost much more. The display quality, human engineering and mechanical integrity all bespeak a product designed to last a long time under heavy-duty, continuous use.

—*Tim Daneliuk*

REVIEW

Stack Chronograph

Should you require any type of timekeeping function as part of your normal computer operations, the Hayes Stack Chronograph should fill the bill nicely. The term *stack* designates the physical format of the device, which is designed to form a stack with the Hayes Smartmodem.

Those familiar with the Hayes Smartmodem will immediately discern

that the Chronograph fits into the "Hayes common language standard." In other words, Smartmodem users should learn how to program the Chronograph in minutes. Newcomers to Hayes equipment might take longer — though not much.

The Hayes Stack Chronograph communicates through an RS-232 port, set up as either DTE (data-terminal equipment) or DCE (data-communications equipment). It gives information on day, date and time via its own blue fluorescent alphanumeric display as well as through the computer.

You can use the Chronograph's alarm feature to direct the computer to control various external devices such as lights, burglar alarms, energy-management systems and sprinkler systems. Used in combination with the Hayes Smartmodem, or any auto-dial modem, the alarm function of the Chronograph can signal the computer to send batch files at hours when phone and connect rates are cheapest.

Other features of the Chronograph include automatic 300/1200 baud-rate detection, automatic parity and word-size detection, automatic leap-year adjustment, a write/protect switch (to prevent inadvertent time and date resets) and battery backup (using three penlight cells that Hayes provides). The clock is crystal controlled and can be operated in 12-hour (A.M./P.M.) or 24-hour mode. Data and time are output in ANSI 3.30- and 3.43-compatible format.

Over a two-month testing period, the Chronograph performed faultlessly, doing everything the operating manual claimed.

For about three weeks we left the clock running strictly on battery power. When we plugged in the power pack, the display came to life displaying the correct time. We repeated this little experiment on several occasions for

InfoWorld Report Card

Stack Chronograph

	Poor	Fair	Good	Excellent
Setup	☐	☐	■	☐
Ease of Use	☐	☐	☐	■
Performance	☐	☐	☐	■
Documentation	☐	☐	☐	■
Serviceability	☐	☐	☐	■

Summary
The Hayes Stack Chronograph performs exactly as claimed and comes with a first-rate manual. If you need timekeeping functions in your computing, you should have little hesitation in buying this product. Its main limitation is that it may not take heavy handling.

Features of unit tested
☐ *Uses Hayes' "standard" interactive protocols*
☐ *Large fluorescent alphanumeric display*
☐ *Matches the Hayes Smartmodem*

Suggested list price: $249

*Hayes Microcomputer Products, Inc.
5923 Peachtree Industrial Blvd.
Norcross, GA 30092
(404) 449-8791*

different lengths of time — always with the same gratifying result.

As for its performance in conjunction with our computer, we can say only that it worked as advertised from the first and has worked the same ever since. If you are planning to connect the unit to an RS-232 DTE interface, you will require no wiring changes in the cabling.

If, on the other hand, you must use a DCE interface, you need to make a special cable. This is a simple matter, for only pins 2, 3 and 7 are required, with pins 2 and 3 cross-connected at the Chronograph end.

To communicate with the Chronograph, you have to write a suitable routine. The operating manual provides sample programs in Apple, TRS-80 and Atari BASICs. The trickiest parts of these routines are those dealing with port initialization and I/O, but they are easy for you to translate from the examples given to whatever BASIC you have available.

Once the computer and the Chronograph are communicating, it is a simple matter to tell the unit what it needs to know. For example, to set the time in the format hours/minutes/ seconds, 12-hour mode, you enter ATST091500A. This entry displays (9:15 A.M.) *AT* is the Hayes command string. *ST* means "set time." The rest of the set functions are just as easy to do. Once you set the clock, you can read the display continuously (unless it is running on battery backup).

To read the setting on the CRT, you simply replace the S(et) command with the R(ead) command. You can specify the separator to be used (colons, slashes or any ASCII characters except a null or carriage return) via the V command. Incidentally, the battery backup system maintains nothing but data controlled by the S command — namely, the time, day and date. You would have to

reprogram the Chronograph's other options if you experienced a power failure.

Because the Hayes Stack Chronograph is, after all, primarily an electronic device and one not subject to the kind of wear associated with, say, a disk drive, it should prove as reliable as the computer it is connected to. It may not survive handling at the post office but a normal jolt or two probably won't bother it.

The case is made of aluminum and has removable plastic panels at each end. Removing the one end panel allows you to slide the circuit-board assembly out for battery maintenance. The board itself is plated only on one side. The component side is neatly screened with part numbers and component outlines. Altogether, it's a clean, stylish piece of work.

Hayes' manuals are among the best in the entire microcomputer industry. The Chronograph manual is no exception. It is spiral bound to lie flat at any page and is printed on heavy stock, semimatte paper.

Print quality is excellent, as are the drawings. The information is presented in a clear, orderly manner. No one who can read should have any problem in using the manual.

Hayes does not expect owners to service the equipment. The manual doesn't even include a schematic. The manual does, however, provide detailed instructions for returning the unit to Hayes should repair be necessary.

The Chronograph is covered by a two-year limited warranty; Hayes will repair or replace, within two years after purchase, any unit that has failed by virtue of either faulty materials or faulty workmanship. Though the conditions are standard, the time period is longer than that offered by most manufacturers.

—*Henry F. Beechhold*

APPENDICES

Company Names and Addresses

A+ magazine
11 Davis Drive
Belmont, CA 94002
(415) 594-2297

Accent Software
3750 Wright Place
Palo Alto, CA 94306
(415) 856-6505

Action-Research Northwest
11442 Marine View Drive, SW
Seattle, WA 98146
(206) 241-1645

Addison-Wesley Publishing Co.
Software Marketing
3 Jacob Way
Reading, MA 01867
(617) 944-3700

Advanced Logic Systems
1195 Arques Avenue
Sunnyvale, CA 94086
(408) 730-0307

Alf Products
1315 Nelson Street, Unit F
Denver, CO 80215
(303) 234-0871

Alison Software Corporation
14937 Ventura Blvd.
Sherman Oaks, CA 91403
(818) 905-8000

Amdek
2201 Lively Blvd.
Elk Grove Village, IL 60007
(312) 364-1180

American Training International
3770 Highland Avenue, Suite 201
Manhattan Beach, CA 90266
(213) 546-4725

Amkey, Inc.
220 Ballardvale Street
Wilmington, MA 01887
(617) 658-7800

Analytical Engines
P.O. Box 26511
Austin, TX 78755-0511
(512) 346-8430

A.P.P.L.E.
21246 68th Avenue S
Kent, WA 98032
(206) 872-2245

Apple Computer Corporation
20525 Mariani Avenue
Cupertino, CA 95014
(408) 996-1010

Apple Orchard
20823 Stevens Creek Blvd.
Building C-3, Suite A
Cupertino, CA 95014
(408) 252-0902

Applied Engineering
P.O. Box 47031
Dallas, TX 75247
(214) 492-2027

Applied Software Technology
170 Knowles Drive
Los Gatos, CA 95030
(408) 370-2662

Arktronics Corporation
520 East Liberty Street
Ann Arbor, MI 48104
(313) 769-7253

Artsci, Inc.
5547 Satsume Avenue
North Hollywood, CA 91601
(818) 985-5763 or 985-2922

Ashton-Tate
10150 West Jefferson Blvd.
Culver City, CA 90230
(213) 204-5570

ASK Micro Incorporated
(formerly: Software Dimensions)
100 Blue Ravine Road
Folsom, CA 95630
(916) 722-8000

Atlantic Data Products
720 — 29th SE
Minneapolis, MN 55414
(612) 623-0293

Axlon
1287 Lawrence Station Road
Sunnyvale, CA 94089
(408) 747-1900

Basis
670 International Parkway, No. 100
Richardson, TX 75081
(214) 699-8980

Beagle Brothers
4315 Sierra Vista
San Diego, CA 92103
(619) 296-6400

Big Pig Software
20152 Viva Circle
Huntington Beach, CA 92646

Blue Chip Software
6744 Eton Avenue
Canoga Park, CA 91303
(818) 346-0730

The Book Company
11223 South Hindry Avenue
Los Angeles, CA 90045
(213) 410-9466

Brady Bookware
Robert J. Brady Company
Route 197
Bowie, MD 20715
(301) 262-6300

Broderbund Software, Inc.
17 Paul Drive
San Rafael, CA 94903
(415) 479-1170

BudgeCo
428 Pala Avenue
Piedmont, CA 94611
(415) 658-8141

Business Solutions, Inc.
60 East Main Street
Kings Park, NY 11754
(516) 269-1120

Byte Publications
70 Main Street
Peterborough, NH 03458
(603) 924-9281

Cavalier Computer
1223 Camino Del Mar
P.O. Box 2032
Del Mar, CA 92014

CBS Software
One Fawcett Place
Greenwich, CT 06836
(203) 622-2503

CDEX
5050 El Camino Real, Suite 200
Los Altos, CA 94022
(415) 964-7600

Central Point Software, Inc.
9700 Southwest Capitol Highway
Suite 100
Portland, OR 97219
(503) 244-5782

Colby Computer
849 Independence Avenue
Mountain View, CA 94043
(415) 493-7788

CompuSource
510 First Avenue North, Suite 408
Minneapolis, MN 55408
(612) 340-1468

Computer Tax Service
P.O. Box 7915
Incline Village, NV 89450
(702) 831-4300

Computer-Advanced Ideas
1442A Walnut Street
Berkeley, CA 94709
(415) 526-9100

Concord Peripheral Systems, Inc.
23152 Verdugo Drive
Laguna Hills, CA 92653
(714) 859-2850

Continental Software
11223 South Hindry Avenue
Los Angeles, CA 90045
(213) 410-3977

Control Data Publishing
P.O. Box 261127
San Diego, CA 92126
(800) 233-3784
(800) 233-3785 (CA)

Corona Data Systems
31324 Via Colinas, Suite 110
Westlake Village, CA 91361
(213) 706-1505

Corvus
2029 O'Toole Avenue
San Jose, CA 95131
(408) 946-7700

Counterpoint Software
5807 Creekridge Circle
Minneapolis, MN 55435
(800) 328-1223

Creative Computer Peripherals Inc.
1044 Lacey Road
Forked River, NJ 08731
(609) 693-0002

Creative Computing
39 East Hanover Avenue
Morris Plains, NJ 07950
(201) 540-0445

Data Transforms
616 Washington Street, No. 106
Denver, CO 80203
(303) 832-1501

Data Trek
621 Second Street
Encinitas, CA 92024
(619) 436-5055

Datamost, Inc.
8943 Fullbright Avenue
Chatsworth, CA 91311
(213) 709-1201

David Data
12021 Wilshire Blvd., Suite 212 B
Los Angeles, CA 90025
(213) 478-7865

Davidson & Associates
6069 Groveoak Place, Suite 12
Rancho Palos Verdes, CA
(213) 378-7826

DesignWare
185 Berry
San Francisco, CA 94107
(415) 546-1866

Diablo Systems
P.O. Box 5030
Fremont, CA 94537
(415) 498-7000

Diversified Software Research, Inc.
5848 Crampton Court
Rockford, IL 61111
(815) 877-1343

Dow Jones Software
P.O. Box 300
Princeton, NJ 08540
(609) 452-2000
(800) 257-5114

Eagle Software Publishing
993 Old Eagle Road, No. 409
Wayne, PA 19087
(215) 964-8660

EduWare/Peachtree
Computer Products
3445 Peachtree Road NE, 8th Floor
Atlanta, GA 30326
(404) 239-3000

8th Dimension Enterprises
P.O. Box 62366
Sunnyvale, CA 94088
(408) 248-3979

Electronic Arts
2755 Campus Drive
San Mateo, CA 94403
(415) 571-7171

Enhancement Technology Company
P.O. Box 1267
100 North Street, Suite 310
Pittsfield, MA 01202
(413) 445-4219

Enter Computer
6867 Nancy Ridge Drive
San Diego, CA 92121
(619) 450-0601

Epson America
3415 Kashiwa Street
Torrance, CA 90505
(213) 534-0360

Epyx/Automated Simulations
1043 Kiel Court
Sunnyvale, CA 94086
(408) 745-0700

Family Computing
730 Broadway
New York, NY 10003
(212) 505-3580

Franklin Computer Corporation
2128 Route 38
Cherry Hill NJ 08002
(609) 482-5900

George Earl
1302 S. General McMullen Drive
San Antonio, TX 78237
(512) 434-3681

Great Plains Software
1701 Southwest 38th Street
Fargo, ND 58103
(701) 281-0550

Harper & Row, Publishers, Inc.
Electronic & Technical Publishing
10 East 53rd Street
New York, NY 10022
(212) 207-7000

Hayden Book Company, Inc.
10 Mulholland Drive
Hasbrouck Heights, NJ 07604
(201) 843-0550

Hayden Software
600 Suffolk
Lowell, MA 08154
(617) 937-0200

Hayes Microcomputer Products
5923 Peachtree Industrial Blvd.
Norcross, GA 30092
(404) 449-8791

Hayes Products
1558 Osage Street
San Marcos, CA 92069
(619) 744-8546

Hewlett-Packard
Personal Software Division
3410 Central Expressway
Santa Clara, CA 95051
(408) 749-9500

High Technology Software Products
P.O. Box 60406
Oklahoma City, OK 73146
(405) 524-4359

Howard W. Sams & Company, Inc.
4300 West 62nd Street
Indianapolis, IN 46206
(317) 298-5566

HowardSoft
8008 Girard Avenue, Suite 310
La Jolla, CA 92037
(619) 454-0121

IJG
1260 West Foothill Blvd.
Upland, CA 91786
(714) 946-5805

Image Computer Products
615 Academy Drive
Northbrook, IL 60062
(312) 564-5060

Infocom
55 Wheeler Street
Cambridge, MA 02138
(617) 492-1031

Information Unlimited Software
2401 Marinship Way
Sausalito, CA 94965
(415) 331-6700

InfoWorld
1060 Marsh Road, Suite C-200
Menlo Park, CA 94025
(415) 328-4602

Insoft
7833 Southwest Cirrus Drive
Beaverton, OR 97005
(503) 641-5223

Interactive Structures
146 Montgomery Avenue
Bala Cynwyd, PA 19004
(215) 667-1713

Kensington Microware Ltd.
251 Park Avenue South
New York, NY 10010
(212) 475-5200

Keytec
P.O. Box 722
Marblehead, MA 01945
(617) 292-6484

Knossos
422 Redwood Avenue
Corte Madera, CA 94925
(415) 924-8528

Koala Technologies Company
3100 Patrick Henry Drive
Santa Clara, CA 95050
(408) 986-8866

KRAFT Systems Company
450 West California Avenue
Vista, CA 92083
(619) 724-7146

Krell Software
1320 Stony Brook Road
Stony Brook, NY 11790
(516) 751-5139

L & S Computerware
880-A Maude Avenue
Mountain View, CA 94043
(415) 962-8686

Laumer Research
1832 School Road
Carrollton, TX 75006

Lazerware
925 Lorna Street
Corona, CA 91720
(714) 735-1041

Leading Edge Products, Inc.
225 Turnpike Street
Canton, MA 02021
(617) 828-8150

The Learning Company
545 Middlefield Road, Suite 170
Menlo Park, CA 94025
(415) 328-5410

Legend Industries
2220 Scott Lake Road
Pontiac, MI 48054
(313) 674-0953

Link Systems
1452 Second Street
Santa Monica, CA 90401
(213) 394-3664

Living Videotext
1000 Elwell Court
Palo Alto, CA 94303
(415) 964-6300

LJK Enterprises, Inc.
7852 Big Bend Blvd.
St. Louis, MO 63119
(314) 962-1855

Lotus Development Corporation
161 First Street
Cambridge, MA 02142
(617) 492-7171

M & R Enterprises
910 George Street
Santa Clara, CA 95050
(408) 980-0160

Macrotech Computer Products Ltd.
1370 Marine Drive
North Vancouver, BC
Canada V7P1T4
(604) 984-9305

Malibu Softcorp
350 North Lantana, Suite 775
Camarillo, CA 93011
(805) 987-6602

MEA Software
P.O. Box 2385, Dept. B
Littleton, CO 80161
(303) 796-7100

Megahaus
5703 Oberlin Drive
San Diego, CA 92121
(619) 450-1230

Micro Ink
P.O. Box 6502
Chelmsford, MA 01824
(617) 256-3649

Microcom
1400A Providence Highway
Norwood, MA 02062
(617) 762-9310

Micromotion
12077 Wilshire Blvd., Suite 506
West Los Angeles, CA 90025
(213) 821-4340

Micro-Sci
2158 South Hathaway Street
Santa Ana, CA 92708
(714) 662-2801

Microsoft Corporation
10700 Northup Way
P.O. Box C-97200
Bellevue, WA 98004
(206) 828-8080

Milton Bradley
443 Shaker Road
East Longmeadow, MA 01028
(413) 525-6411

Monogram
8295 South La Cienega Blvd.
Inglewood, CA 90301
(213) 215-0529

Mountain Computer
300 El Pueblo Road
Scotts Valley, CA 95066
(408) 438-6650

Multi-Tech Systems, Inc.
82 Second Avenue SE
New Brighton, MN 55112
(612) 631-3550

Muse Software
347 North Charles Street
Baltimore, MD 21201
(301) 659-7212

NEC Home Electronics
1401 Estes Avenue
Elk Grove Village, IL 60007
(312) 228-5900

Nibble
P.O. Box 325
Lincoln, MA 01773
(617) 259-9710

Novation
20409 Prairie Street
Chatsworth, CA 91311
(818) 996-5060

Okidata Corporation
532 Fellowship Road
Mt. Laurel, NJ 08054
(609) 235-2600

Omega Microware, Inc.
222 South Riverside Plaza
Chicago, IL 60606
(312) 648-4844

Orange Micro
1400 North Lakeview Avenue
Anaheim, CA 92807
(714) 779-2772

Osborne/McGraw-Hill
2600 Tenth Street
Berkeley, CA 94710
(415) 548-2805

Panasonic Industrial Company
One Panasonic Way
Secaucus, NJ 07094
(201) 348-7000

Passport Designs, Inc.
625 Miramontes Street, Suite 103
Half Moon Bay, CA 94019
(415) 726-0280

Peelings
P.O. Box 699
Las Cruces, NM 88004
(505) 526-8364

Penguin Software
P.O. Box 311
830 Fourth Avenue
Geneva, IL 60134
(312) 232-1984

Personal Computer Products, Inc.
11590 West Bernardo Court
San Diego, CA 92127
(619) 485-8411

Personal Computing
10 Mulholland Drive
Hasbrouck Heights, NJ 07604
(201) 393-6000

Personal Software
10 Mulholland Drive
Hasbrouck Heights, NJ 07604
(201) 393-6000

Popular Computing
70 Main Street
Peterborough, NH 03458
(603) 924-9281

Practical Peripherals
31304 Via Colinas
Westlake Village, CA 91362
(213) 991-8200

PrimeSoft
Box 50
Cabin John, MD 20818
(301) 229-4229

Princeton Graphic Systems
1101-I State Road
Princeton, NJ 08540
(609) 683-1660

Prometheus Products Inc.
45277 Fremont Blvd.
Fremont, CA 94538
(415) 490-2370

Proximity Designs Corp.
1261 Oakmead Parkway
Sunnyvale, CA 94086
(408) 749-9191

Quadram Corporation
4355 International Blvd.
Norcross, GA 30093
(404) 923-6666

Quality Software
21601 Marilla Street
Chatsworth, CA 91311
(818) 709-1721

Quark Inc.
2525 West Evans Avenue, Suite 220
Denver, CO 80219
(303) 934-2211

Quinsept, Inc.
P.O. Box 216
Lexington, MA 02173
(617) 862-0404

Qwerty
952 Chesapeake Drive, Suite 600
San Diego, CA 92123
(619) 569-5283

Rana Systems
21300 Superior Street
Chatsworth, CA 91311
(818) 709-5484

Reston Publishing Company, Inc.
11480 Sunset Hills Road
Reston, VA 22090
(703) 437-8900

Reward Books
See Reston

Roger Wagner Publishing
10761 Woodside Avenue, Suite E
Santee, CA 92071
(619) 562-3670

Sanyo Electric
1200 West Artesia Blvd.
Compton, CA 90220
(213) 537-5830

Scarborough Systems, Inc.
25 North Broadway
Tarrytown, NY 10591
(914) 332-4545

Science Research Associates, Inc.
155 North Wacker Drive
Chicago, IL 60606
(312) 984-7000

Scott, Foresman and Company
1900 East Lake Avenue
Glenview, IL 60025
(312) 729-3000

Sensible Software, Inc.
24011 Seneca
Oak Park, MI 48237
(313) 399-8877

Sentient Software
P.O. Box 4929
Aspen, CO 81612
(303) 925-9293

Sierra On-Line, Inc.
Sierra On-Line Building
Coarsegold, CA 93614
(209) 683-6858

Silicon Valley Systems, Inc.
1625 El Camino Real, Suite 4
Belmont, CA 94002
(415) 593-4344

Sirius Software
10364 Rockingham Drive
Sacramento, CA 95827
(916) 366-1195

Sir-tech Software, Inc.
6 Main Street
Ogdensburg, NY 13669
(315) 393-6633

Smith Micro Software, Inc.
P.O. Box 604
Sunset Beach, CA 90742
(213) 592-1032

Soft Images
200 Route 17
Mahwah, NJ 07430
(201) 529-1440
(800) 526-9042

Softalk
P.O. Box 60
North Hollywood, CA 91603
(818) 980-5074

Softkey Publishing
P.O. Box 44549
Tacoma, WA 98444
(206) 581-6038

Softronics
3639 New Getwell Road, Suite 10
Memphis, TN 38118
(901) 683-6850

Software Publishing Corporation
1901 Landings Drive
Mountain View, CA 94043
(415) 962-8910

Southeastern Software
7743 Briarwood Drive
New Orleans, LA 70128
(504) 246-8438

Spectrum Software
690 West Fremont Avenue, Suite D
Sunnyvale, CA 94087
(408) 738-4387

Spinnaker Software
1 Kendal Square
Cambridge, MA 02139
(617) 494-1200

Star Micronics, Inc.
P.O. Box 612186
Dallas/Ft. Worth Airport, TX 75261
(214) 456-0052

Stellation Two
The Lobero Building
P.O. Box 2342
Santa Barbara, CA 93120
(805) 966-1140

Stoneware
50 Belvedere Street
San Rafael, CA 94901
(415) 454-6500

Street Electronics Corporation
1140 Mark Avenue
Carpinteria, CA 93013
(805) 684-4593

Strobe
897 Independence Avenue
Building 5A
Mountain View, CA 94043
(415) 969-5130

Sublogic Corporation
713 Edgebrook Drive
Champaign, IL 61820
(217) 359-8482

SUNCOM
650E Anthony Trail
Northbrook, IL 60062
(312) 291-9780

Sweet Micro Systems
50 Freeway Drive
Cranston, RI 02910
(800) 341-8001

Sybex
2344 Sixth Street
Berkeley, CA 94710
(415) 848-8233

Synergistic Software
830 North Riverside Drive, Suite 201
Renton, WA 98055
(206) 226-3216

Synetix, Inc.
10635 Northeast 38th Place
Kirkland, WA 98033
(206) 828-4884

Syntauri Corporation
1670 South Amphlett Blvd.
Suite 116
San Mateo, CA 94402
(415) 574-3335

Taxan
18005 Cortney Court
City of Industry, CA 91748
(818) 810-1291
(800) 772-7491

Tencal, Inc.
9525 Desoto Avenue
Chatsworth, CA 91311
(818) 998-4850

TG Products
1104 Summit Avenue, Suite 110
Plano, TX 75074
(214) 424-8568

Thunderware, Inc.
19 G Orinda Way
Orinda, CA 94563
(415) 254-6581

Titan Technologies Inc.
P.O. Box 8050
310 West Ann Street
Ann Arbor, MI 48104
(313) 662-8542

Trackhouse
625 Trailwood Court
Garland, TX 75043
(214) 270-0922

Transend Corporation
2190 Paragon Drive
San Jose, CA 95131
(408) 946-7400

United Software Industries
1880 Century Park East, Suite 311
Los Angeles, CA 90067
(213) 556-2211

USI International
150 North Hill Drive
Brisbane, CA 94005
(415) 468-4900

Videx, Inc.
897 Northwest Grant Avenue
Corvallis, OR 97330
(503) 758-0521

Virtual Combinatics
P.O. Box 755
5 School Street
Rockport, MA 01966
(617) 546-6553

Vista
1317 East Edinger
Santa Ana, CA 92705
(714) 953-0523

The Voice Connection
1000 South Grand Avenue
Santa Ana, CA 92705
(714) 541-0454

Wadsworth Electronic
Publishing Company
10 Davis Drive
Belmont, CA 94002
(415) 594-1900

John Wiley & Sons
605 Third Avenue
New York, NY 10158
(212) 850-6000

Xerox Education Publications
245 Long Hill Road
Middletown, CT 06457
(203) 347-7251

XPS, Inc.
323 York Road
Carlisle, PA 17013
(717) 243-5373

Zenith Data Systems
1000 Milwaukee Avenue
Glenview, IL 60025
(312) 391-7000

Zoom Telephonics
207 South Street
Boston, MA 02111
(800) 631-3116

Apple's Macintosh

Apple is betting it has a winner in the Macintosh, a 20-pound, 32-bit computer.

The Macintosh's black-and-white, 9-inch monitor generates a bit-mapped display of 512×342 dots, a resolution so crisp that individual dots are difficult to discern. The Macintosh (or Mac) comes with 128K of random-access memory (RAM) and 64K of machine-language read-only memory (ROM), which contains the most advanced software environment ever designed for a personal computer.

The Macintosh doesn't run IBM PC software, and it won't run it anytime soon, either. So far, the lack of PC compatibility is not a deterrent to the Mac's projected success.

For all the clamor over the Macintosh, it is a deceptively small and simple-looking piece of office furniture. The main console, which weighs about 16 pounds, contains a black-and-white monitor, a printed-circuit board containing the entire memory and power supply of the machine, and a single 3½-inch Sony microfloppy-disk drive that holds about 400,000 characters of information on one disk.

The Mac also has a detached keyboard connected to the console by a phone cord and a digital mouse that plugs into the back.

The primary storage medium is a 3½-inch-diameter floppy disk that can fit in a shirt pocket. This disk and its drive, which are also being used in new computers from Hewlett-Packard, Apricot and others, were developed by Sony Corporation of Japan. It is a major departure from the 5¼-inch floppy-disk standard set by the Apple II, the IBM PC, Commodore and most other micro-computers introduced since 1980.

The software for the Macintosh, which resembles the software for the Lisa machine introduced last year, reduces the basic operation of the computer to moving the mouse, pointing at different symbols on the screen and clicking the mouse's button.

Apple's own software for the Mac includes a disk containing MacWrite, an easy-to-use, though limited, word processor; and MacPaint, which turns the Mac's mouse into a fancy paintbrush.

Most critics agree that the new Apple software for the Macintosh, including MacWrite and MacPaint, is a great improvement over the Lisa software, such as LisaWrite and LisaDraw, although, unlike the Lisa, the Macintosh can only call up one program at a time.

Equally impressive, according to observers, are the adaptations of existing software being developed for the Mac. Microsoft's Multiplan runs twice as fast on the Mac as it does on the IBM PC, and all commands are fully implemented by the mouse and the Mac's pull-down menus.

Macintosh BASIC, also developed by Microsoft and available this summer, is even more striking. It runs ten times faster than Microsoft BASIC on the IBM PC and is incrementally compiled. This means that every time the user types a line of code and presses Return, the code is compiled into a pseudocode to run faster. Mac BASIC users can also run subroutines concurrently, or watch a program execute in one window while observing and modifying their program in another.

Other Macintosh software includes MacTerminal, a $99 communications package that emulates VT100 or VT52 or glass CRT emulation to permit the Macintosh to communicate over telephone lines with other computers. Appleline, a hardware expansion box, lets the computer connect to an IBM controller, allowing the Mac to emulate full-screen terminals such as the IBM 3278.

Also planned for release this summer are MacProject (a derivative of LisaProject), MacDraw, Mac Assembler/Debugger and Macintosh Logo.

According to Jonathan Rotenberg, president of the Boston Computer Society, the bulk of outstanding Macintosh software will not be available until Apple upgrades the computer to 512K RAM, a move expected some time in late 1984. He notes other minor problems, including the awkwardness of transporting both the Mac and the second Sony drive necessary to make disk copying efficient.

Another question mark punctuating the Macintosh's fortunes hinges on Sony's development of a double-sided 3½-inch disk drive. When Sony delivers that drive, the Macintosh's storage capacity will double, going to 800K.

The list of software companies writing Macintosh applications reads like a who's who of the industry, including Lotus Development Corporation (1-2-3), Ashton Tate (dBASE II), Continental Software (The Home Accountant), Digital Research (DR Logo), Harvard Associates (MacManager), Infocom (Zork, Infidel,

Deadline), Living Videotext (ThinkTank), the Minnesota Educational Computing Consortium, Simon & Schuster, Software Publishing Corporation (PFS series) and many others.

Hardware companies will manufacture accessories for the Mac, as will Apple: a second 3½-inch disk drive and the Imagewriter dot-matrix printer, released last December for the Lisa and capable of reproducing any Lisa or Mac screen displays.

Apple is also making a numeric keypad for the Mac; a carrying case that holds the Mac, its keyboard and cables; and a Security Kit, a cable that loops through the Mac to secure it to a table or desk. A modem, with price to be announced, will also be sold.

All of the Macintosh's memory and processing power is on one board running along one side of the main box. On this board are the 8-MHz Motorola 68000 processor; 128K of RAM; 64K of ROM; and connectors to the mouse, an external floppy-disk drive and serial ports for the Macintosh's printer and modem.

The Macintosh also has a built-in clock calendar, kept going by an AA battery, and a four-voice sound synthesizer with a built-in speech chip.

The 64K of ROM on the main board contains some of the Macintosh's most interesting technology. A third of the ROM is loosely referred to as the Mac's operating system, which includes input/output and memory control. The second third of the ROM contains Quickdraw, a routine that quickly generates almost all of the screen graphics. The final third of the ROM is the Macintosh Developer's Toolbox, which contains 480 additions to the 68000 instruction set that let programmers quickly use Macintosh routines.

Another innovative part of the Toolbox is called the resource manager. This manager keeps the code of a Macintosh program separate from the data that goes with that code, such as user prompts or error messages. Programmers can get at this separated data and quickly convert programs to suit different needs. Apple's manager of international marketing, Joanna Hoffman, says the resource manager will let programmers quickly convert Mac software into foreign languages, bypassing the often lengthy lead time necessary for foreign-language program conversions. — Scott Mace, *InfoWorld* Senior Writer

Glossary

Access. (1) *V*, means to read, write or update information, usually on an external memory such as a disk. It also can mean being able to get at the data to perform a read or write. *N*, means a single one of these read or write operations.

Acoustic coupler. A device that couples a terminal or computer system to the telephone system through sound waves. A computer or terminal hooks up to a modem, which translates computer signals into tone signals suitable for sending over the telephone line. To get those tones into and out of the telephone system, you can either plug the modem into the phone wires, or you can place the handset of an ordinary phone into a pair of cups containing a speaker and microphone — that's the acoustic coupler. Connecting the modem with an acoustic coupler works mostly on older modems or ones intended for portable use. The cups are generally built into the top of the modem case.

Alphanumeric. Data consisting of letters and digits. In some contexts, punctuation marks are also included.

Amber screen. A monochrome (one-color) monitor that shows text and graphics as amber and black. Some people prefer these to black-and-white monitors or green screens (which are green and black), and they are popular in Europe.

Applesoft. The version of the BASIC computer language for the Apple that allows you to use full decimal numbers (including decimal fractions). It also features a set of commands for graphics.

Application software. Programs that you use for some task other than running your computer or developing other programs — for example, financial programs and word-processing programs, appointment-schedule programs and so on.

Archive. To make a copy of information on a hard disk, in case the hard disk is erased or fails. Because hard disks store so much more information than floppy disks, hard disks are usually archived on tape. Alternatively, you can archive sections of the hard disk marked as changed on the floppy disks.

ASCII. (ASS-key) an acronym for American Standard Code for Information Interchange, the method that almost all personal and small computers use for encoding letters, digits and other symbols into computer bit strings.

Assembly language. A type of language that requires a programmer to specify exactly which machine operations the computer must perform. Using assembly language can result in fast, compact and efficient programs, but the detail involved may require a great deal of progamming time and be difficult to test and debug. Since the operations are based on a particular processor, this kind of program must be extensively rewritten if you want to use it with a different type of computer. Most programs that do not require the fastest possible execution are now written in a high-level langauge, where a single program line can specify many machine operations.

Asynchronous communication. A method of transferring data in which the information need not be sent at a constant pace. It is the standard method of communication used on most personal-computer networks where you need to read or send information, including public communications networks, bulletin boards and information utilities such as The Source or CompuServe. Except for a few special programs designed to link the Lisa and the Macintosh to big-computer networks, asynchronous communication is the method used to let Apples communicate by phone with other computers, including other Apples.

Backup. A copy that you make of a file or program in case anything goes wrong with the original. Because computers can erase information more quickly than they can process it, regular backups are an essential part of any serious application.

Bar chart. A chart that shows the relationship between amounts as a series of horizontal and vertical bars.

BASIC (beginner's all-purpose symbolic instruction code). A computer language designed for the easy, interactive development of programs. Because the computer

translates and executes a BASIC program line by line, it can show you any problems it has in understanding your commands, and you can quickly fix them and try again. See *Applesoft* and *Integer BASIC*.

Baud. A measure of data-transmission speed. In the context of personal computers, it is ten times the amount of characters transferred per second or the number of bits exchanged per second. Common rates include 300 and 1200 baud by telephone, and up to 19,200 baud between the computer and a terminal or printer.

Binary. Referring to files, in a form suitable for loading directly into the computer's memory. Program files in binary can be BRUN, meaning run without translation. High-resolution graphic images can be saved in binary form, then reloaded and shown directly.

Bit. The smallest unit of information that a computer can store. It can represent a single digit of 0 or 1, a single yes/no answer, a light or dark spot on the screen or one of two sets of colors. The word is a contraction of binary digit.

Board. Commonly used to mean a printed circuit board with the circuitry to perform some computer function. Apple users usually refer to them as cards — for example, a "disk-controller card."

Boot. To start up DOS, Pascal or another operating system. On early Apples, you had to instruct the Apple to start reading in the disk — but on newer models, the computer automatically boots when you turn on the power or press Reset.

Bulletin board. A computer system that you can call up when you want to leave or read messages. Most

bulletin boards are free, run as personal hobbies or used for goodwill by businesses and organizations.

Bus. A group of signal lines carrying address, data or control information. The term is also loosely used to refer to the connections to the signal lines, such as the slots that allow cards to plug into the Apple. (The S-100 is a type of bus.)

Byte. A group of 8 bits. A byte can represent a single character, a computer instruction, part of an address or part of a number.

Cable. In general, a wire that runs between various devices. Most cables consist only of the wire and the connectors at each end, but some have special shielding or circuitry inside. Cables are often not included in the advertised prices of a system, but are necessary for the operation of any added devices.

Central processing unit (CPU). The part of the computer that intreprets instructions, does calculations and issues orders to store and retrieve data. On most personal computers, it is a card or section of the main board containing a microprocessor chip plus some supporting circuits.

Color monitor. A display device much like a color TV but without the tuner. Because the video signal doesn't have to be changed to a television signal and back, color monitors can show finer detail (including more characters per line) than can TV sets.

Compiler. A software package that converts a complete program or module from the high-level language written by people into machine-language instructions that the computer can execute. Once the compiled program is saved in machine-language form, you can run it without having to compile it each time.

Composite video. A video signal that has the picture, synchronization and any color information all combined in a single signal. Composite video requires only one signal wire, but combining and then splitting the various parts of the signal causes a loss in fidelity compared to separate sync and picture or color information.

Coprocessor. An added microprocessor chip or complete board that either helps with specialized tasks or substitutes for the main processor for running certain programs. The most common coprocessor used with the Apple is the Z80, used for running programs under the CP/M operating system.

Copy protection. One of the various methods that attempts to let the computer read and run a program but not make copies. Manufacturers would like to copy-protect their software to prevent unauthorized copying, but users want to be able to make backup copies in case something goes wrong with their disk.

CP/M. A trademark of Digital Research, Inc., for its disk-operating systems. As applied to the Apple, it generally refers to the version that runs on computers using the Z80 chip as the central processor — since the Apple normally uses a 6502 chip, you must add a special Z80 card to the Apple so it can run CP/M.

Dedicated. Referring to the Apple's slots, one that is normally reserved for a particular type of card. For example, almost all Apple software requires the disk controller to be in slot 6.

Disk, diskette. External forms of storage that retain data as magnetic patterns on a coated disk. Disks come in hard varieties, also called rigid and Winchester, and flexible, also called floppy disks and diskettes. See *floppy disk* and *hard disk*.

Disk controller. The plug-in card that passes information to and from the disk drive in the Apple. A single disk controller can manage up to two drives.

Disk drive. The recorder/player mechanism that reads and writes information on disks. A disk drive must match both the kind and size of disk you are using, as well as the disk controller that connects it to the rest of the computer.

Disk-operating system (DOS). A set of programs that tells the computer how to read and write information from the disks, read and execute programs and interact with the user through the keyboard and screen. The most popular version for the Apple II family is called DOS, but you can also run the UCSD p-Code operating system, the new ProDos or several varieties of Forth.

Diskette. Another term for floppy, or flexible, disk. See *floppy disk*.

Diskette holder. A plastic box used for holding diskettes (floppy disks) while they are not being used. The most popular are like covered trays and hold from 20 to 100 disks.

DOS. See *disk operating system*.

Dot-matrix printer. A printer that forms each letter out of a pattern of small dots arranged in a grid. Especially if made out of a small number of dots, letters produced this way are less attractive than those produced by printers using fully

formed characters. Dot-matrix printers, however, tend to be less expensive, faster and more durable.

Double sided. Diskettes and drives capable of reading and writing on both sides of a diskette, thereby storing twice as much information. Standard Apple II-family drives are single sided, but you can buy double-sided drives for the Apple from other companies.

80-column display. A display that can show up to 80 characters per line. Most business applications and serious word-processing programs need such a display. On the Apple II, II Plus and IIe, you must add an 80-column card available either from Apple or outside vendors.

Electronic bulletin board. A computer system that you can call up to leave or read messages. See *bulletin board*.

Expansion bus. One term for the slots on the Apple into which you can plug cards to give you additional functions or interfaces.

Expansion slot. One of the slots inside the Apple into which you can plug additional boards carrying increased memory, interfaces, coprocessors or other added circuits.

EPROM. Memory chips that normally are only read from and retain their data even when the power is turned off. You can, however, erase and reprogram them, using moderately simple equipment.

Field. A group of characters that together are considered a single value or the space for entering the value — for example, a blank line in a display for entering your name, or a part of a disk record holding the last date accessed.

File. A collection of data stored under a single name. It can be equivalent to either a single file folder or to an entire drawer or file cabinet. Files are made up of records equivalent to single forms or entries. When you use a CAT (Catalog command), you see a list of the files on the disk.

Floppy disk. A form of computer storage much like a cross between audio recording tape and records. The data is recorded in a magnetic coating that rides on a flexible round sheet of Mylar, which is encased in a stiff but flexible, square plastic envelope. As with recording tape, you can record, read and rewrite the floppy disk many times; as with a record, you don't have to play the entire disk to reach information at the end or any other point. Floppy disks are also called flexible disks or diskettes.

Floppy-disk drive. A mechanism for recording and playing back information on floppy disks. Drives come in models for each of the standard disk sizes and in single- and double-sided varieties (meaning they record on one or both sides of each disk).

40-column display. A standard Apple II computer produces a maximum of 24 lines with 40 characters to a line. You can add an 80-column card and get twice as many characters per line — generally required for most word processing and most business use.

Graphics software. Programs that either make graphs and charts from existing data, or programs that let you draw or sketch on the screen.

Green screen. A monochrome (one-color) monitor that shows text and graphics as green and black. Some people prefer these to black-and-

white monitors, because they seem to have less flicker and contain less glaring contrasts.

Half duplex. In data communciations in general, it means that data can flow alternately in each direction but not both ways at the same time. Applied to terminals and terminal-software, it means the way characters typed on the keyboard are also displayed on the screen, along with any sent back from the other system.

Hard disk. A type of storage that retains data as magnetic patterns on a coated rigid disk. Until recently, hard disks for personal computers were all permanently mounted in their disk drives, but they are now available in removable models as well. Hard disks hold more data and transfer it faster than do floppy disks, but they are substantially more expensive.

Hardware. The chips, circuits, board and cabinets that make up a computer, as distinguished from the software that the computer reads in to tell it what to do.

Hex. An abbreviation for hexadecimal, the number system with base 16. This system uses the digits 0 through 9 plus the letters A through F to give a total of 16 possible digits. Hex is used to write out numbers that computers use internally because it converts easily to the binary numbers that the computer uses and is also easy for people to read and work with.

High-level language. A language for writing computer programs that is based on stating the logical operations desired instead of the exact steps the machine needs to take to accomplish the instructions. A single high-level language instruction may cause the machine

to execute dozens or even hundreds of machine instructions. High-level languages must be translated into machine language for the computer to execute them, a task performed by programs called compilers and interpreters.

High-order language. Another term for high-level language, used mostly ' in Europe and by academic experts in this country. *See high-level language.*

High resolution. A method of display in which a program specifies whether every dot the hardware can make on the screen is on or off. On the Apple, this method is more commonly known as hi res, and it can show up to 240 dots across and 192 dots high.

Hi res. The common Apple term for the High Resolution screen-display mode. In this mode, the Apple can show a picture of up to 240 dots wide and 192 dots high.

Horizontal. As applied to software or markets for personal computers, pertaining to an activity that's generally part of a wide range of business or leisure activities — for example, writing; data bases and other information storage and retrieval; and arithmetic calculation. Software or complete systems designed for horizontal markets must be more general and may not solve any particular problem as efficiently as a targeted solution. Owing to their bigger potential market, however, their cost may be lower, and you can use the knowledge you gain in learning a single package for several applications.

IC. The common abbreviation for *integrated circuit*, a combination of logic or memory circuits on a single piece of semiconductor material. The greatly increased power of ICs and their falling relative prices have made personal computers possible.

Integer BASIC. The original form of BASIC offered on the Apple II. In this form, numbers could only be integers (no fractions or decimal points), but processing was fast. Although Integer BASIC is still available, most new programs are written in Applesoft, which Apple developed later.

Integrated program, integrated software. A program or series of programs that accomplishes several standard functions and shares data and general command structures among the various modes. Most popular are those that contain some combination of spreadsheets, word processing, data bases and graphing.

Interface. (1) *V,* to form the connection between two systems or units that cannot be directly connected. (2) *N,* a program circuit or card that performs the function. One of the commonest uses of the term is for the serial and parallel interfaces, cards or circuits that translate data between the internal form that the computer uses and the form needed for communicating with printers, modems, networks and other external circuits. See *parallel* and *serial.*

Interpreter. A software package that translates a program from a higher-level language to machine form by translating each line in turn and executing it. Interpreters make it easy for you to write and debug programs, since you can build them up from small parts and test them easily, but they take the time to re-translate the program every time it is run, even if the program contains no errors.

Joystick. A type of game-control input device that looks somewhat like a floor-mounted stick shift in a small box. You can use it as a direction-pointing input for games and graphic programs.

K. In general, short for 1024 (a binary thousand). When used in reference to the size of programs, memory, disks or other forms of storage, it means multiples of 1024 bytes (characters) long.

Kilobyte. 1024 bytes. A common measure of program length, memory size or disk capacity.

Language. A vocabulary and set of rules for constructing expressions that you can understand. Computer languages such as BASIC and Pascal have a restricted vocabulary and a formal set of syntax rules. Natural languages such as English and Spanish are more open-ended and ambiguous.

Language card. A 16K memory card that gives Apple IIs and II Pluses the added space they need to work with programs written in languages other than the BASIC they contain in ROM.

Light pen. An input device that looks like a pen with a wire trailing from the top. You can use it to point to locations on the screen, allowing programs to read the indicated position. Light pens are used for drawing programs, for selecting from menus and for computer-aided design programs.

Lowercase modification. The original Apple II and II Plus did not provide lowercase letters. You can, however, get these letters by making some minor circuit changes, and kits are available for this purpose.

Machine language. The sequence of 1s and 0s that the computer uses as instructions for executing a program. All other languages are translated into machine language before the computer runs them. Machine language is also called binary form.

Modem. A device that changes computer data back and forth into forms that can be more easily transmitted by telephone or other communications link. The most common type used for personal computers connects an RS-232 line (a serial port) to the telephone network.

Monitor. (1) A display unit much like a TV but without the tuner. The Apple can use either a monochrome (one-color) or a full-color monitor. (2) The simple program stored in the Apple's permanent memory that lets you examine and change memory, load programs and work with the numbers that comprise the 6502 processor's machine language.

Monochrome. Meaning one-color, it refers to displays that produce one color and black — including black-and-white, amber (amber on black) and green screens (green on black). Monochrome displays are less expensive than color ones and usually show a sharper image.

Mouse. A palm-size device that you slide or roll around on a desktop to move a corresponding point around on the computer display. Most mice also have one or more buttons so that you can tell the computer to select or act upon whatever is shown on the screen at the spot the mouse indicates.

Network. A system that lets computers exchange information and share the use of expensive devices such as large disk drives or printers.

Wide-area networks (WANs) or telecommunications networks are linked by phone lines or other long data links. Local-area networks (LANs) are intended for computers at a single location.

Numeric keypad. A separate small keyboard that contains the digits from 0 through 9, usually arranged as three rows of three plus a zero key on the bottom. Those who enter a lot of numbers (for bookkeeping or other financial work) often add these accessory units to speed data entry.

132-column display. A display that shows up to 132 characters per line — just what you may need if you spend much time working with large spreadsheets. You can buy a plug-in board for an Apple to produce such a display.

Parallel. Referring to connections between the Apple and printers or other devices, sending data as groups of eight bits at a time, each bit carried by an individual wire. Printers with parallel input are generally inexpensive, and parallel connections are usually easy to set up. Many companies make parallel cards for the Apple.

Pie chart. A chart that shows the relative values of various quantities as portions of a total pie. It is one of the most popular displays in many business graphics packages.

Pixel. The smallest dot the screen can display. All screen images, including both text and graphics, are made up of combinations of pixels. The more pixels per screen, the finer the images that can be drawn. The word is a contraction of picture element.

Power-line filter. A device into which you plug the computer and which you then plug into a power outlet. Most filters consist mainly of special clipper circuits that chop off the tops of any noise spikes that may come over the power line. The manufacturers of these devices claim that power-line noise is a major cause of unexplained computer-system crashes.

Processor. The part of the computer that interprets the commands, does the arithmetic and logic operations and controls the flow of data. One way of classifying the processors used in personal computers is by noting how many bits the processor expects for most of its arithmetic and logic operations. The 6502 used on the Apple is an 8-bit processor, as is the Z80 used in most CP/M computers. The 8088 used in the IBM PC is a 16-bit processor, and the 6800 used in the Apple Lisa and Macintosh is a 32-bit device.

Protocol. A set of rules governing how information is exchanged over a computer network. Personal-computer data networks generally use simple protocols meant originally for teletypewriters, a public-domain protocol called XMODEM or various protocols included in proprietary software packages.

Radio-frequency interference (RFI). Disturbance in TV or radio reception, sometimes caused by computers or peripherals such as printers. Newer computers must stay within certain limits for radiating the offending signals, but problems may arise with older units or in cases where TV or radio reception is difficult.

Random-access memory (RAM). Memory that the computer can both read from and write into. The random-access part of the name indicates that the various locations can be read or written in any order, not just from bottom to top.

Read-only memory (ROM). Memory that the Apple can read from but not change. The ROM chips also keep their contents intact when the power is turned off. On the Apple, the ROMs contain a simple version of BASIC, instructions on how to read in DOS from the disks and various short utility routines.

Record. A single complete unit of information stored to read from a disk. A physical record is the chunks of data that the disk reads and stores. A logical record indicates how the information is assembled for use in programs, and it can be smaller or larger than a physical record. Typically, a logical record represents a single filled-in form, the work hours of one employee, a single sale in a retail data base and so on. Records are made up of individual fields and are combined into files.

Reverse video. Images in which the background is the brighter color, and the text or graphic is darker (the opposite of the usual computer display of light on dark). It is used for emphasis in many programs.

RF modulator. A small device that takes the video signal that the computer produces and changes it to the form that a normal TV set expects from its antenna. Due to limitations in the fidelity of encoding and decoding the video signal, the TV set cannot show as clear a picture as that produced by a monitor.

RGB monitor. A type of video display that accepts signals representing the red, green and blue colors on individual wires within the connecting cable, rather than combining all the color information in one signal as on composite monitors. Generally, RGB monitors produce better colors and sharper images and can show more characters per line. Apples produce the right signal internally for these monitors but need a special adapter to bring the signal out for connection.

RS-232. The most common standard for connecting computers, terminals, modems and other equipment using a serial connection. Although a complete standard for this type of connection exists, most computer connections use only some of the half-dozen or so control lines — you may need some expertise and work to get two of these "standard" connections to work together.

Serial. Applied to data exchanges, refers to sending each character or group of bits one after another down the same wire. Characters are distinguished either by timing methods or by special, longer, start- and stop-bit patterns.

Serial card. A plug-in card that provides a serial port for running a printer or modem from an Apple.

Serial interface. On a printer, modem or other device, a connection that expects to communicate with a computer by passing data down one wire in each direction. On the computer, the matching circuit and connector that sends and receives data in that fashion.

Sieve of Eratosthenes. A mathematical calculation often used as a test for the speed of computers and programs because it involves a great deal of multiplication and division. The Sieve finds prime numbers by attempting to divide a prospective value by a series of smaller numbers.

Slot. The connector and chassis space on the Apple where you can plug in a board such as a disk controller or printer card. The

connectors at the bottom of the slots are tied to the Apple's expansion bus.

Software. The programs and instructions that are not built permanently into a computer, but that are instead read in from disks or tapes, or entered from the keyboard.

Source code. The text of a program as written by a person. Either a compiler or an interpreter program then translates the source code into machine-language form.

Starter package. One of the standard combinations of Apple computers and accessories that authorized dealers offer. Each package includes all the items you need to take an Apple home and start using it.

Terminal. A unit that combines a display screen, keyboard and the electronic circuits for transforming keystrokes into signals and signals into images. You enter data into the computer through the keyboard and see the results on the screen. Apples generally do not use terminals, as these functions are built into the computer.

Terminal files. Files containing text that can be shown upon a screen or printed on a printer. They are marked with a T in catalog listings.

Touchpad. A device about the size of a book that you touch or draw on with a stylus to send a position signal to the computer. Touchpads are especially good for drawing programs, for picking among choices and for playing some types of games.

Track. An invisible magnetic circle pattern written onto a disk as a guide to where to store and read information. Standard Apple II-family disks have 35 of these

concentric circles, with track 0 being closest to the outside of the disk. Apple drives can also read and write between tracks — many types of copy protection use this half-tracking feature.

Users' group. An association of users of a particular computer software package, or those interested in a particular application of computers. Some users' groups are sponsored by manufacturers, but most rely either on volunteers or entrepreneurs to keep them moving. Users' groups commonly have regular meetings and publish newsletters, both of which are important methods for learning about the performance of various systems and software.

Utility. A program that does "housekeeping" or maintenance work, rather than one that produces a result useful for an external activity — for example, the programs that format blank disks and copy files. The DOS 3.3 system master disk includes some of these programs.

Vertical. As applied to software or markets for personal computers, pertaining to a specific type of business or leisure activity — for example, farming, medical practice or pawnshops. Software or complete systems designed for a particular vertical market can be tailored to the needs of that application, but are likely to be more costly than products intended for a wider, horizontal, market.

Wire-Wrap. A method for connecting electronic components on a board by using individual wires instead of printer circuits. The name is a trademark of Gardner-Denver, Cooper Electronics.

Word processing. Using a computer to edit, store and print out text. In the past, word processing was done only on special systems, but personal computers can now do it well with the right software.

Workstation. A fancy word for a computer or terminal suited for use by one person at a time.

Z80. The processing chip used on most computers that run the CP/M operating system. A CP/M card or Z80 card includes one of these chips so that an Apple can also run CP/M programs. The Z80 is an 8-bit computer and can directly keep track of 64,000 bytes of information at a time.

The glossary in this book is based in part on Rosenthal's Personal Computer Glossary, *to be published by Prentice-Hall. Portions of the glossary have appeared previously in* InfoWorld. Rosenthal's Personal Computer Glossary © *1983 Steve Rosenthal.*

Index